United Kingdom

From Early Centuries, the History.
[Part One]

Author
Michael Booth

Copyright Notice

Copyright © 2017 Global Print Digital
All Rights Reserved

Digital Management Copyright Notice. This Title is not in public domain, it is copyrighted to the original author, and being published by **Global Print Digital**. No other means of reproducing this title is accepted, and none of its content is editable, neither right to commercialize it is accepted, except with the consent of the author or authorized distributor. You must purchase this Title from a vendor who's right is given to sell it, other sources of purchase are not accepted, and accountable for an action against. We are happy that you understood, and being guided by these terms as you proceed. Thank you

First Printing: 2017.

ISBN: 978-1-912483-20-4

Publisher: Global Print Digital.
Arlington Row, Bibury, Cirencester GL7 5ND
Gloucester
United Kingdom.
Website: www.homeworkoffer.com

Table of Content

Introduction 1
Land 4
    Relief 5
        The highland zone 6
        The lowland zone 11
    Drainage 13
    Soils 14
    Climate 15
    Plant and animal life 16
People 20
    Ethnic groups 20
    Languages 21
    Religion 22
    Settlement patterns 24
        Rural settlement 24
        Urban settlement 25
    Demographic trends 27
        Population growth 27
        Migration patterns 28
Economy 33
    Agriculture, forestry, and fishing 34
        Agriculture 34
        Forestry 35
        Fishing 36
    Resources and power 36
        Minerals 36
        Energy 37
    Manufacturing 38
    Finance 40
    Trade 42
    Services 43
    Labour and taxation 44
Government and Society 47
    Constitutional framework 47
        Regional government 49
    Local government 50
    Justice 53
    Political process 55

Security	58
Health and welfare	59
Cash benefits	61
Housing	63
Education	63
Private schools	64
Higher education	65
Cultural	**67**
Daily life and social customs	68
The arts	68
Cultural institutions	70
Sports and recreation	70
Media and publishing	72
Newspapers	72
Broadcasting	73
History	**76**
Ancient Britain	76
Pre-Roman Britain	77
Neolithic Period	77
Iron Age	79
Roman Britain	80
The conquest	80
Condition of the province	84
Army and frontier	84
Administration	85
Roman society	86
Economy	87
Towns	89
Villas	89
Religion and culture	90
The decline of Roman rule	91
Anglo-Saxon England	94
The social system	95
The conversion to Christianity	97
The golden age of Bede	99
The heptarchy	101
The great age of Mercia	103
The church and scholarship in Offa's time	105
The decline of Mercia and the rise of Wessex	106
The period of the Scandinavian invasions	106
Viking invasions and settlements	106

Alfred's government and his revival of learning	108
The achievement of political unity	109
The reconquest of the Danelaw	109
The kingdom of England	109
The church and the monastic revival	112
The Anglo-Danish state	113
The Danish conquest and the reigns of the Danish kings	113
The reign of Edward the Confessor and the Norman Conquest	115
The Normans (1066–1154)	117
Resistance and rebellion	117
The introduction of feudalism	118
Government and justice	118
Church–state relations	121
William's accomplishments	121
The sons of William I	122
Henry I (1100–35)	123
The period of anarchy (1135–54)	126
Civil war	127
England in the Norman period	128
The early Plantagenets	129
Government of England	130
Struggle with Thomas Becket	131
Rebellion of Henry's sons and Eleanor of Aquitaine	132
Richard I (1189–99)	133
John (1199–1216)	134
Loss of French possessions	134
Struggle with the papacy	135
Revolt of the barons and Magna Carta	136
Economy and society	137
The 13th century	138
Henry III (1216–72)	139
Early reign	139
The county communities	140
Simon de Montfort and the Barons' War	141
Later reign	142
Edward I (1272–1307)	143
Law and government	143
Finance	144
The growth of Parliament	144
Edward's wars	145
Domestic difficulties	148

Social, economic, and cultural change	148
The 14th century	**149**
Edward II (1307–27)	150
Edward III (1327–77)	153
Domestic achievements	155
Law and order	156
The crises of Edward's later years	157
Richard II (1377–99)	158
The Peasants' Revolt (1381)	158
Political struggles and Richard's deposition	160
Economic crisis and cultural change	163
Lancaster and York	**164**
Henry IV (1399–1413)	165
The rebellions	165
Henry and Parliament	166
Henry V (1413–22)	167
The French war	167
Domestic affairs	168
Henry VI (1422–61 and 1470–71)	168
Domestic rivalries and the loss of France	168
Cade's rebellion	169
The beginning of the Wars of the Roses	170
Edward IV (1461–70 and 1471–83)	172
Richard III (1483–85)	174
England under the Tudors	**176**
Economy and society	178
Dynastic threats	180
Financial policy	182
The administration of justice	184
Henry VIII (1509–47)	186
The king's "Great Matter"	188
The Reformation background	189
The break with Rome	191
The consolidation of the Reformation	192
Henry's last years	196
Edward VI (1547–53)	199
Mary I (1553–58)	203
Elizabeth I (1558–1603)	205
The Tudor ideal of government	206
Elizabethan society	208
Mary, Queen of Scots	212

The clash with Spain	212
Internal discontent	215
The early Stuarts and the Commonwealth	**220**
Government and society	224
James I (1603–25)	227
Triple monarchy	228
Religious policy	229
Finance and politics	230
Factions and favourites	232
Charles I (1625–49)	235
The politics of war	235
Peace and reform	238
Religious reform	239
The Long Parliament	241
Civil war and revolution	245
Commonwealth and Protectorate	251
The later Stuarts	**256**
War and government	258
The Popish Plot	260
The exclusion crisis and the Tory reaction	261
James II (1685–88)	263
The Revolution of 1688	265
William III (1689–1702) and Mary II (1689–94)	266
A new society	267
The sinews of war	268
Anne (1702–14)	272
Whigs and Tories	272
Tories and Jacobites	274
18th-century Britain, 1714–1815	**276**
Britain from 1715 to 1742	278
Robert Walpole	281
George II and Walpole	282
Foreign policy	283
Religious policy	284
Economic policies	285
The electoral system	286
Walpole's loss of power	288
Britain from 1742 to 1754	289
The Jacobite rebellion	291
The rule of the Pelhams	294
Domestic reforms	295

British society by the mid-18th century 296
Urban development 298
Change and continuity.. 300
The revolution in communications... 302
Britain from 1754 to 1783 303
Conflict abroad 304
Political instability in Britain 306
The American Revolution 308
Domestic responses to the American Revolution 310
Britain from 1783 to 1815 312
William Pitt the Younger 313
Economic growth and prosperity 314
The Industrial Revolution 315
Britain during the French Revolution 317
The Napoleonic Wars 320
    Imperial expansion 323
Great Britain, 1815–1914 324
    The political situation 327
    Early and mid-Victorian Britain... 331
    The political situation 335
    Chartism and the Anti-Corn Law League 337
    Peel and the Peelite heritage 338
    Palmerston 340
    Gladstone and Disraeli... 341
    Economy and society... 346
    Cultural change... 350
    Religion 354
    Leisure 357
    Late Victorian Britain 360
    The political situation 364
    The Irish question 366
    Split of the Liberal Party 367
    Imperialism and British politics 368
    The return of the Liberals 372
    The international crisis 375
    Economy and society... 376
    Family and gender 380
    Mass culture 383

Introduction

United Kingdom is an island Nation located off the northwestern coast of mainland Europe. The United Kingdom comprises the whole of the island of Great Britain which contains England, Wales, and Scotland as well as the northern portion of the island of Ireland. The name Britain is sometimes used to refer to the United Kingdom as a whole. The capital is London, which is among the world's leading commercial, financial, and cultural centres. Other major cities include Birmingham, Liverpool, and Manchester in England, Belfast and Londonderry in Northern Ireland, Edinburgh and Glasgow in Scotland, and Swansea and Cardiff in Wales.

The origins of the United Kingdom can be traced to the time of the Anglo-Saxon king Athelstan, who in the early 10th century ce secured the allegiance of neighbouring Celtic kingdoms and became "the first to rule what previously many kings shared between them," in the words of a contemporary chronicle. Through subsequent conquest over the following centuries, kingdoms lying farther afield came under English dominion. Wales, a congeries of Celtic kingdoms lying in Great Britain's southwest, was formally united with England by the Acts of Union of 1536 and 1542. Scotland, ruled from London since 1603, formally was joined with England and Wales in 1707 to form the United Kingdom of Great Britain

(The adjective "British" came into use at this time to refer to all the kingdom's peoples.) Ireland came under English control during the 1600s and was formally united with Great Britain through the Act of Union of 1800. The republic of Ireland gained its independence in 1922, but six of Ulster's nine counties remained part of the United Kingdom as Northern Ireland. Relations between these constituent states and England have been marked by controversy and, at times, open rebellion and even warfare. These tensions relaxed somewhat during the late 20th century, when devolved assemblies were introduced in Northern Ireland, Scotland, and Wales. Nonetheless, even with the establishment of a power-sharing assembly after referenda in both Northern Ireland and the Irish republic, relations between Northern Ireland's unionists (who favour continued British sovereignty over Northern Ireland) and nationalists (who favour unification with the republic of Ireland) remained tense into the 21st century.

The United Kingdom has made significant contributions to the world economy, especially in technology and industry. Since World War II, however, the United Kingdom's most prominent exports have been cultural, including literature, theatre, film, television, and popular music that draw on all parts of the country. Perhaps Britain's greatest export has been the English language, now spoken in every corner of the world as one of the leading international mediums of cultural and economic exchange.

The United Kingdom retains links with parts of its former empire through the Commonwealth. It also benefits from historical and cultural links with the United States and is a member of the North Atlantic Treaty Organization (NATO). Moreover, the United Kingdom became a member of the European Union in 1973. Many Britons, however, were sometimes reluctant EU members, holding to the sentiments of the great wartime prime minister Winston Churchill, who sonorously remarked, "We see nothing but good and hope in a richer, freer, more contented European commonalty. But we have our own dream and our own task. We are with Europe, but not of it. We are linked, but not comprised. We are interested and associated, but not absorbed." Indeed, in June 2016, in a referendum on whether the United Kingdom should remain in the EU, 52 percent of British voters chose to leave. That set the stage for the U.K. to become the first country to do so, pending the negotiations between the U.K. and the EU on the details of the separation.

Michael Booth

Land

The United Kingdom comprises four geographic and historical parts England, Scotland, Wales, and Northern Ireland. The United Kingdom contains most of the area and population of the British Isles the geographic term for the group of islands that includes Great Britain, Ireland, and many smaller islands. Together England, Wales, and Scotland constitute Great Britain, the larger of the two principal islands, while Northern Ireland and the republic of Ireland constitute the second largest island, Ireland. England, occupying most of southern Great Britain, includes the Isles of Scilly off the southwest coast and the Isle of Wight off the southern coast. Scotland, occupying northern Great Britain, includes the Orkney and Shetland islands off the northern coast and the Hebrides off the northwestern coast. Wales lies west of England and includes the island of Anglesey to the northwest.

Apart from the land border with the Irish republic, the United Kingdom is surrounded by sea. To the south of England and between the United Kingdom and France is the English Channel. The North Sea lies to the east. To the west of Wales and northern England and to the southeast of Northern Ireland, the Irish Sea separates Great Britain from Ireland, while southwestern England, the northwestern coast of Northern Ireland, and western Scotland face the Atlantic Ocean. At its widest the United Kingdom is 300 miles (500 km) across. From the northern tip of Scotland to the southern coast of England, it is about 600 miles (1,000 km). No part is more than 75 miles (120 km) from the sea. The capital, London, is situated on the tidal River Thames in southeastern England.

The archipelago formed by Great Britain and the numerous smaller islands is as irregular in shape as it is diverse in geology and landscape. This diversity stems largely from the nature and disposition of the underlying rocks, which are westward extensions of European structures, with the shallow waters of the Strait of Dover and the North Sea concealing former land links. Northern Ireland contains a westward extension of the rock structures of Scotland. These common rock structures are breached by the narrow North Channel.

On a global scale, this natural endowment covers a small area approximating that of the U.S. state of Oregon or the African country of Guinea and its internal diversity, accompanied by rapid changes of often beautiful scenery, may convey to visitors from larger countries a striking sense of compactness and consolidation. The peoples who, over the centuries, have hewed an existence from this Atlantic extremity of Eurasia have put their own imprint on the environment, and the ancient and distinctive palimpsest of their field patterns and settlements complements the natural diversity.

Relief

Great Britain is traditionally divided into a highland and a lowland zone. A line running from the mouth of the River Exe, in the southwest, to that of the Tees, in the northeast, is a crude expression of this division. The course of the 700-foot (213-metre) contour, or of the boundary separating the older rocks of the north and west from the younger southeastern strata, provides a more accurate indication of the extent of the highlands.

The highland zone

The creation of the highlands was a long process, yet elevations, compared with European equivalents, are low, with the highest summit, Ben Nevis, only 4,406 feet (1,343 metres) above sea level. In addition, the really mountainous areas above 2,000 feet (600 metres) often form elevated plateaus with relatively smooth surfaces, reminders of the effects of former periods of erosion.

Scotland's three main topographic regions follow the northeast-to-southwest trend of the ancient underlying rocks. The northern Highlands and the Southern Uplands are separated by the intervening rift valley, or subsided structural block, called the Midland Valley (or Central Lowlands). The core of the Highlands is the elevated, worn-down surface of the Grampian Mountains, 1,000–3,600 feet (300–1,100 metres) above sea level, with the Cairngorm Mountains rising to elevations of more than 4,000 feet (1,200 metres). This majestic mountain landscape is furrowed by numerous wide valleys, or straths. Occasional large areas of lowland, often fringed with long lines of sand dunes, add variety to the east.

The Buchan peninsula, the Moray Firth estuarine flats, and the plain of Caithness all low-lying areas contrast sharply with the mountain scenery and show smoother outlines than do the glacier-scoured landscapes of the west, where northeast-facing hollows, or corries, separated by knife-edge ridges and deep glens, sculpt the surfaces left by earlier erosion. The many freshwater lochs (lakes) further enhance a landscape of wild beauty. The linear Glen Mor where the Caledonian Canal now threads the chain of lakes that includes Loch Ness is the result of a vast structural sideways tear in the whole mass of the North West Highlands.

To the northwest of Glen Mor stretches land largely divided among agricultural smallholdings, or crofts; settlement is intermittent and mostly coastal, a pattern clearly reflecting the pronounced dissection of a highland massif that has been scored and plucked by the Ice Age glaciers. Many sea-drowned, glacier-widened river valleys (fjords) penetrate deeply into the mountains, the outliers of which rise from the sea in stately, elongated peninsulas or emerge in hundreds of offshore islands.

In comparison with the Scottish Highlands, the Southern Uplands of Scotland present a more subdued relief, with elevations that never exceed 2,800 feet (850 metres). The main hill masses are the Cheviots, which reach 2,676 feet (816 metres) in elevation, while only Merrick and Broad Law have elevations above the 2,700-foot (830-metre) contour line. Broad plateaus separated by numerous dales characterize these uplands, and in the west most of the rivers flow across the prevailing northeast-southwest trend, following the general slope of the plateau, toward the Solway Firth or the Firth of Clyde. Bold masses of granite and the rugged imprint of former glaciers occasionally engender mountainous scenery. In the east the valley network of the River Tweed and its many tributaries forms a broad lowland expanse between the Lammermuir and Cheviot hills.

The Midland Valley lies between great regular structural faults. The northern boundary with the Highlands is a wall-like escarpment, but the boundary with the Southern Uplands is sharp only near the coast. This vast trench is by no means a continuous plain, for high ground often formed of sturdy, resistant masses of volcanic rock meets the eye in all directions, rising above the low-lying areas that flank the rivers and the deeply penetrating estuaries of the Firth of Clyde and the Firth of Forth.

In Northern Ireland, structural extensions of the Scottish Highlands reappear in the generally rugged mountain scenery and in the peat-covered summits of the Sperrin Mountains, which reach an elevation of 2,241 feet (683 metres). The uplands in the historic counties Down and Armagh are the western continuation of Scotland's Southern

Uplands but reach elevations of more than 500 feet (150 metres) only in limited areas; the one important exception is the Mourne Mountains, a lovely cluster of granite summits the loftiest of which, Slieve Donard, rises to an elevation of 2,789 feet (850 metres) within 2 miles (3.2 km) of the sea. In the central region of Northern Ireland that corresponds to Scotland's Midland Valley, an outpouring of basaltic lavas has formed a huge plateau, much of which is occupied by the shallow Lough Neagh, the largest freshwater lake in the British Isles.

The highland zone of England and Wales consists, from north to south, of four broad upland masses: the Pennines, the Cumbrian Mountains, the Cambrian Mountains, and the South West Peninsula. The Pennines are usually considered to end in the north at the River Tyne gap, but the surface features of several hills in Northumberland are in many ways similar to those of the northern Pennines. The general surface of the asymmetrically arched backbone (anticline) of the Pennines is remarkably smooth because many of the valleys, though deep, occupy such a small portion of the total area that the windswept moorland between them appears almost featureless.

This is particularly true of the landscape around Alston, in Cumbria (Cumberland), which cut off by faults on its north, west, and south sides stands out as an almost rectangular block of high moorland plateau with isolated peaks (known to geographers as monadnocks) rising up above it. Farther south, deep and scenic dales (valleys) dissect the Pennine plateau. The dales' craggy sides are formed of millstone grit, and beneath them flow streams stepped by waterfalls. The most southerly part of the Pennines is a grassy upland. More than 2,000 feet (610 metres) above sea level in places, it is characterized by the dry valleys, steep-sided gorges, and underground streams and caverns of a limestone drainage system rather than the bleak moorland that might be expected at this elevation. At lower levels the larger dales are more richly wooded, and the trees stand out against a background of rugged cliffs of white-gray rocks. On both Pennine flanks, older rocks disappear beneath younger layers, and the uplands merge into flanking coastal lowlands.

The Cumbrian Mountains, which include the famous Lake District celebrated in poetry by William Wordsworth and the other Lake poets, constitute an isolated, compact mountain group to the west of the northern Pennines. Many deep gorges, separated by narrow ridges and sharp peaks, characterize the northern Cumbrian Mountains, which consist of tough slate rock. Greater expanses of level upland, formed from thick beds of lava and the ash thrown out by ancient volcanoes, lie to the south. The volcanic belt is largely an irregular upland traversed by deep, narrow valleys, and it includes England's highest point, Scafell Pike, with an elevation of 3,210 feet (978 metres), and Helvellyn, at 3,116 feet (950 metres). Nine rivers flowing out in all directions from the centre of this uplifted dome form a classic radial drainage pattern. The valleys, often containing long, narrow lakes, have been widened to a U shape by glacial action, which has also etched corries from the mountainsides and deposited the debris in moraines. Glacial action also created a number of "hanging valleys" by truncating former tributary valleys.

The Cambrian Mountains, which form the core of Wales, are clearly defined by the sea except on the eastern side, where a sharp break of slope often marks the transition to the English lowlands. Cycles of erosion have repeatedly worn down the ancient and austere surfaces. Many topographic features derive from glacial processes, and some of the most striking scenery stems largely from former volcanism. The mountain areas above 2,000 feet (610 metres) are most extensive in North Wales. These include Snowdonia named for Snowdon (Yr Wyddfa), the highest point in Wales, with an elevation of 3,560 feet (1,085 metres) and its southeastern extensions, Cader Idris and Berwyn. With the exception of Plynlimon and the Radnor Forest, central Wales lacks similar high areas, but the monadnocks of South

Wales notably the Black Mountains and the Brecon Beacons stand out in solitary splendour above the upland surfaces.

There are three such surfaces: a high plateau of 1,700 to 1,800 feet (520 to 550 metres); a middle peneplain, or worn-down surface, of 1,200 to 1,600 feet (370 to 490 metres); and a low peneplain of 700 to 1,100 feet (210 to 340 metres). These smooth, rounded, grass-covered moorlands present a remarkably even skyline. Below 700 feet (210 metres) lies a further series of former wave-cut surfaces. Several valleys radiate from the highland core to the coastal regions. In the west these lowlands have provided a haven for traditional Welsh culture, but the deeply penetrating eastern valleys have channeled English culture into the highland. A more extensive lowland physically and structurally an extension of the English lowlands borders the Bristol Channel in the southeast. The irregularities of the 600-mile (970-km) Welsh coast show differing adjustments to the pounding attack of the sea.

The South West England's largest peninsula has six conspicuous uplands: Exmoor, where Dunkery Beacon reaches an elevation of 1,704 feet (519 metres); the wild, granite uplands of Dartmoor, which reach 2,038 feet (621 metres) at High Willhays; Bodmin Moor; Hensbarrow; Carn Brea; and the Penwith upland that forms the spectacular extremity of Land's End. Granite reappears above the sea in the Isles of Scilly, 28 miles (45 km) farther southwest. Despite the variation in elevation, the landscape in the South West, like that of so many other parts of the United Kingdom, has a quite marked uniformity of summit heights, with a high series occurring between 1,000 and 1,400 feet (300 and 430 metres), a middle group between 700 and 1,000 feet (210 and 300 metres), and coastal plateaus ranging between 200 and 400 feet (60 and 120 metres). A network of deep, narrow valleys alternates with flat-topped, steplike areas rising inland. The South West derives much of its renowned physical attraction from its peninsular nature; with both dramatic headlands and magnificent drowned estuaries created by sea-level changes, the coastline is unsurpassed for its diversity.

The lowland zone

Gauged by the 700-foot (210-metre) contour line, the lowland zone starts around the Solway Firth in the northwest, with a strip of low-lying ground extending up the fault-directed Vale of Eden (the valley of the River Eden). Southward the narrow coastal plain bordering the Lake District broadens into the flat, glacial-drift-covered Lancashire and Cheshire plains, with their slow-flowing rivers. East of the Pennine ridge the lowlands are continuous, except for the limestone plateau north of the River Tees and, to the south, the North York Moors, with large exposed tracts that have elevations of more than 1,400 feet (430 metres). West of the North York Moors lies the wide Vale of York, which merges with the east Midland plain to the south. The younger rocks of the Midlands terminate at the edge of the Cambrian Mountains to the west.

The lowland continues southward along the flat landscapes bordering the lower River Severn, becomes constricted by the complex Bristol-Mendip upland, and opens out once more into the extensive and flat plain of Somerset. The eastern horizon of much of the Midland plain is the scarp face of the Cotswolds, part of the discontinuous outcrop of limestones and sandstones that arcs from the Dorset coast in southern England as far as the Cleveland Hills on the north coast of Yorkshire. The more massive limestones and sandstones give rise to noble 1,000-foot (300-metre) escarpments, yet the dip slope is frequently of such a low angle that the countryside resembles a dissected plateau, passing gradually on to the clay vales of Oxford, White Horse, Lincoln, and Pickering. The flat, often reclaimed landscapes of the once-marshy Fens are also underlain by these clays, and the next scarp, the western-facing chalk outcrop (cuesta), undergoes several marked directional changes in the vicinity of the Wash, a shallow arm of the North Sea.

The chalk scarp is a more conspicuous and continuous feature than the sandstone and limestone outcrops farther west. It begins in the north with the open rolling country known as the Yorkshire Wolds, where elevations of 750 feet (230 metres) occur. It is breached by the River Humber and then continues in the Lincolnshire Wolds. East of the Fens the scarp is very low, barely attaining 150 feet (45 metres), but it then rises gradually to the 807-foot (246-metre) Ivinghoe Beacon in the attractive Chiltern Hills. Several wind gaps, or former river courses, interrupt the scarp, and the River Thames actually cuts through it in the Goring Gap. Where the dip slope of the chalk is almost horizontal, as in the open Salisbury Plain, the landscape forms a large dissected plateau with an elevation of 350 to 500 feet (110 to 150 metres). The main valleys contain rivers, while the other valleys remain dry.

The chalk outcrop continues into Dorset, but in the south the chalk has been folded along west-to-east lines. Downfolds, subsequently filled in by geologically recent sands and clays, now floor the London and Hampshire basins. The former, an asymmetrical synclinal (or structurally downwarped) lowland rimmed by chalk, is occupied mainly by gravel terraces and valley-side benches and has relatively little floodplain; the latter is similarly cradled by a girdle of chalk, but the southern rim, or monocline, has been cut by the sea in two places to form the scenic Isle of Wight.

Between these two synclinal areas rises the anticlinal, or structurally upwarped, dome of the Weald of Kent and Sussex. The arch of this vast geologic upfold has long since been eroded away, and the bounding chalk escarpments of the North and South Downs are therefore inward-facing and enclose a concentric series of exposed clay vales and sandstone ridges. On the coast the waters of the English

Channel have undermined and eroded the upfold to produce a dazzling succession of chalk cliffs facing the European mainland, 21 miles (34 km) distant at the Strait of Dover, the narrowest part of the English Channel.

Drainage

The main drainage divide in Great Britain runs from north to south, keeping well to the west until the basin of the River Severn. Westward-flowing streams empty into the Atlantic Ocean or Irish Sea over relatively short distances. The Clyde in Scotland, the Eden and Mersey in northwestern England, and the Dee, Teifi, and Tywi in Wales are the only significant westward-flowing rivers north of the Severn estuary. The drainage complex that debouches into the Severn estuary covers a large part of Wales and the South West and West Midlands of England. To the south the Avon (flowing through Bristol) and the Parret watershed extend somewhat to the east, but subsequently, with the exception of the Taw and Torridge valleys, they run very close to the western coast in Devon and Cornwall.

The rivers draining east from the main divide are longer, and several coalesce into wide estuaries. The fast-flowing Spey, Don, Tay, Forth, and Tweed of eastern Scotland run generally across impermeable rocks, and their discharges increase rapidly after rain. From the northern Pennines the Tyne, Wear, and Tees flow independently to the North Sea, but thereafter significant estuary groupings occur. A number of rivers including the Ouse, Aire, and Trent drain into the Humber after they leave the Pennines. To the south another group of rivers (including the Ouse, Welland, and Nene) enters the Wash after sluggishly draining a large, flat countryside. The large drainage complex of the River Thames dominates southeastern England. Its source is in the Cotswolds, and, after receiving many tributaries as it flows over the Oxford Clay, the mainstream breaches the chalk escarpment in the Goring Gap. A number of tributaries add their discharges farther downstream, and the total area draining into the Thames estuary is nearly 4,000 square miles (10,000 square km). The important rivers flowing into the English Channel are the Tamar, Exe, Avon, Test, Arun, and Ouse. The major rivers in Northern Ireland are the Erne, Foyle, and Bann.

Soils

The regional pattern of soil formation correlates with local variations of relief and climate. Although changes are gradual and soils can vary locally, a division of Britain into four climatic regimes largely explains the distribution of soils.

At the higher altitudes of the highland zone, particularly in Scotland, the weather is characterized by a cold, wet regime of more than 40 inches (1,000 mm) rainfall and less than 47 °F (8 °C) mean temperature annually; these areas have blanket peat and peaty podzol soils, with their organic surface layer resting on a gray, leached base. A regime similarly wet but with a mean annual temperature exceeding 47 °F characterizes most of the remainder of the highland zone, particularly on the lower parts of the Southern Uplands, the Solway Firth–Lake District area, the peripheral plateaus of Wales, and most of southwestern England. These areas are covered by acid brown soils and weakly podzolized associates. On the lower-lying areas within the highland zone, particularly in eastern Scotland and the eastern flanks of the Pennines, a relatively cold, dry regime gives rise to soils intermediate between the richer brown earths and the podzols.

Over the entire lowland zone, which also has a mean annual temperature above 47 °F but less than 40 inches of rainfall, leached brown soils are characteristic. Calcareous, and thus alkaline, parent materials are widespread, particularly in the southeast, so acid soils and podzols are confined to the most quartz-laden parent materials. In Northern Ireland at elevations of about 460 feet (140 metres), brown earths give way to semipodzols, and these grade upslope into more intensively leached podzols, particularly in the Sperrins and the Mournes. Between these mountains in the Lough Neagh lowland, rich brown earth soils predominate.

Climate

The climate of the United Kingdom derives from its setting within atmospheric circulation patterns and from the position of its landforms in relation to the sea. Regional diversity does exist, but the boundaries of major world climatic systems do not pass through the country. Britain's marginal position between the European landmass to the east and the ever-present relatively warm Atlantic waters to the west exposes the country to air masses with a variety of thermal and moisture characteristics. The main types of air masses, according to their source regions, are polar and tropical; by their route of travel, both the polar and tropical may be either maritime or continental. For much of the year, the weather depends on the sequence of disturbances within the midlatitude westerlies that bring in mostly polar maritime and occasionally tropical maritime air. In winter occasional high-pressure areas to the east allow biting polar continental air to sweep over Britain. All of these atmospheric systems tend to fluctuate rapidly in their paths and to vary both in frequency and intensity by season and also from year to year. Variability is characteristic of British weather, and extreme conditions, though rare, can be very important for the life of the country.

The polar maritime winds that reach the United Kingdom in winter create a temperature distribution that is largely independent of latitude. Thus, the north-to-south run of the 40 °F (4 °C) January isotherm, or line of equal temperature, from the coast in northwestern Scotland south to the Isle of Wight betrays the moderating influence of the winds blowing off the Atlantic Ocean. In summer polar maritime air is less common, and the 9° difference of latitude and the distance from the sea assume more importance, so that temperatures increase from north to south and from the coast inland. Above-average temperatures usually accompany tropical continental air, particularly in anticyclonic, or high-pressure, conditions. On rare occasions these southerly or southeasterly airstreams can bring heat waves to southern England with temperatures of 90 °F (32 °C). The mean annual temperature ranges from 46 °F (8 °C) in the Hebrides to 52 °F (11 °C) in southwestern England. In spring and autumn a variety of airstreams and temperature conditions may occur.

Rain-producing atmospheric systems arrive from a westerly direction, and some of the bleak summits of the highest peaks of the highland zone can receive as much as 200 inches (5,100 mm) of rainfall per year. Norfolk, Suffolk, and the Thames estuary, in contrast, can expect as little as 20 inches (510 mm) annually. Rain is fairly well distributed throughout the year. June, on average, is the driest month throughout Britain; May is the next driest in the eastern and central parts of England, but April is drier in parts of the west and north. The wettest months are typically October, December, and August, but in a given year almost any month can prove to be the wettest, and the association of Britain with seemingly perpetual rainfall (a concept popularly held among foreigners) is based on a germ of truth. Some precipitation falls as snow, which increases with altitude and from southwest to northeast. The average number of days with snow falling can vary from as many as 30 in blizzard-prone northeastern Scotland to as few as five in southwestern England. Average daily hours of sunshine vary from less than three in the extreme northeast to about four and one-half along the southeastern coast

Plant and animal life

Except for northern Scotland, the highest hills of the north and west, the saturated fens and marshes, and the seacoast fringes, the natural vegetation of the British Isles is deciduous forest dominated by oak. Human occupation has left only scattered woodlands and areas of wild or seminatural vegetation outside the enclosed cultivated fields. Few of the fine moorlands and heathlands, wild though they may appear, can lay claim to any truly natural plant communities. Nearly all show varying degrees of adjustment to grazing, swaling (controlled burning), or other activities. Woodland now covers less than one-tenth of the country, and, although the Forestry Commission has been active since its creation in 1919, nearly two-thirds of this woodland remains in private hands. The largest areas of woodland now stand in northeastern Scotland, Kielder and other forests in Northumberland, Ashdown Forest in Sussex, Gwynedd in Wales, and Breckland in Norfolk.

The moorlands and heathlands that occupy about one-fourth of the total area of the United Kingdom consist of arctic-alpine vegetation on some mountain summits in Scotland and the much more extensive peat moss, heather, bilberry, and thin Molinia and Nardus grass moors of the highland zone. Similar vegetation exists on high ground in eastern Northern Ireland and on the Mournes, and there are considerable areas of peat moss vegetation on the mountains of Antrim. In the lowland zone, where light sandy soils occur, the most common plant of the moorlands is the common heather whose deep purple adds a splash of colour to the autumn countryside but these areas also contain bilberry and bell heather. A strip of land immediately bordering the coastline has also largely escaped exploitation by humans and domesticated animals, so that patches of maritime vegetation often appear in approximately their natural state.

The survival of the wild mammals, amphibians, and reptiles of the United Kingdom depends on their ability to adapt to the changing environment and to protect themselves from attacks by their enemies, the most dangerous of whom are human. British mammals survive in a greater range of habitats than do amphibians or reptiles. Most of the formerly abundant larger mammals such as boars, reindeer, and wolves have become extinct, but red deer survive in the Scottish Highlands and in Exmoor Forest and roe deer in the wooded areas of Scotland and southern England. Smaller carnivores (badgers, otters, foxes, stoats, and weasels) thrive in most rural areas. Rodents (rats, squirrels, mice) and insectivores (hedgehogs, moles, shrews) are also widely distributed. Rabbits are widespread, and their numbers are increasing. The other nocturnal vegetarian, the brown hare, lives in open lowland country, while the mountain hare is native to Scotland. Amphibians include three species of newt and five species of frogs and toads, while reptiles comprise three species of snakes, of which only the adder is venomous, and three species of lizards. There are no snakes in Northern Ireland.

In many respects the British Isles are an ornithologist's paradise. The islands lie at the focal point of a migratory network, and the coastal, farmland, and urban habitats for birds are diverse. Some 200 species of birds occur in the United Kingdom, of which more than one-half are migratory. Many species are sufficiently versatile to adapt to changing conditions, and it is estimated that suburban gardens have a higher bird density than any kind of woodland. The most common game birds are the wild pigeon, pheasant, and grouse. Most numerous are the sparrow, blackbird, chaffinch, and starling.

Marshland reclamation has displaced waterfowl to various bird sanctuaries. A continuous effort by ornithological organizations has promoted and encouraged research and conservation. It also has led to the creation of bird refuges, sanctuaries, and reserves. These developments, along with a more sympathetic and enlightened attitude, may help to redress some of the worst effects of environmental changes on bird life.

Many British rivers, once renowned for their salmon, trout, roach, perch, pike, and grayling, have become polluted, and inland fisheries have consequently declined. Freshwater fishing is now largely for recreation and sport. The Dogger Bank in the North Sea, one of the richest fishing grounds in the world, has provided excellent fishing for centuries. Other good waters for fishing lie in the Irish Sea and also off the western coast of Scotland. Chief offshore species are cod, haddock, whiting, mackerel, coalfish, turbot, herring, and plaice.

People
Ethnic groups

For centuries people have migrated to the British Isles from many parts of the world, some to avoid political or religious persecution, others to find a better way of life or to escape poverty. In historic times migrants from the European mainland joined the indigenous population of Britain during the Roman Empire and during the invasions of the Angles, Saxons, Jutes, Danes, and Normans. The Irish have long made homes in Great Britain. Many Jews arrived in Britain toward the end of the 19th century and in the 1930s.

After 1945 large numbers of other European refugees settled in the country. The large immigrant communities from the West Indies and South Asia date from the 1950s and '60s. There are also substantial groups of Americans, Australians, and Chinese, as well as various other Europeans, such as Greeks, Russians, Poles, Serbs, Estonians, Latvians, Armenians, Turkish Cypriots, Italians, and Spaniards. Beginning in the early 1970s, Ugandan Asians (expelled by Idi Amin) and immigrants from Latin America, Southeast Asia, and Sri Lanka have sought refuge in Britain. People of Indian, Pakistani, and Bangladeshi origin account for more than half of the total ethnic minority population, and people of West Indian origin are the next largest group. The foreign-born element of the population is disproportionately concentrated in inner-city areas, and more than half live in Greater London.

Languages

All the traditional languages spoken in the United Kingdom ultimately derive from a common Indo-European origin, a tongue so ancient that, over the millennia, it has split into a variety of languages, each with its own peculiarities in sounds, grammar, and vocabulary. The distinct languages in what became the United Kingdom originated when languages from the European continent developed independently in the British Isles, cut off from regular communication with their parent languages.

Of the surviving languages the earliest to arrive were the two forms of Celtic: the Goidelic (from which Irish, Manx, and Scottish Gaelic derive) and Brythonic (from which the old Cornish language and modern Welsh have developed). Among the contemporary Celtic languages Welsh is the strongest: about one-fifth of the total population of Wales are able to speak it, and there are extensive interior upland areas and regions facing the Irish Sea where the percentage rises to more than half. Scottish Gaelic is strongest among the inhabitants of the islands of the Outer Hebrides and Skye, although it is still heard in the nearby North West Highlands. Because less than 2 percent of Scots are able to speak Gaelic, it has long since ceased to be a national language, and even in northwestern areas, where it remains the language of religion, business, and social activity, Gaelic is losing ground. In Northern Ireland very little Irish is spoken. Similarly, Manx no longer has any native speakers, although as late as 1870 it was spoken by about half the people of the Isle of Man. The last native speakers of Cornish died in the 18th century.

The second link with Indo-European is through the ancient Germanic language group, two branches of which, the North Germanic and the West Germanic, were destined to make contributions to the English language. Modern English is derived mainly from the Germanic dialects spoken by the Angles, Saxons, and Jutes (who all arrived in

Britain in the 5th century ad) and heavily influenced by the language of the Danes (Vikings), who began raiding the British Isles about 790 and subsequently colonized parts of northern and eastern England. The Humber became an important linguistic as well as a geographic boundary, and the English-speaking territory was divided into a Northumbrian province (roughly corresponding to the kingdom of Northumbria) and a Southumbrian province (in which the most important kingdoms were Mercia, Wessex, and Kent). In the 8th century Northumbria was foremost in literature and culture, followed for a short time by Mercia; afterward Wessex predominated politically and linguistically until the time of King Edward the Confessor.

Although the French-speaking Normans were also of Viking stock, the English population initially regarded them as much more of an alien race than the Danes. Under the Norman and Angevin kings, England formed part of a continental empire, and the prolonged connection with France retained by its new rulers and landlords made a deep impression on the English language. A hybrid speech combining Anglo-Saxon and Norman French elements developed and remained the official language, sometimes even displacing Latin in public documents, until the mid-14th century, when late Middle English, a language heavily influenced by Norman French, became the official language. This hybrid language subsequently evolved into modern English. Many additions to the English language have been made since the 14th century, but the Normans were the last important linguistic group to enter Britain.

Religion

The various Christian denominations in the United Kingdom have emerged from schisms that divided the church over the centuries. The greatest of these occurred in England in the 16th century, when Henry VIII rejected the supremacy of the pope. This break with Rome facilitated the adoption of some Protestant tenets and the founding of the Church of England, still the state church in England, although Roman Catholicism has retained adherents. In Scotland the Reformation gave rise to the Church of Scotland, which was governed by presbyteries local bodies composed of ministers and elders rather than by bishops, as was the case in England. Roman Catholicism in Ireland as a whole was almost undisturbed by these events, but in what became Northern Ireland the Anglican and Scottish (Presbyterian) churches had many adherents. In the 17th century further schisms divided the Church of England as a consequence of the Puritan movement, which gave rise to so-called Nonconformist denominations, such as the Baptists and the Congregationalists, that reflected the Puritan desire for simpler forms of worship and church government. The Society of Friends (Quakers) also originated at that time. Religious revivals of the mid-18th century gave Wales a form of Protestantism closely linked with the Welsh language; the Presbyterian Church of Wales (or Calvinistic Methodism) remains the most powerful religious body in the principality. The great Evangelical revivals of the 18th century, associated with John Wesley and others, led to the foundation of Methodist churches, particularly in the industrial areas. Northumberland, Durham, and Yorkshire in northeastern England and Cornwall in the southwestern peninsula still have the largest percentages of Methodists. In the 19th century the Salvation Army and various fundamentalist faiths developed. Denominations from the United States also gained adherents, and there was a marked increase in the practice of Judaism in Britain. In 1290 Jews were expelled from Britain, as they would be from other countries in the 14th and 15th centuries, a reflection of medieval anti-Semitism. The first Jewish community to be reestablished in Britain was in London in the 17th century, and in the 19th century Jews also settled in many of the large provincial cities. More than half of all British Jews live in Greater London, and nearly all the rest are members of urban communities. Britain now has the second largest Jewish community in Europe.

The British tradition of religious tolerance has been particularly important since the 1950s, when immigrants began to introduce a great variety of religious beliefs. There are large and growing communities that practice Islam, Hinduism, and Sikhism. The largest number of Muslims came from Pakistan and Bangladesh, with sizable groups from India, Cyprus, the Arab world, Malaysia, and parts of Africa. The large Sikh and Hindu communities originated in India. There are also many Buddhist groups.

Settlement patterns

British culture preserves regional variations, though they have become more muted over time. Still, the cultural identities of the Northern Irish, Scottish, Welsh, and Cornish to say nothing of the rivalry between a North and South Walian or a Highland and Lowland Scot are as distinct as the obvious geographic identities of these parts of the highland zone.

Rural settlement

The diverse forms and patterns of settlement in the United Kingdom reflect not only the physical variety of the landscape but also the successive movements of peoples arriving as settlers, refugees, or conquerors from continental Europe, along with the changing economic contexts in which settlement has occurred. Social and economic advantages led some people to cluster, whereas others had an equally strong desire for separateness. Both tendencies mark settlement forms in Britain from very early times, and regional contrasts in the degree of dispersion and nucleation are frequent.

Single farmsteads, the many surviving old clachans (clusters or hamlets), and occasional villages and small towns still characterize much of the highland zone. Some nucleated settlement patterns, however, have undergone radical change. In Wales hamlets began to disappear in the late Middle Ages through the related processes of consolidation and enclosure that accompanied the decline in the size of the bond (feudally tied) population. The Black Death of 1349, which spread quickly among poorer inhabitants, reinforced this trend. Many surviving bondsmen fled their servile obligations amid the turmoil of the nationalistic uprising led by Owain Glyn Dŵr. Thus, many Welsh hamlets had fallen into decay by 1410, when the rebellion was crushed. In Scotland great changes accompanied the late 18th-century Highland clearances, in which landlords forcibly evicted tenants and converted their holdings to sheep pastures. As late as the 1880s many clachans disappeared in Northern Ireland as part of a deliberate policy of reallocating land to new dispersed farmsteads. Great changes have also occurred in the lowland zone, where the swing to individual ownership or tenancy from the medieval custom of landholding in common brought about not only dispersion and deserted villages but the enclosure of fields by hedges and walls. Villages remain remarkably stable features of the rural landscape of Britain, however, and linear, round, oval, and ring-shaped villages survive, many with their ancient greens still held in common by the community.

Urban settlement

By any standard the United Kingdom is among the most urbanized of countries, for towns not only typify the national way of life but are unusually significant elements in the geography of the country. The greatest overall change in settlement was, in fact, the massive urbanization that accompanied Britain's early industrial development. The increasing percentage of employees in offices and service industries ensures continued urban growth. Of every 10 people in the United Kingdom, about eight live in towns more than three of them in one of the country's 10 largest metropolitan areas. The Greater London metropolitan area the greatest port, the largest centre of industry, the most important centre of office employment, and the capital city is by far the largest of these. The need for accommodating business premises has displaced population from Inner London, and this outward movement, in part, has led to the development of new towns outside the 10-mile- (16-km-) wide Green Belt that surrounds London's built-up area.

Large metropolitan areas also formed in industrial areas during the 19th and early 20th centuries. Although coalfields or textile manufacture underpinned the initial growth of many of these urban areas, coal mining had virtually ceased in all of them by the end of the 20th century, and the economic predominance of heavy industry and textile production had given way to a more diverse blend of manufacturing and service activities. Birmingham dominates the extensive built-up area of the West Midlands metropolitan area, but the industrial Black Country named for its formerly polluted skies and grimy buildings also has several large and flourishing towns. In Greater Manchester, with a similar number of inhabitants, urbanization accompanied the mechanization of the cotton textile industry.

Across the Pennines similar mechanization of wool textiles created the West Yorkshire metropolitan area, with Leeds and Bradford as its twin centres. The metropolitan area of Tyne and Wear (centred on Newcastle upon Tyne) and the Greater Glasgow metropolitan area are also located on coalfields. Greater Glasgow houses about one-third of Scotland's people. Merseyside (centred on Liverpool) has traditionally served as a seaport and distribution centre for Greater Manchester and the rest of Lancashire. Other large metropolitan areas in Great Britain include South Yorkshire (centred on Sheffield), Nottingham, and Bristol. About one-fifth of Northern Ireland's population live in Belfast. In addition to these large metropolitan areas, there are many other minor urban agglomerations and large towns, several of which line the coast.

With so much urban and suburban concentration, the problems of air, water, and noise pollution have attracted much concern in the United Kingdom. Clean-air legislation has brought considerable progress in controlling air pollution, partly by establishing smoke-control areas in most cities and towns, and there has been a shift from coal to cleaner fuels. Pollution of the rivers remains a large problem, particularly in the highly industrialized parts of the United Kingdom, but vigilance, research, and control by the National River Authorities and general public concern for the environment are encouraging features of contemporary Britain. Several statutory and voluntary organizations support measures to protect the environment. They aim to conserve the natural amenity and beauty not only of the countryside but also of the towns and cities.

Demographic trends

Population growth

The population of the United Kingdom has been increasing since at least 1086, the date of Domesday Book, which provides the earliest reasonable estimate of England's population (the survey did not cover other areas). This growth has continued despite some setbacks, by far the most serious of which was the Black Death of the mid-14th century, in which it is estimated that about one-third of the population died. There is little concrete information, however, concerning birth or death rates, immigration, or emigration until 1801, the date of the first official census. The assumption is that a population of about three million lived in what became the United Kingdom at the end of the 11th century and that this figure had increased to about 12 million by 1801.

This slow growth rate, in contrast with that of more modern times, resulted mainly from the combination of a high birth rate with an almost equally high death rate. Family monuments in old churches show many examples of men whose "quivers were full" but whose hearths were not crowded. It is estimated that in the first half of the 18th century three-fourths of the children born in London died before they reached puberty. Despite the appalling living conditions it produced, the Industrial Revolution resulted in an acceleration of the birth rate. Gradually the greater medical knowledge, improved nutrition, and concern for public health that characterized the 19th and 20th centuries yielded a lower mortality rate and an overall increase in population, even as birth rates began to drop.

Since the 1930s the population has experienced a complete cycle in its pattern of growth. A low rate of increase during the 1930s was followed by a post-World War II marriage boom that accelerated the rate of growth, culminating in a peak during the mid-1960s. After 1964 a considerable fall in the birth rate brought about a dramatic decline in growth, with a small absolute decline in population between 1974 and 1978. However, modest population growth resumed during the 1980s, and the population of the United Kingdom rose from 56 million in 1980 to about 60 million by the end of the 20th century. The main cause of these abrupt shifts was the erratic nature of the birth rate, with the interaction of two opposing trends: on one hand, a long-term general decline in fertility and, on the other, a rising longevity and a decline in death rates. Such processes also have affected the age composition of the population, which has grown decidedly older. There has been a decline in the proportion of youths and an increase in the proportion of older people, especially those age 85 and older.

Migration patterns

Beginning in the 1950s, the immigration of nonwhite ("New Commonwealth") people from such developing nations as India, Pakistan, and the countries of the West Indies became significant, and from 1957 until 1962 there was a net migration gain. Since then restriction on the entry of New Commonwealth citizens has lessened the primary inflow, but dependents of immigrants already in the United Kingdom are still admitted. The reasons for restricting entry were in part economic but were also associated with the resistance of the existing population to the new arrivals. Nevertheless, the United Kingdom continues to gain people from the New Commonwealth.

Although historical records refer to emigration to North America in the 17th and 18th centuries, there is little quantitative information about such movements before the middle of the following century. The greatest numbers appear to have left Great Britain in the 1880s and between 1900 and the outbreak of World War I. Emigration, particularly to Canada, Australia, and New Zealand ("Old Commonwealth" countries), continued at a high rate after the war until 1930, when unfavourable economic conditions in the British Empire and in the United States reversed the movement. During the same years, there also was an influx of refugees from Europe. After World War II both inward and outward movements were considerable.

Emigration to the countries of the Old Commonwealth and, to a lesser degree, to the United States continued, but until 1951 immigration into Britain roughly equaled British emigration to the rest of the world. Since the mid-1960s there has been a slackening of emigration, as Canada and Australia no longer maintain an open-door policy to citizens of the United Kingdom, accepting only those whose skills are in demand. Nevertheless, the United Kingdom continues to be an exporter of population, albeit on a declining scale, to the Old Commonwealth, while emigration to the nations of the European Union and other foreign countries has increased.

Migration within the United Kingdom has at times been sizable. Until 1700 the relatively small population was sparsely distributed and largely rural and agricultural, much as it had been in medieval times. From the mid-18th century, scientific and technological innovations created the first modern industrial state. At the same time, agriculture underwent technical and tenurial changes that allowed increased production with a smaller workforce, and revolutionary improvements in transport facilitated the movement of materials and people. As a result, by the late 19th century a theretofore mainly rural population had largely become a nation of industrial workers and town dwellers.

The rural exodus was a long process. The breakdown of communal farming started before the 14th century. Subsequently enclosures advanced steadily, especially after 1740, until a century later open fields had virtually disappeared from the landscape. Many of the displaced landless agricultural labourers were attracted to the better employment opportunities and the higher wage levels of the growing industries. Meanwhile, a rapid rise in the birth rate had produced a growing population of young people in the countryside who faced little prospect of agricultural employment. These groups contributed to a high volume of internal migration toward the towns.

Industry, as well as the urban centres that inevitably grew up around it, concentrated near the coalfields, while the railway network, which grew rapidly after 1830, enhanced the commercial importance of many towns. The migration of people, especially young people, from the country to industrialized towns took place at an unprecedented rate in the early railway age, and such movements were relatively confined geographically. Migration from agricultural Ireland provided an exception, for, when the disastrous potato disease of 1845–49 led to widespread famine, large numbers moved to Great Britain to become urban workers in Lancashire, Clydeside (the Glasgow region), and London. The rural exodus continued, but on a greatly reduced scale, after 1901.

Soon after World War I, new interregional migration flows commenced when the formerly booming 19th-century industrial and mining districts lost much of their economic momentum. Declining or stagnating heavy industry in Clydeside, northeastern England, South Wales, and parts of Lancashire and Yorkshire swelled the ranks of the unemployed, and many migrated to the relatively more prosperous Midlands and southern England. This movement of people continued until it was arrested by the relatively full employment conditions that obtained soon after the outbreak of World War II.

In the 1950s opportunities for employment in the United Kingdom improved with government-sponsored diversification of industry, reducing the volume of migration to the south. The decline of certain northern industries coal mining, shipbuilding, and cotton textiles in particular had nevertheless reached a critical level by the late 1960s, and the emergence of new growth points in the West Midlands and southeastern England made the drift to the south a continuing feature of British economic life. During the 1960s and '70s the areas of most rapid growth were East Anglia, the South West, and the East Midlands, partly because of limitations on growth in Greater London and the development of peripheral new towns in surrounding areas.

During the 1980s the government largely abandoned subsidies for industry and adopted a program of rationalization and privatization. The result was the collapse of coal mining and heavy industry in the north and the West Midlands of England and in the Lowlands of Scotland and a similar loss of heavy industry in Northern Ireland; this unleashed a wave of migration from these regions to the more prosperous south of England, especially East Anglia, the East Midlands, and the South West. As the economy stabilized during the 1990s, migration from Scotland, Northern Ireland, and northern England subsided. While the South East (including Greater London) was the chief destination of external immigrants into Britain, this region, along with the West Midlands, produced a growing internal migration to surrounding regions of England during the 1990s. This pattern reflected a larger trend of migration out of older urban centres throughout Britain to surrounding rural areas and small towns at the end of the 20th century.

Economy

The United Kingdom has a fiercely independent, developed, and international trading economy that was at the forefront of the 19th-century Industrial Revolution. The country emerged from World War II as a military victor but with a debilitated manufacturing sector. Postwar recovery was relatively slow, and it took nearly 40 years, with additional stimulation after 1973 from membership in the European Economic Community (ultimately succeeded by the European Union [EU]), for the British economy to improve its competitiveness significantly. Economic growth rates in the 1990s compared favourably with those of other top industrial countries. Manufacturing's contribution to gross domestic product (GDP) has declined to about one-fifth of the total, with services providing the source of greatest growth.

The United Kingdom's chief trading ties have shifted from its former empire to other members of the EU, which account for more than half its trade in tangible goods. The United States is a major investment and trading partner, and Japan has become a significant investor in local production. American and Japanese companies often choose the United Kingdom as their European base. In addition, other fast-developing East Asian countries with export-oriented economies include the United Kingdom's open market among their important outlets.

During the 1980s the Conservative government of Margaret Thatcher pursued the privatization, or denationalization, of publicly owned corporations that had been nationalized by previous governments. Privatization, accompanied by widespread labour unrest, resulted in the loss of tens of thousands of jobs in the coal-mining and heavy industrial sectors. Although there was some improvement in the standard of living nationally, in general there was greater prosperity in the South East, including London, than in the heavily industrialized regions of the West Midlands, northern England, Clydeside, and Belfast, whose economies suffered during the 1980s. During the 1980s and '90s, income disparity also increased. Unemployment and inflation rates were gradually reduced but remained high until the late 1990s. The country's role as a major world financial centre remained a source of economic strength. Moreover, its exploitation of offshore natural gas since 1967 and oil since 1975 in the North Sea has reduced dependence on coal and imported oil and provided a further economic boost.

Agriculture, forestry, and fishing

Agriculture

The United Kingdom is unusual, even among western European countries, in the small proportion of its employed population (about 2 percent) engaged in agriculture. With commercial intensification of yields and a high level of mechanization, supported initially by national policy and subsequently by the Common Agricultural Policy (CAP) of the EU, the output of some agricultural products has exceeded demand. Employment in agriculture has declined gradually, and, with the introduction of policies to achieve reduction of surpluses, the trend is likely to continue. Efforts have been made to create alternative employment opportunities in rural areas, some of which are remote from towns. The land area used for agriculture (about three-quarters of the total) has also declined, and the arable share has fallen in favour of pasture.

Official agricultural policy conforms to the CAP and has aimed to improve productivity, to ensure stable markets, to provide producers a fair standard of living, and to guarantee consumers regular food supplies at reasonable prices. To achieve these aims, the CAP provides a system of minimum prices for domestic goods and levies on imports to support domestic prices. Exports are encouraged by subsidies that make up the difference between the world market price and the EU price. For a few products, particularly beef and sheep, there are additional payments made directly to producers. More recent policies have included milk quotas, land set-asides (to compensate farmers for taking land out of agricultural use), and reliance on the price mechanism as a regulator.

The most important farm crops are wheat, barley, oats, sugar beets, potatoes, and rapeseed. While significant proportions of wheat, barley, and rapeseed provide animal feed, much of the remainder is processed for human consumption through flour milling (wheat), malting and distilling (barley), and the production of vegetable oil (rapeseed). The main livestock products derive from cattle and calves, sheep and lambs, pigs, and poultry. The United Kingdom has achieved a high level of self-sufficiency in the main agricultural products except for sugar and cheese.

Forestry

About one-tenth of the United Kingdom's land area is devoted to productive forestry. The government-supported Forestry Commission manages almost half of these woodlands, and the rest are in private hands. Domestic timber production supplies less than one-fifth of the United Kingdom's demand. The majority of new plantings are of conifers in upland areas, but the commission encourages planting broad-leaved trees where appropriate.

Fishing

Although the United Kingdom is one of Europe's leading fishing countries, the industry has been in long-term decline. Fishing limits were extended to 200 nautical miles (370 km) offshore in the mid-1970s, and, because a significant part of the area fished by other EU members lies within British waters, it has been necessary to regulate catches on a community-wide basis. Meanwhile, the United Kingdom has lost opportunities to fish in some more-distant waters (e.g., those off Iceland), and this has reduced its total catch more than those of other countries of the EU. The United Kingdom's fishing industry now supplies only half the country's total demand. The most important fish landed are cod, haddock, mackerel, whiting, and plaice, as well as shellfish, including Nephrops (Norway lobsters), lobsters, crabs, and oysters. Estuarine fish farming mainly of trout and salmon has expanded considerably.

Resources and power

Minerals

The United Kingdom has relatively limited supplies of economically valuable mineral resources. The once-important extraction of iron ore has dwindled to almost nothing. Other important metals that are mined include tin, which supplies about half the domestic demand, and zinc. There are adequate supplies of nonmetallic minerals, including sand and gravel, limestone, dolomite, chalk, slate, barite, talc, clay and clay shale, kaolin (china clay), ball clay, fuller's earth, celestine, and gypsum. Sand, gravel, limestone, and other crushed rocks are quarried for use in construction.

Energy

By contrast, the United Kingdom has larger energy resources including oil, natural gas, and coal than any other EU member. Coal, the fuel once vital to the British economy, has continued to decrease in importance. Compared with its peak year of 1913, when more than one million workers produced more than 300 million tons, current output has fallen by more than four-fifths, with an even greater reduction in the labour force. Power stations are the major customers for coal, but, with growth in the use of other fuels and the increasing closing of pits that have become uneconomical to operate, the industry remains under considerable pressure.

The discovery of oil in the North Sea and the apportionment of its area to surrounding countries led to the rapid development of oil exploitation. Since the start of production in 1975, the quantities brought ashore have grown each year, and the United Kingdom has become virtually self-sufficient in oil and even an exporter. With an average output of nearly three million barrels per day at the beginning of the 21st century, the country was one of the world's largest producers. The balance of payments has benefited considerably from oil revenues, and a substantial proportion has been invested abroad to offset diminishing oil income in the future. Proven reserves were estimated at around 700 million tons in the late 1990s.

Since offshore natural gas supplies from the North Sea began to be available in quantity in 1967, they have replaced the previously coal-based supplies of town gas. A national network of distribution pipelines has been created. Proven reserves of natural gas were estimated at 26.8 trillion cubic feet (760 billion cubic metres) in the late 1990s.

Self-sufficiency in oil and natural gas and the decline of coal mining has transformed Britain's energy sector. Nuclear fuel has slightly expanded its contribution to electricity generation, and hydroelectric power contributes a small proportion (mainly in Scotland), but conventional steam power stations provide most of the country's electricity.

Manufacturing

The manufacturing sector as a whole has continued to shrink both in employment and in its contribution (now around one-fifth) to the GDP. The decline in manufacturing largely accounted for the rapid rise in unemployment in the early 1980s. Once economic growth returned, however, there was great improvement in productivity and profits in British manufacturing.

In terms of their relative importance to the GDP, the most important manufacturing industries are engineering; food, beverages (including alcoholic beverages), and tobacco; chemicals; paper, printing, and publishing; metals and minerals; and textiles, clothing, footwear, and leather. The fastest-growing sectors have been chemicals and electrical engineering. Within the chemical industry, pharmaceuticals and specialty products have shown the largest increases. Within the engineering industry, electrical and instrument engineering and transport engineering including motor vehicles and aerospace equipment have grown faster than mechanical engineering and metal goods, and electronic products have shown the fastest growth.

On the other hand, the growth in motor vehicle production has occurred among foreign-owned, especially Japanese, companies investing in the United Kingdom. British automobile manufacturers have been in decline since the 1970s. After a period of restructuring during the 1980s, the British steel industry substantially increased its productivity, output, and exports during the 1990s. However, food, beverages, tobacco, leather, and engineering as a whole have had below-average growth. Textiles, clothing, and footwear have been in absolute decline because British companies have faced increasing difficulty competing with imports, especially from Asia.

During the 1980s imports of manufactured products increased dramatically, and, although exports of finished manufactured products increased in value, the surplus in the balance of trade disappeared and was transformed into a large deficit. Nevertheless, after a period of restructuring in the 1980s, Britain's manufacturing sector increased its productivity and competitiveness, and the trade balance improved and stabilized during the 1990s.

Construction in Britain stagnated during the 1990s because of a decline in prices and in demand for new housing and because of decreased government investment in infrastructure during the first half of the decade. About half the labour force in construction is self-employed. More than half of all construction work is on new projects, the remainder on repair and maintenance. There has been a marked switch from housing funded and owned by public authorities toward private development. Considerable efforts have also been made to encourage tenants of publicly owned rented houses to become owner-occupiers, with the result that the proportion of owner-occupied homes has grown considerably since the early 1970s.

The supply of privately rented accommodations became scarcer because of statutory rent controls that discouraged new construction, but changes during the 1980s both in the economic climate and in official policy began to stimulate the supply. The average price of a new house, particularly in London and the South East, has generally continued to increase more rapidly than the prevailing rate of inflation, although prices have fluctuated considerably. In turn, the rising price of new homes has created considerable pressure on the land available for housing, which has been relatively tightly controlled. Here, too, public policy has been changing in favour of greater permissiveness.

Private industrial and commercial construction and public projects account for the remainder of construction. During the 1980s and '90s the United Kingdom embarked on a series of major infrastructure projects, including the Channel Tunnel between Britain and France, the rebuilding of large parts of London's traditional Docklands as a new commercial centre, and extensions to London's rail and Underground systems.

Finance

The United Kingdom, particularly London, has traditionally been a world financial centre. Restructuring and deregulation transformed the sector during the 1980s and '90s, with important changes in banking, insurance, the London Stock Exchange, shipping, and commodity markets. Some long-standing distinctions between financial institutions have become less clear-cut. For example, housing loans used to be primarily the responsibility of building societies, but increasingly banks and insurance companies have entered this area of lending. Two related developments have occurred: the transformation of building-society branch offices into virtual banks with personal cashing facilities and the diversification of all three of these types of institutions into real estate services. Building societies also participate to a limited extent in investment services, insurance, trusteeship, executorship, and land services.

At the end of the 20th century, the financial services industry employed more than one million people and contributed about one-twelfth of the GDP. Although financial services have grown rapidly in some medium-sized cities, notably Leeds and Edinburgh, London has continued to dominate the industry and has grown in size and influence as a centre of international financial operations. Capital flows have increased, as have foreign exchange and securities trading. Consequently, London has more foreign banks than any other city in the world. Increased competition and technological developments have accelerated change. The International Stock Exchange was reorganized, and the historical two-tier structure of brokers, who executed investors' instructions to buy and sell stocks and shares, and jobbers, who "made" markets in these securities, was abolished. As a result, new companies link British and foreign banks with former brokers and jobbers. The Financial Services Act of 1986, the Building Societies Act of 1987, and the Banking Act of 1987 regulate these new financial organizations.

In 1997 the government established the Financial Services Authority (FSA) to regulate the financial services industry; it replaced a series of separate supervisory organizations, some of them based on self-regulation. Among other tasks, the FSA took over the supervision of the United Kingdom's commercial banks from the Bank of England. The FSA was widely criticized for its response to the financial crisis that erupted in 2008 and led to a government bailout for a number of prominent British banks. As a result, the Financial Services Act of 2012 abolished the FSA, and the "tripartite" system of financial regulation (the FSA, the Bank of England, and the Treasury) was replaced in 2013 with three new bodies the Financial Conduct Authority (FCA), mandated with regulating financial service firms and protecting consumers, the Financial Policy Committee (FPC), and the Prudential Regulation Authority (PRA) the last two of which were embedded in the Bank of England, to which the supervision and regulation of banks were returned.

The Bank of England retains the sole right to issue banknotes in England and Wales (banks in Scotland and Northern Ireland have limited rights to do this in their own areas). In 1997 the Bank of England was given the power to set the "repo," or benchmark, interest rate, which influences the general structure of interest rates. The bank's standing instruction from the government is to set an interest rate that will meet a target inflation rate of 2.5 percent per annum. The bank also intervenes actively in foreign exchange markets and acts as the government's banker. The pound sterling is a major internationally traded currency.

A variety of institutions, including insurance companies, pension funds, and investment and unit trusts, channel individual savings into investments. Finance houses are the primary providers of home mortgages and corporate lending and leasing. There are also companies that finance the leasing of business equipment; factoring companies that provide immediate cash to creditors and subsequently collect the corporate debts owed; and finance corporations that provide venture capital funding for innovations or high-risk companies and that supplement the medium- and long-term capital markets, otherwise supplied by the banks or the Stock Market.

The United Kingdom has a number of organized financial markets. The securities markets comprise the International Stock Exchange, which deals in officially listed stocks and shares (including government issues, traded options, stock index options, and currency options); the Unlisted Securities Market, for smaller companies; and the Third Market, for small unlisted companies. Money market activities include the trading of bills, certificates of deposit, short-term deposits, and, increasingly, sterling commercial paper. Other markets are those dealing in Eurocurrency, Eurobonds, foreign exchange, financial futures, gold, ship brokerage, freight futures, and agricultural and other commodity futures.

The share of invisible trade (receipts and payments from financial services; interest, profits, and dividends; and transfers between the United Kingdom and other countries) has been rising steadily since the 1960s from about one-third to one-half of the country's total foreign earnings. Within this area, service transactions have grown rapidly, and financial services have grown the fastest.

Trade

Trade has long been pivotal to the United Kingdom's economy. The total value of imports and exports represents nearly half the country's GDP. (By comparison, the value of foreign trade amounts to about one-fifth of the GDP of the United States.) The volume of both the exports and the imports of the United Kingdom has grown steadily in recent years. Principal British exports include machinery, automobiles and other transport equipment, electrical and electronic equipment (including computers), chemicals, and oil. Services, particularly financial services, are another major export and contribute positively to Britain's trade balance. The country imports about one-tenth of its foodstuffs and about one-third of its machinery and transport equipment.

An increasing share of the United Kingdom's trade is with other developed countries. Joining the European Economic Community caused a major reorientation of trade flows. More than half of all trade is now with European partners, although at the beginning of the 21st century the United States remained the United Kingdom's single largest export market and a major supplier. Germany was the leading supplier and the second most important export market.

The United Kingdom's current overall balance of payments (including trade in services and transfer payments), which historically had been generally favourable, fell into deficit from the mid-1980s until the late 1990s because visible imports (i.e., tangible goods imported) exceeded visible exports. Meanwhile there was considerable overseas investment, and foreign earnings grew. The government has supported trade liberalization and participated in international trade organizations. By the late 1990s the steady growth in exports of goods and services and in foreign earnings had produced the first balance-of-payments surplus in more than a decade.

Services

The most remarkable economic development in the United Kingdom has been the growth of service industries, which now provide about two-thirds of the GDP and three-fourths of total employment. This reflects the rise in real personal incomes, changes in patterns of consumer expenditure, and the elaboration and increasing outsourcing of business services. Although some services for example, public transportation, laundries, and movie theatres have declined in favour of privately owned goods such as automobiles, washing machines, and television sets this has stimulated increased demand for the related services that distribute, maintain, and repair such products. Other growing service industries include hotels and catering, air travel and other leisure-related activities, distribution (particularly retailing), and finance. Especially rapid growth has occurred in other business-support services, including computing systems and software, management consultancy, advertising, and market research, as well as the provision of exhibition and conference facilities. Britain is also the base for some of the world's leading art auction houses.

The United Kingdom's many cultural treasures e.g., its historic castles, museums, and theatres make it a popular tourist destination. The tourism industry is a leading sector in the British economy, and each year more than 25 million tourists visit the country. London is among the world's most-visited cities.

Labour and taxation

Government revenues are derived from several main sources, including income taxes, corporate taxes, taxes on the sale of goods and services, and national insurance contributions. After World War II the government adopted individual income tax rates that were among the highest in Europe. During the last two decades of the 20th century, individual income tax rates dropped, and corporate tax rates increased slightly. A value-added tax, which levies a 20 percent tax on purchases, generates nearly one-third of government revenues.

During the 1980s the Thatcher government adopted policies that placed limits on the power and influence of trade unions and provided training for those entering the workforce or changing careers. The Labour government of the late 1990s retained many of Thatcher's policies, but they abandoned the Conservative objective of unlimited tax reduction and instead sought to stabilize the overall burden of taxation at about 37 percent of GDP.

Just under half the total population is in the labour force, including a small but expanding proportion who are self-employed. About three-tenths of workers are members of a trade union, a share that dropped significantly with the adoption of legislation restricting trade union rights in the last two decades of the 20th century. Among the various influential trade organizations are the public-sector union UNISON and the general-services unions Unite and GMB. Although manufacturing once dominated employment, it now involves less than one-sixth of all workers. In contrast, the service sector employs more than two-thirds of employees, with financial services and distribution the two largest components.

Transportation and telecommunications

The United Kingdom, which is relatively small in area and has a fairly high population density, has undergone considerable change in its patterns of transport. The growth of automobile ownership (by the turn of the 21st century, nearly two-thirds of all households had one automobile, and some had two or more), the decline in the use of local buses, and the transfer of much internal freight from rail to road increased the importance of maintaining and developing road networks, particularly motorways (superhighways) and trunk roads. Intercity rail services have been improved, as have commuter services in major metropolitan areas. Similarly, air traffic has grown, particularly international flights. Although there has been a downward trend in shipping and sea travel, most foreign trade still moves by sea.

However, the opening of the Channel Tunnel rail link between England and France in 1994 had a big impact on cross-Channel passenger and freight patterns. At peak periods the tunnel accommodates up to four passenger and four freight shuttletrains per hour in each direction. By the end of the decade, these trains carried about half of the car traffic and more than one-third of the coach and truck traffic on the Dover/Folkestone–Calais route the principal artery linking Britain to mainland Europe. In addition, the tunnel accommodates through freight trains and high-speed passenger trains between London and Paris or Brussels. Substantial passenger and cargo traffic moves by sea between the ports of the United Kingdom, Ireland, and Europe. Oil and natural gas, each of which has a national bulk-distribution pipeline system, do not rely on the road and rail networks.

Investment in transportation has sometimes failed to meet rising demand for example, the M25 motorway around London showed signs of overload soon after it was opened in 1986; there is overcrowding on commuter rail services, including London's Underground; congested traffic moves at a snail's pace in cities; and there is continuous pressure to build more motorways and airports to serve London.

During the 1980s British Telecom (BT) was privatized, and the government subsequently deregulated the country's telecommunications sector. Although BT has continued to be the largest telecommunications company, several additional operators provide extensive service for cable, wireless, fibre-optic, and other telecommunications services. An independent regulatory agency, the Office of Communications (Ofcom), oversees the sector.

Government and Society
Constitutional framework

The United Kingdom is a constitutional monarchy and a parliamentary democracy. The country's head of state is the reigning king or queen, and the head of government is the prime minister, who is the leader of the majority political party in the House of Commons.

The British constitution is uncodified; it is only partly written and is flexible. Its basic sources are parliamentary and European Union legislation, the European Convention on Human Rights, and decisions by courts of law. Matters for which there is no formal law, such as the resignation of office by a government, follow precedents (conventions) that are open to development or modification. Works of authority, such as Albert Venn Dicey's Lectures Introductory to the Study of the Law of the Constitution (1885), are also considered part of the constitution.

The main elements of the government are the legislature, the executive, and the judiciary. There is some overlap between the branches, as there is no formal separation of powers or system of checks and balances. For example, the lord chancellor traditionally was a member of all three branches, serving as a member of the cabinet (executive branch), as the government's leader in the House of Lords (legislative branch), and as the head of the country's judiciary (judicial branch). However, constitutional reforms enacted in 2005 (and entering into force in 2006) stripped the office of most of its legislative and judicial functions, with those powers devolving to the lord speaker and the lord chief justice, respectively. That reform also created the Supreme Court, which in October 2009 replaced the Appellate Committee of the House of Lords as the venue of last resort in the British legal system.

Sovereignty resides in Parliament, which comprises the monarch, the mainly appointive House of Lords, and the elected House of Commons. The sovereignty of Parliament is expressed in its legislative enactments, which are binding on all, though individuals may contest in the courts the legality of any action under a specific statute. In certain circumstances individuals may also seek protection under European law. Until 1999 the House of Lords consisted mainly of hereditary peers (or nobles). Since then it has comprised mainly appointed peers, selected by successive prime ministers to serve for life. As of March 2016, of 815 lords, 701 were life peers, 88 were hereditary peers, and another 26 were archbishops and bishops. Each of the 650 members of the House of Commons (members of Parliament; MPs) represents an individual constituency (district) by virtue of winning a plurality of votes in the constituency.

All political power rests with the prime minister and the cabinet, and the monarch must act on their advice. The prime minister chooses the cabinet from MPs in his political party. Most cabinet ministers are heads of government departments. The prime minister's authority grew during the 20th century, and, alone or with one or two colleagues, the prime minister increasingly has made decisions previously made by the cabinet as a whole. Prime ministers have nevertheless been overruled by the cabinet on many occasions and must generally have its support to exercise their powers.

Because the party with a majority in the House of Commons supports the cabinet, it exercises the sovereignty of Parliament. The royal right of veto has not been exercised since the early 18th century, and the legislative power of the House of Lords was reduced in 1911 to the right to delay legislation. The cabinet plans and lays before Parliament all important bills. Although the cabinet thus controls the lawmaking machinery, it is also subject to Parliament; it must expound and defend its policy in debate, and its continuation in office depends on the support of the House of Commons.

The executive apparatus, the cabinet secretariat, was developed after World War I and carries out the cabinet's decisions. It also prepares the cabinet's agenda, records its conclusions, and communicates them to the government departments that implement them.

Regional government

Within the United Kingdom, national assemblies in Scotland, Wales, and Northern Ireland took power in 1999 and assumed some powers previously held exclusively by the central Parliament at Westminster, to which they remain subordinate. The central Parliament retains full legislative and executive control over England, which lacks a separate regional assembly.

Scotland's Parliament has wide powers over such matters as health, education, housing, transport, the environment, and agriculture. It also has the power to increase or decrease the British income tax rate within Scotland by up to three percentage points. The central Parliament retains responsibility for foreign affairs, defense, social security, and overall economic policy. Unlike the members of the House of Commons, members of the Scottish Parliament are chosen under a system of proportional representation. Scotland has a distinct legal system based on Roman law. In 2011 the Scottish National Party formed Scotland's first majority government, which pledged an independence forum by 2015.

Since 1999 Wales has also had its own assembly, but only in 2011 did that National Assembly gain direct lawmaking power. It broadly administers the same services as the Scottish Parliament. Like Scottish legislators, members of the Welsh assembly are elected by proportional representation.

The Northern Ireland Assembly gained limited legislative and executive power at the end of 1999. Its members, like those of the other regional assemblies, are elected by proportional representation. It has power over matters concerning agriculture, economic development, education, the environment, health, and social services, but the Westminster government retains control over foreign affairs, defense, general economic policy, taxation, policing, and criminal justice. Divisions between unionist (Protestant) and nationalist (Roman Catholic) factions in the Northern Ireland Assembly, however, have threatened its future. If either faction withdraws from the assembly, the region could return to the system of direct rule by the central government that prevailed in Northern Ireland from 1973 to 1999.

Local government

Each part of the United Kingdom has a distinct system of local government. (For a full account of local government in each part of the United Kingdom, see the discussions of local government in the articles on England, Wales, Scotland, and Northern Ireland.) Local governments have very few legislative powers and must act within the framework of laws passed by the central Parliament (and by the Scottish Parliament in Scotland). Nevertheless, they do have the power to enact regulations and to levy council taxes (property taxes) within limits set by the central government. They are funded by the council taxes that they levy, by business rates (taxes levied on nonresidential properties, such as stores, offices, factories, and warehouses), by fees for services, and by grants from the central government.

Local governments in the United Kingdom are responsible for a range of community services, including environmental matters, education, highways and traffic, social services, firefighting, sanitation, planning, housing, parks and recreation, and elections. In Scotland and Wales regional governments handle some of these functions, and local governments handle the remainder. In Northern Ireland the Northern Ireland Assembly is responsible for many of these functions. The responsibilities of local governments in Northern Ireland are limited to environmental matters, sanitation, and recreation.

Parts of the United Kingdom have as many as three levels, or tiers, of local government, each with its own responsibilities, whereas other areas have only a single tier or two tiers. Throughout England, parish and town councils form the lowest tier of local government. (Parishes are civil subdivisions, usually centred on a village or small town, that are distinct from church bodies.) They have the power to assess "precepts" (surcharges) on the local rates and a range of rights and duties, including maintenance of commons, recreational facilities, and environmental quality and participation in the planning process. Community councils perform a similar role in Wales, whereas community councils in Scotland are voluntary and consultative bodies with few statutory powers. This lowest level of local government has no counterpart in Northern Ireland.

The next tier of local government is usually known in England and Northern Ireland as a district, borough, or city. In Northern Ireland this is the only level of local government. In Scotland and Wales this second tier is the only one with broad powers over major local government functions. In Wales these local government areas are known as either counties or county boroughs, while in Scotland they are variously known as council areas or local government authorities or, in some cases, cities. In some areas of England this second tier of local government is the only one with broad statutory and administrative powers.

These areas are known in England as unitary authorities (since they form a single tier of local government above the parishes and towns) or metropolitan boroughs (which are functionally equivalent to unitary authorities but form part of a larger metropolitan county). In other areas of England, districts, boroughs, and cities form an intermediate tier of local government between the towns and parishes on the one hand and administrative counties on the other. Administrative counties, which cover much of England, are the highest tier of local government where they exist.

In Greater London, boroughs form the lowest tier of local government and are responsible for most local government functions. However, in 2000 a new Greater London Authority (GLA) was established with very limited revenue-gathering powers but with responsibility for public transport, policing, emergency services, the environment, and planning in Greater London as a whole. The GLA consists of a directly elected mayor (a constitutional innovation for the United Kingdom, which had never previously filled any executive post by direct election) and a 25-member assembly elected by proportional representation.

Whereas the administrative counties of England and the counties and county boroughs of Wales have statutory and administrative powers, there are other areas throughout the United Kingdom that are called counties but lack administrative power. In England, metropolitan counties cover metropolitan areas; they serve as geographic and statistical units, but since 1986 their administrative powers have belonged to their constituent metropolitan boroughs. Moreover, in England there is a unit known variously as a ceremonial county or a geographic county.

These counties also form geographic and statistical units. In most cases they comprise an administrative county and one or more unitary authorities. In other cases they comprise one or more unitary authorities without an administrative county. Greater London and each of the metropolitan counties also constitute ceremonial and geographic counties. These areas are known as ceremonial counties because each has a lord lieutenant and a high sheriff who serve as the representatives of the monarch in the county and who represent the county at the ceremonial functions of the monarchy.

Finally, every part of the United Kingdom lies within what is known as a historic county. The historic counties have formed geographic and cultural units since the Middle Ages, and they historically had a variety of administrative powers. The Local Government Act of 1888 regularized the administrative powers of counties and reassigned them to new administrative counties with the same names as the historic counties but with different boundaries in some cases. Successive local government reorganizations in the 1970s and '90s redrew the boundaries of administrative units in the United Kingdom so that no remaining administrative unit corresponds directly to a historic county, although many administrative and geographic counties and other local government units carry the names of historic counties. Still, even though they lack administrative power, historic counties remain important cultural units. They serve as a focus for local identity, and cultural institutions such as sporting associations are often organized by historic county.

Justice

Recruited from successful practicing lawyers, judges in the United Kingdom are appointed and virtually irremovable. The courts alone declare the law, but the courts accept any act of Parliament as part of the law. As courts in the United Kingdom do not possess the power of judicial review, no court can declare a statute invalid.

An accused person is presumed innocent until proved guilty. The courts strictly enforce a law of contempt to prevent newspapers or television from prejudicing the trial of the accused before a jury. Verdicts in criminal cases rest on a majority vote of the jury (in Scotland a simple majority, in England, Wales, and Northern Ireland with no more than two dissenting votes). Capital punishment was abolished in 1965. Almost all defendants in criminal cases in the Crown Courts (in Scotland the High Court of Justiciary), which deal with all serious cases, are granted publicly funded legal aid.

More than 90 percent of criminal cases in England and Wales are tried and determined by about 30,000 justices of the peace, who are unpaid laypersons, or by the more than 60 stipendiary (paid) magistrates, who are trained lawyers. More serious crimes also come initially before a magistrate's court. The system is similar in Northern Ireland, but in Scotland district and sheriff courts try most criminal cases. The police must bring an arrested person before a magistrate within 36 hours, but the magistrate can authorize further detention without charge for up to 96 hours. Only 1 percent of suspects are held without charge for more than 24 hours, however. The magistrate decides whether the accused should be held on bail or in custody.

The vast majority of civil actions in England, Wales, and Northern Ireland are tried in local county courts, whose jurisdiction is limited by the nature of the action and the amount of money at stake. In Scotland, sheriff courts and the Court of Session try all civil actions.

Appeals in civil and criminal matters move from the High and Crown courts to the Court of Appeal, from which for centuries cases of legal importance could be appealed to the Appellate Committee of the House of Lords, better known as the Law Lords. In October 2009, however, as a result of constitutional reform, the Appellate Committee was abolished and replaced by a newly constituted Supreme Court of the United Kingdom, made up of 12 independently appointed justices. At the same time, the Supreme Court also assumed the devolution jurisdiction previously held by the Judicial Committee of the Privy Council. In Scotland only civil matters may be appealed to the House of Lords.

Political process

All citizens aged 18 or older are eligible to vote in parliamentary and local elections as well as in elections to the European Parliament. All other public posts are filled by appointment. Each member of the House of Commons represents one parliamentary constituency. Constituency populations historically have varied considerably, with those in Scotland and Wales being much smaller than those in England. This overrepresentation for Scotland and Wales dates from the 18th century and the 1940s, respectively; however, because of the wide array of powers vested in the Scottish Parliament, the disparity in constituency size between England and Scotland was eliminated at the May 2005 election, when Scotland's seats in the House of Commons were reduced from 72 to 59. Constituencies in Northern Ireland are slightly smaller than those in England. As there are no residency requirements, many members of Parliament reside outside the constituency that they represent.

Registration of voters is compulsory and carried out annually. Candidates for election to Parliament or a local council are normally chosen by the local parties. There are no primary elections along U.S. lines, for example, nor would such a system be easy because the timing of general elections is unpredictable.

The House of Commons is elected for a maximum term of five years. Traditionally, at any time during those five years, the prime minister had the right to ask the monarch to dissolve Parliament and call a general election. However, the Fixed-term Parliaments Act 2011 mandated a five-year period between elections and proscribed early elections except under special circumstances: (1) if a motion for an early general election is agreed upon either by at least two-thirds of the whole House of Commons or without division (that is, when a voice vote is sufficient to determine the will of the House of Commons) or (2) if a motion of no confidence is passed and no alternative government is confirmed by the House of Commons within 14 days. Parliamentary candidates' campaign spending is strictly limited.

Since 2000, national party expenditure, which was previously unrestricted, has been limited to a maximum of £20 million per party. In addition, each party is allocated free election broadcasts on the main television channels. Televised debates between the leaders of the principal parties (de facto candidates for prime minister) were a part of the campaign process for the first time in the 2010 general election. No paid political advertising is permitted on television or radio. These provisions and the uncertainty about the timing of an election produce campaigns that are, by international standards, unusually brief and relatively inexpensive.

A two-party system has existed in the United Kingdom since the late 17th century. Since the mid-1920s the dominant groupings have been the Conservative Party and the Labour Party. However, several smaller parties e.g., the Liberal Democrats, the United Kingdom Independence Party, the Scottish National Party, Plaid Cymru (the Welsh Nationalist Party), and loyalist (unionist) and republican (nationalist) political parties in Northern Ireland have gained representation in Parliament, especially since the 1970s. The two-party system is one of the outstanding features of British politics and generally has produced firm and decisive government.

The practice of simple plurality voting in single-member constituencies (commonly referred to a "first past the post") has tended to exaggerate the majority of the winning party and to diminish the representation and influence of third parties, except for those with a geographic base of support (e.g., Plaid Cymru). When the 2010 general election resulted in a "hung parliament" (no party with enough seats to form a majority government), the Liberal Democrats who were courted as coalition partner by both the Conservatives (who captured the most seats) and Labour (which finished a distant second) used as a bargaining chip the possibility of changing to a system of proportional representation that would benefit third parties.

The two-party system, together with uncertainty about the timing of a general election, has produced the British phenomenon of the official opposition. Its decisive characteristic is that the main opposition party forms an alternative, or "shadow," government, ready at any time to take office, in recognition of which the leader of the opposition receives an official salary.

Despite several high-profile female monarchs and politicians, men have dominated politics in the United Kingdom for centuries. In 2011, however, centuries-old succession laws stipulating that the heir to the throne be the first-born son of the monarch and that sons take precedence over daughters in succession were slated for change to remove gender as a qualification. Nevertheless, while women have made strong political gains in much of western Europe, especially in Scandinavia, breakthroughs for women in British national elections have been rare. Throughout much of the 20th century, only a few women won elections; before the 1980s the high point for female representation in the House of Commons was 29 in 1964. Indeed, many women who were able to win election to the House of Commons were of aristocratic stock or widows of influential politicians.

One such exception was Margaret Thatcher, who was first elected to Parliament in 1959 and became Britain's first female prime minister in 1979. However, during the 1980s women began to make gains, with

60 female candidates winning seats in Parliament in 1992. In order to increase its appeal to women and increase the number of women MPs, the Labour Party adopted a policy of all-women shortlists for half of its "target seats" (i.e., seats where an existing Labour MP was standing down or where Conservative MPs had small majorities) for the 1997 election, and, though the policy subsequently was ruled in violation of equal rights laws, 120 women 101 from the Labour Party were elected to the House of Commons. Even with the law invalidated, 118 women won election in 2001. In addition to women, minorities have had some success in national elections. There consistently have been several Jewish members of the House of Commons, and Sikh and Muslim candidates also have had limited success.

Security

The United Kingdom has no national police force nor any minister exclusively responsible for the police. Each provincial force is overseen by an elected police and crime commissioner (PCC), whose performance is scrutinized by police and crime panels. PCCs are responsible for the totality of policing, answerable to the communities they serve, and charged with holding accountable the chief constable and police force.

The commissioner of London's Metropolitan Police has a status similar to that of a chief constable. Scotland Yard (the criminal investigation department of the Metropolitan Police) assists other police forces and handles the British responsibilities of the International Criminal Police Organization (Interpol).

The British police, popularly known as "bobbies," wear a uniform that is nonmilitary in appearance. Their only regular weapon is a short, wooden truncheon, which they keep out of sight and may not employ except in self-defense or to restore order. Police on a dangerous mission may carry firearms for that specific occasion.

Responsibility for national defense rests with the prime minister and the cabinet. The secretary of state for defense formulates defense policy. His ministry has responsibility for the armed forces. The secretary of state is advised by the chief of the defense staff, aided by the chiefs of the three services the army, navy, and air force. Britain has been an active member of the North Atlantic Treaty Organization (NATO), deploying its troops in various theatres of conflict. Internal security and intelligence are handled by the MI5 government agency, and foreign intelligence services are carried out by MI6.

Health and welfare

The National Health Service

The National Health Service (NHS) provides comprehensive health care throughout the United Kingdom. The NHS provides medical care through a tripartite structure of primary care, hospitals, and community health care. The main element in primary care is the system of general practitioners (family doctors), who provide preventive and curative care and who refer patients to hospital and specialist services. All consultations with a general practitioner under the NHS are free.

The other major types of primary medical care are dentistry and pharmaceutical and opthalmic services. These are the only services of the NHS for which charges are levied, though persons under age 16, past retirement, or with low incomes are usually exempt. Everyone else must pay charges that are below the full cost of the services involved.

Under the Department of Health in England are four regional health directors who oversee area health authorities, whose major responsibility is to run the hospital service. (Overseeing the health authorities in Scotland, Wales, and Northern Ireland is the responsibility of their respective parliament or assembly.) Hospitals absorb more than two-thirds of the NHS budget. All hospital treatment under the NHS is free, including consultations with doctors, nursing, drugs, and intensive care, whatever the type of medical problem and however long the hospital stay. Hospital doctors are paid a salary rather than a fee for service but can combine salaried work for the NHS with a private practice.

The Community Health Service has three functions: to provide preventive health services; to act as a liaison with local government, especially over matters of public health; and to cooperate with local government personal social service departments to enable health and personal care to be handled together whenever possible.

Individuals can register with any NHS general practitioner in their area who is prepared to add them to his or her list of patients. Anyone who wishes to change to another doctor may do so. Except in emergencies, patients are referred to a hospital by their general practitioner, allowing patients an element of choice.

Apart from the charges mentioned above, treatment under the NHS is free to the patient. The service is almost entirely funded by government revenues, with less than 5 percent of NHS revenue coming from charges. This arrangement is unique among industrialized countries. There is no substantial reliance on private medical insurance (as, for example, in the United States).

The NHS budget, like that for any other government service, is determined by negotiations between the Treasury and the spending departments, as modified by subsequent discussion in the cabinet. The resulting figure is a budget for the NHS as a whole. The division of money throughout the United Kingdom is partly constrained by a formula designed to improve the geographic distribution of medical resources. Each regional authority divides its total funds among the area health authorities.

Alongside the NHS is a system of private medical care both for primary care and for hospital treatment. Although it grew somewhat in the 1980s and '90s, the sector absorbs only about one-tenth of the total expenditure on doctors and hospital inpatient care. Most private care is financed by voluntary private medical insurance.

Although the NHS is a popular institution, it is not without problems: resources are scarce, many hospital buildings are old, there are waiting lists for nonurgent conditions, the distribution of health care by social class and by region is less equal than many would wish, and management needs to be improved. The advantages, however, are enormous. The NHS is very inexpensive by international standards; in the late 1990s, for example, the United Kingdom spent about half the percentage of GDP on health care as the United States. Despite such low spending, health in the United Kingdom, measured in terms of infant mortality and life expectancy, matches that in comparable countries. The variation in the quality and quantity of treatment by income level is smaller than in most other countries. The system is able to direct resources toward specific regions and specific types of care. Treatment is free, whatever the extent and duration of illness, no one is denied care because of low income, and no one fears financial ruin as a result of treatment.

Cash benefits

The current system of cash benefits, though substantially modified since its introduction in 1946, is based on the 1942 "Beveridge Report." Every employed person pays a national insurance contribution, which since 1975 has taken the form of a percentage of earnings, although contributions are due only on amounts up to about 150 percent of nationwide average earnings. Employers collect the contribution, and there is also an employer contribution. Separate arrangements exist for the self-employed. The revenue from contributions goes into the National Insurance Fund.

Insured individuals are entitled to unemployment compensation, cash benefits during sickness or disability, and a retirement pension. There are also benefits for individuals injured in work-related accidents and for widows. Whether or not they receive an insurance benefit, all are eligible for a noncontributory benefit. Employees who lose their jobs through no fault of their own receive lump-sum redundancy, or severance, payments, whose cost is met in part by their employers and in part from a general levy on employers.

The major noncontributory benefits, paid out of general tax revenues, offer poverty relief to individuals and families whose income and savings fall below some prescribed level. The benefit of last resort is income support (formerly called the supplementary benefit); it is payable to individuals whose entitlement to insurance benefits has been exhausted or has left them with a very low income and to those who never had any entitlement to an insurance benefit. Other means-tested benefits assist low-paid working families with children and help people on low incomes with their housing costs. An important class of noncontributory benefits is not means-tested, the major example being the child benefit, a weekly tax-free payment for each child, usually payable to the mother.

The 1946 system has changed substantially over the years, with a burst of reform in the mid-1970s, including an increase in earnings-related pensions, and another in the late 1990s. In the late 1990s a working-families tax credit replaced income support for low-paid working households with children, and the government introduced a national minimum wage. The government also introduced a children's tax credit to provide additional support to low- and middle-income families. There was a review of the benefit system in 1985 that changed the detailed workings of several benefits in 1988 but left the basic structure intact.

Housing

During the mid-20th century, local governments developed council houses (public housing estates) throughout the United Kingdom. At public housing's peak, about 1970, local governments owned 30 percent of all housing in the country. Under the Housing (Homeless Persons) Act of 1977 (which amended older legislation), local governments have a statutory obligation in certain circumstances to find housing for homeless families. Partly for that reason, they keep a substantial stock of housing for rent, maintain waiting lists, and allocate housing according to need. Following the introduction of "right to buy" legislation in 1980, many tenants became owner-occupiers. By the beginning of the 21st century, the proportion of homes owned by local governments had almost halved.

Education

Overall responsibility for education and children's services in England rests with the Department of Education, which is accountable to Parliament. Separate departments of education are headed by ministers who answer to the assemblies in Scotland (Education and Lifelong Learning Department), Wales (Department of Education and Skills), and Northern Ireland (Department for Education). State-funded primary and secondary education are a local responsibility, generally overseen by the local authority. There is also a small private sector.

Primary education is free and compulsory from age 5 to 11. Secondary education is organized in a variety of ways for children aged 11 to 19 and is free and compulsory to age 16. In most parts of the United Kingdom, secondary schools are comprehensive; that is, they are open to pupils of all abilities. Pupils may stay on past the minimum school-leaving age of 16 to earn a certificate or take public examinations that qualify them for higher education.

The state finances primary and secondary education out of central and local tax revenues. Most expenditures take place at the local level, though about half of local revenues derive from the central government. Under the government of Prime Minister Tony Blair, a new type of school was introduced academies, which receive their funding directly from the central government (though they are eligible for some local funding and were initially required to have private sponsors). Academies operate independently of the local authority and have greater freedom than traditional ("maintained") state schools over their curriculum and finance, as well as teachers' pay and conditions. Academies generally arise from underperforming schools that have been given over to a new provider, whereas free schools, another new type of institution, operate as academies do but differ from them in that they are wholly new schools. Although the Conservative–Liberal Democrat coalition government led by David Cameron pushed for a significant expansion of academies and free schools, in the early 2010s they still constituted only a small percentage of state-funded schools.

Private schools

Alongside the state sector, a small number of private schools (often called "public schools") provide education for a small percentage of children. Their existence is controversial. It is argued that private schools divert gifted children and teachers and scarce financial resources from state schools and that they perpetuate economic and social divisions (an argument that some have extended to include academies and free schools). The counterarguments focus on their high quality, the beneficial effects of competition, and parents' freedom of choice.

Higher education

Universities historically have been independent and self-governing; however, they have close links with the central government because a large proportion of their income derives from public funds. Higher education also takes place in other colleges.

Students do not have a right to a place at a university; they are carefully selected by examination performance, and the dropout rate is low by international standards. Most students receive state-funded grants inversely related to their parents' income to cover the tuition fees. In addition, most students receive state-funded loans to cover living expenses. Foreign students and British students taking a degree at an overseas university are not generally eligible for public funding.

Public funds flow to universities through recurrent grants and in the form of tuition fees; universities also derive income from foreign students and from various private-sector sources. After a major expansion in the 1960s, the system came under pressure in the 1980s. Public funding became more restricted, and the grant system no longer supported students adequately. The government introduced the present system of student loans to replace dwindling grants for living expenses and established higher-education funding councils in each part of the United Kingdom (England, Wales, Scotland, and Northern Ireland) to coordinate state support of higher education. In 2010, in the interest of budget reduction, the government raised the maximum level of tuition for higher educational institutions in England to £9,000 (about $11,600) per year. In 2016 that limit was raised to £9,250 (about $11,900), with plans to allow further increases to keep up with inflation.

The Open University a unique innovation in higher education is a degree-granting institution that provides courses of study for adults through television, radio, and local study programs. Applicants must apply for a number of places limited at any time by the availability of teachers.

Cultural

English culture tends to dominate the formal cultural life of the United Kingdom, but Scotland, Wales, and Northern Ireland have also made important contributions, as have the cultures that British colonialism brought into contact with the homeland. Scotland, Wales, and Northern Ireland share fully in the common culture but also preserve lively traditions that predate political union with England.

Widespread changes in the United Kingdom's cultural life occurred after 1945. The most remarkable was perhaps the emergence first of Liverpool and then of London in the 1960s as a world centre of popular culture. The Beatles were only the first and best-known of the many British rock groups to win a world following. British clothing designers for a time led the world as innovators of new styles of dress for both men and women, and the brightly coloured outfits sold in London's Carnaby Street and King's Road shops briefly became more symbolic of Britain than the traditionally staid tailoring of Savile Row.

Underlying both this development and a similar if less-remarked renewal of vigour in more traditional fields were several important social developments in the decades after World War II. Most evident was the rising standard of education. The number of pupils going on to higher education increased dramatically after World War II and was matched by a major expansion in the number of universities and other institutions of higher education. In society in general there was a marked increase in leisure. Furthermore, immigration, particularly from the West Indies and South Asia, introduced new cultural currents to the United Kingdom and contributed to innovation in music, film, literature, and other arts.

Daily life and social customs

The United Kingdom's cultural traditions are reflective of the country's heterogeneity and its central importance in world affairs over the past several centuries. Each constituent part of the United Kingdom England, Scotland, Wales, and Northern Ireland maintains its own unique customs, traditions, cuisine, and festivals. Moreover, as Britain's empire spanned the globe, it became a focal point of immigration, especially after the independence of its colonies, from its colonial possessions. As a result, immigrants from all corners of the world have entered the United Kingdom and settled throughout the country, leaving indelible imprints on British culture. Thus, at the beginning of the 21st century, age-old English, Irish, Scottish, and Welsh customs stood alongside the rich traditions of Afro-Caribbean, Asian, and Muslim immigrants, placing the United Kingdom among the world's most cosmopolitan and diverse countries.

The arts

From the plays of William Shakespeare to the music of the Sex Pistols, British art has had a tremendous impact on world culture. Writers from every part of the United Kingdom, joined by immigrants from parts of the former British Empire and the Commonwealth, have enriched the English language and world literature alike with their work. British studios, playwrights, directors, and actors have been remarkable pioneers of stage and screen. British comedians have brought laughter to diverse audiences and been widely imitated; British composers have found devoted listeners around the world, as have various contemporary pop groups and singer-songwriters; and British philosophers have had a tremendous influence in shaping the course of scientific and moral inquiry. From medieval time to the present, this extraordinary flowering of the arts has been encouraged at every level of society. Early royal patronage played an important role in the development of the arts in Britain, and since the mid 20th century the British government has done much to foster their growth.

The independent Arts Council of Great Britain, which was founded in 1946, supported many kinds of contemporary creative and performing arts until 1994, when it devolved into the Arts Council of England (which became Arts Council England in 2003 after joining with the Regional Arts Boards), the Arts Council of Wales, and the Scottish Arts Council (the last becoming Creative Scotland 2010, when it consolidated with Scottish Screen). Having developed separately from the Arts Council of Great Britain, the Arts Council of Northern Ireland reorganized in 1995.

The state-owned British Broadcasting Corporation (BBC) and privately owned Channel Four Television are also major patrons of the arts, especially music and film. The work of filmmakers and actors throughout the United Kingdom is supported by the Film Council, a government board that helps fund productions and secure film-related services. This support has contributed to the great expansion of the market for cultural goods and of audiences for the arts generally. As in many other highly developed countries, the clash of tastes and values between generations and, to some extent, between social classes has occasionally been sharp, as it was in the 1960s and '70s. However, the overall effect of social and financial diversity has been to make culture a major British industry, which employs more than a million people and commands one-sixth of the world's cultural exports, three times greater than Britain's share of world trade overall.

Cultural institutions

The United Kingdom contains many cultural treasures. It is home to a wide range of learned societies, including the British Academy, the Royal Geographical Society, and the Royal Society of Edinburgh. The British Museum in London houses historical artifacts from all parts of the globe. London is also home to many museums (e.g., the National Gallery, the National Portrait Gallery, the Tate galleries, the Imperial War Museum, and the Victoria and Albert Museum) and theatres (e.g., the Royal National Theatre and those in the world-renowned West End theatre district). Cultural institutions also abound throughout the country. Among the many libraries and museums of interest in Scotland, Wales, and Northern Ireland are the Royal Museum, the Museum of Scotland, and the Writers' Museum in Edinburgh, the Museum of Scottish Country Life in Glasgow, the National Museum of Wales in Cardiff, and the Ulster Museum in Belfast.

Sports and recreation

The global spread of sports that had their origins in Britain was central to the development of modern sports in the 18th and 19th centuries and is one of the British Empire's important cultural legacies. The modern game of football (soccer) is generally accepted to have originated in England. The Football Association, the game's first organization, was founded in England in 1863, and the first football match played between England and Scotland the oldest rivalry in the sport was at Glasgow in 1872. English football fans can follow three national divisions and the celebrated premiership, which includes such legendary clubs as Manchester United, Arsenal, and Liverpool FC. Scotland has three national divisions as well and a premiership that features the Celtic and Rangers clubs of Glasgow; Wales and Northern Ireland also have national leagues. The Scottish and English national teams regularly appear in international competitions. In 1966 England hosted and won the World Cup; it was the third host nation to win the championship.

Rugby and cricket have also long enjoyed great popularity in Britain. According to tradition, rugby began in 1823 at Rugby School in England. In 1871 the Rugby Football Union was formed as the English governing body, and the rival Rugby Football League was founded in 1895. England, Scotland, and Wales all have club competitions in both union and league versions of the game. The three also send national teams to the Six Nations Championship and to World Cup tournaments. Cricket's origins may date to 13th-century England, and county competition in England was formally organized in the 19th century. International matches, known as tests, began in 1877 with a match between England and Australia.

Great Britain has attended every modern Olympic Games, beginning with the first competition in Athens, Greece, in 1896. Britain has hosted the Games three times in London, in 1908, 1948, and 2012. At the 1896 Games weight lifter Launceston Elliot was the first Briton to win a gold medal, and in 1908 figure skater Madge Cave Syers became the first female athlete to win a medal in the Winter Games. British athletes have won hundreds of medals over the years, making especially strong showings in athletics, tennis, rowing, yachting, and figure skating. Several British athletes have put forth memorable performances in track-and-field events, including sprinter Harold Abrahams in the 1920s, middle-distance runners Sebastian Coe and Steve Ovett, and two-time decathlon gold medalist Daley Thompson in the 1970s and '80s. At the 2000 Summer Games rower Steve Redgrave accomplished the rare feat of earning gold medals in five consecutive Games. At the 2012 Games in London, athletes representing the United Kingdom claimed 65 medals.

Britain is home to several important international sports competitions. The Open Championship also known, outside of Britain, as the British

Open is a golf tournament held annually, often at the world-renowned course at St. Andrews in Scotland. The All-England (Wimbledon) Championships is one of the world's leading tennis competitions. Celebrated horse-racing events include the Royal Ascot, the Derby, and the Grand National steeplechase. The Henley Royal Regatta is the world's premiere rowing championship.

Although the United Kingdom's climate often rewards staying indoors, the British are enthusiasts of outdoor leisure activities and are well served by an extensive network of hiking and bicycling paths, national parks, and other amenities. Especially popular are the Lake District, which preserves a scenic area commemorated in many works by English poets; the rugged Scottish Highlands and Inner Hebrides islands; and the mountainous Welsh region of Snowdonia National Park, a magnet for climbers from around the world.

Media and publishing

The communications media press, publishing, broadcasting, and entertainment reach audiences ranging from the millions for television, radio, and national newspapers to small minorities for local papers, specialist periodicals, or experimental theatre and film. In addition to their presence in print, most newspapers disseminate information through the Internet, to which access grew rapidly during the late 1990s. By the early 21st century about one-third of all households had personal computers with access to the Internet.

Newspapers

In both sales and reputation the national papers published in London dominate. Within the national newspaper business in the United Kingdom, a distinction has developed between popular papers (often tabloids) with multimillion circulation and quality broadsheet papers with relatively small sales. Four "populars" account for about five-sixths of the total morning paper circulation. Generally, British newspapers are not formally tied to specific political parties. However, most display clear political sympathies that are usually determined by their proprietors. The tabloid Daily Mail and the broadsheet The Daily Telegraph have consistently supported the Conservative Party, while the tabloid The Daily Mirror and the broadsheet The Guardian (published in both London and Manchester) have normally supported Labour.

The Times of London is one of the world's oldest newspapers. The United Kingdom's biggest-selling newspaper, The Sun whose popularity since it was bought by Rupert Murdoch's News International company in 1969 has stemmed from a diet of sensational personality-based news stories, show-business gossip, lively sports reporting, and pictures of scantily dressed young women supported Labour in the early 1970s, switched to the Conservative Party under Margaret Thatcher in 1979, and switched back again to Labour in the late 1990s. In England there are also several regional dailies and weeklies and national weeklies some targeting particular ethnic communities.

The Welsh press includes several daily papers (e.g., the Western Mail and the South Wales Echo) as well as a number of weekly English-language, bilingual, or Welsh-language newspapers. Scotland has national daily newspapers based in Edinburgh and Glasgow with wide circulation (e.g., The Scotsman, the Daily Record, and The Herald) and a number of regional weeklies as well. Northern Ireland's daily papers (e.g., the Belfast Telegraph and The Irish News) are all published in Belfast. There is a large periodical press in the United Kingdom that ranges from such traditional publications as The Economist, The Spectator, and New Statesman to more specialized and, often, more mercurial journals.

Broadcasting

The BBC, which had been established as an independent public corporation in 1927, held a monopoly of both radio and television broadcasting until 1954, when the Independent Television Authority (ITA) was established to provide the facilities for commercial television companies. The ITA's successor today is the Office of Communications (Ofcom). Created by the Communications Act of 2003, Ofcom is responsible for regulating all commercial radio and television services, including satellite and cable, as well as all wired, wireless, and broadband telecommunications. Commercial television broadcasters include Channel Four and the ITV network. Almost every household receives the terrestrial television channels, and by the early 21st century about one in four households also could receive several dozen additional channels by satellite or cable. The satellite and cable market is dominated by Sky PLC (formerly BSkyB), which is partly owned by Murdoch's News International. Sky, which serves Austria, Germany, Ireland, and Italy as well as the United Kingdom, also operates a 24-hour news channel and several sports channels.

A new 11-year charter for the BBC was enacted in 2016. Under it the BBC continues to draw its revenue from license fees (on a scale fixed by the government) from persons owning television sets. Its governance, however, shifted from the external BBC Trust and internal BBC Executive to a new "unitary board," the majority of whose members are appointed by the BBC. The board also includes members nominated by the government whose involvement guarantees that the individual interests of England, Scotland, Wales, and Northern Ireland are represented. Whereas regulation of the BBC was formerly provided by the BBC Trust, that responsibility now falls to Ofcom and its governing board, which also license and regulate commercial television companies, which earn revenue by selling advertising time and (in the case of some satellite and cable companies) subscription and pay-per-view channels.

The BBC operates two terrestrial television channels, and Ofcom operates three. On its second television channel, the BBC tends to offer programs of above-average intellectual and cultural interest competition that the Channel Four commercial channel meets with its own cultural programs. The BBC also provides a 24-hour news service and a channel devoted to live proceedings of Parliament to people able to receive satellite, cable, or digital television services. In addition, BBC Radio operates a comprehensive external service, broadcasting around the world in more than 40 languages, as well as a world service in English 24 hours a day.

Both the BBC and terrestrial commercial channels supply educational programs for schools and for adult studies. The Open University, offering degree courses to people who lack formal academic qualifications, uses educational programs that are broadcast by the BBC; these programs are backed by correspondence courses.

The BBC and Ofcom are public bodies that in the last resort can be controlled by the government, and Parliament can alter the terms of their authority. The government has the statutory power to veto a broadcast, but only rarely does it interfere with the day-to-day management of the BBC or Ofcom. There are more than 30 BBC local radio stations and more than 200 commercial local radio stations serving the United Kingdom.

For a more-detailed discussion of cultural life in England, Scotland, Wales, and Northern Ireland, see the cultural life sections of the articles England, Scotland, Wales, and Northern Ireland.

History

This discussion encompasses the history of England and Great Britain. Histories of the other three constituent parts of the United Kingdom can be found in Northern Ireland, Scotland, and Wales.

Ancient Britain

Archaeologists working in Norfolk in the early 21st century discovered stone tools that suggest the presence of humans in Britain from about 800,000 to 1 million years ago. These startling discoveries underlined the extent to which archaeological research is responsible for any knowledge of Britain before the Roman conquest (begun ad 43). Britain's ancient history is thus lacking in detail, for archaeology can rarely identify personalities, motives, or exact dates or present more than a general overview. All that is available is a picture of successive cultures and some knowledge of economic development. But even in Roman times Britain lay on the periphery of the civilized world, and Roman historians, for the most part, provide for that period only a framework into which the results of archaeological research can be fitted. Britain truly emerged into the light of history only after the Saxon settlements in the 5th century ad.

Until late in the Mesolithic Period, Britain formed part of the continental landmass and was easily accessible to migrating hunters.

The cutting of the land bridge, c. 6000–5000 bc, had important effects: migration became more difficult and remained for long impossible to large numbers. Thus Britain developed insular characteristics, absorbing and adapting rather than fully participating in successive continental cultures. And within the island geography worked to a similar end; the fertile southeast was more receptive of influence from the adjacent continent than were the less-accessible hill areas of the west and north. Yet in certain periods the use of sea routes brought these too within the ambit of the continent.

From the end of the Ice Age (c. 11,000 bc), there was a gradual amelioration of climate leading to the replacement of tundra by forest and of reindeer hunting by that of red deer and elk. Valuable insight on contemporary conditions was gained by the excavation of a lakeside settlement at Star Carr, North Yorkshire, which was occupied for about 20 successive winters by hunting people in the 8th millennium bc.

Pre-Roman Britain

Neolithic Period

A major change occurred c. 4000 bc with the introduction of agriculture by Neolithic immigrants from the coasts of western and possibly northwestern Europe. They were pastoralists as well as tillers of the soil. Tools were commonly of flint won by mining, but axes of volcanic rock were also traded by prospectors exploiting distant outcrops. The dead were buried in communal graves of two main kinds: in the west, tombs were built out of stone and concealed under mounds of rubble; in the stoneless eastern areas the dead were buried under long barrows (mounds of earth), which normally contained timber structures. Other evidence of religion comes from enclosures (e.g., Windmill Hill, Wiltshire), which are now believed to have been centres of ritual and of seasonal tribal feasting. From them developed, late in the 3rd millennium, more clearly ceremonial ditch-enclosed earthworks known as henge monuments. Some, like Durrington Walls, Wiltshire, are of great size and enclose subsidiary timber circles. British Neolithic culture thus developed its own individuality.

Early in the 2nd millennium or perhaps even earlier, from c. 2300 bc, changes were introduced by the Beaker folk from the Low Countries and the middle Rhine. These people buried their dead in individual graves, often with the drinking vessel that gives their culture its name. The earliest of them still used flint; later groups, however, brought a knowledge of metallurgy and were responsible for the exploitation of gold and copper deposits in Britain and Ireland. They may also have introduced an Indo-European language. Trade was dominated by the chieftains of Wessex, whose rich graves testify to their success. Commerce was far-flung, in one direction to Ireland and Cornwall and in the other to central Europe and the Baltic, whence amber was imported. Amber bead spacers from Wessex have been found in the shaft graves at Mycenae in Greece. It was, perhaps, this prosperity that enabled the Wessex chieftains to construct the remarkable monument of shaped sarsens (large sandstones) known as Stonehenge III. Originally a late Neolithic henge, Stonehenge was uniquely transformed in Beaker times with a circle of large bluestone monoliths transported from southwest Wales.

Little is known in detail of the early and middle Bronze Age. Because of present ignorance of domestic sites, these periods are mainly defined by technological advances and changes in tools or weapons. In general, the southeast of Britain continued in close contact with the continent and the north and west with Ireland.

From about 1200 bc there is clearer evidence for agriculture in the south; the farms consisted of circular huts in groups with small oblong fields and stock enclosures. This type of farm became standard in Britain down to and into the Roman period. From the 8th century onward, British communities developed close contacts with their continental European neighbours. Some of the earliest hill forts in Britain were constructed in this period (e.g., Beacon Hill, near Ivinghoe, Buckinghamshire; or Finavon, Angus); though formally belonging to the late Bronze Age, they usher in the succeeding period.

Iron Age

Knowledge of iron, introduced in the 7th century, was a merely incidental fact: it does not signify a change of population. The centuries 700–400 bc saw continued development of contact with continental Europe. Yet the greater availability of iron facilitated land clearance and thus the growth of population. The earliest ironsmiths made daggers of the Hallstatt type but of a distinctively British form. The settlements were also of a distinctively British type, with the traditional round house, the "Celtic" system of farming with its small fields, and storage pits for grain.

The century following 600 bc saw the building of many large hill forts; these suggest the existence of powerful chieftains and the growth of strife as increasing population created pressures on the land. By 300 bc swords were making their appearance once more in place of daggers. Finally, beginning in the 3rd century, a British form of La Tène Celtic art was developed to decorate warlike equipment such as scabbards, shields, and helmets, and eventually also bronze mirrors and even domestic pottery. During the 2nd century the export of Cornish tin, noted before 300 by Pytheas of Massalia, a Greek explorer, continued; evidence of its destination is provided by the Paul (Cornwall) hoard of north Italian silver coins. In the 1st century bc this trade was in the hands of the Veneti of Brittany; their conquest (56 bc) by Julius Caesar, who destroyed their fleet, seems to have put an end to it.

By 200 Britain had fully developed its insular "Celtic" character. The emergence, however, of the British tribes known to Roman historians was due to limited settlement by tribesmen from Belgic Gaul. Coin finds suggest that southeast Britain was socially and economically bound to Belgic Gaul. The result was a distinctive culture in southeast Britain (especially in Kent and north of the Thames) which represented a later phase of the continental Celtic La Tène culture. Its people used coins and the potter's wheel and cremated their dead, and their better equipment enabled them to begin the exploitation of heavier soils for agriculture.

Roman Britain

The conquest

Julius Caesar conquered Gaul between 58 and 50 bc and invaded Britain in 55 or 54 bc, thereby bringing the island into close contact with the Roman world. Caesar's description of Britain at the time of his invasions is the first coherent account extant. From about 20 bc it is possible to distinguish two principal powers: the Catuvellauni north of the Thames led by Tasciovanus, successor of Caesar's adversary Cassivellaunus, and, south of the river, the kingdom of the Atrebates ruled by Commius and his sons Tincommius, Eppillus, and Verica. Tasciovanus was succeeded in about ad 5 by his son Cunobelinus, who, during a long reign, established power all over the southeast, which he ruled from Camulodunum (Colchester). Beyond these kingdoms lay the Iceni in what is now Norfolk, the Corieltavi in the Midlands, the Dobuni (Dobunni) in the area of Gloucestershire, and the Durotriges in that of Dorset, all of whom issued coins and probably had Belgic rulers. Behind these again lay further independent tribes the Dumnonii of Devon, the Brigantes in the north, and the Silures and Ordovices in Wales. The Belgic and semi-Belgic tribes later formed the civilized nucleus of the Roman province and thus contributed greatly to Roman Britain.

The client relationships that Caesar had established with certain British tribes were extended by Augustus. In particular, the Atrebatic kings welcomed Roman aid in their resistance to Catuvellaunian expansion. The decision of the emperor Claudius to conquer the island was the result partly of his personal ambition, partly of British aggression. Verica had been driven from his kingdom and appealed for help, and it may have been calculated that a hostile Catuvellaunian supremacy would endanger stability across the Channel. Under Aulus Plautius an army of four legions was assembled, together with a number of auxiliary regiments consisting of cavalry and infantry raised among warlike tribes subject to the empire.

After delay caused by the troops' unwillingness to cross the ocean, which they then regarded as the boundary of the human world, a landing was made at Richborough, Kent, in ad 43. The British under Togodumnus and Caratacus, sons and successors of Cunobelinus, were taken by surprise and defeated. They retired to defend the Medway crossing near Rochester but were again defeated in a hard battle. The way to Camulodunum lay open, but Plautius halted at the Thames to await the arrival of the emperor, who took personal command of the closing stages of the campaign. In one short season the main military opposition had been crushed: Togodumnus was dead and Caratacus had fled to Wales.

The rest of Britain was by no means united, for Belgic expansion had created tensions. Some tribes submitted, and subduing the rest remained the task for the year 44. For this purpose smaller expeditionary forces were formed consisting of single legions or parts of legions with their auxilia (subsidiary allied troops). The best-documented campaign is that of Legion II under its legate Vespasian starting from Chichester, where the Atrebatic kingdom was restored; the Isle of Wight was taken and the hill forts of Dorset reduced. Legion IX advanced into Lincolnshire, and Legion XIV probably across the Midlands toward Leicester. Colchester was the chief base, but the fortresses of individual legions at this stage have not yet been identified.

By the year 47, when Plautius was succeeded as commanding officer by Ostorius Scapula, a frontier had been established from Exeter to the Humber, based on the road known as the Fosse Way; from this fact it appears that Claudius did not plan the annexation of the whole island but only of the arable southeast. The intransigence of the tribes of Wales, spurred on by Caratacus, however, caused Scapula to occupy the lowlands beyond the Fosse Way up to the River Severn and to move forward his forces into this area for the struggle with the Silures and Ordovices. The Roman forces were strengthened by the addition of Legion XX, released for this purpose by the foundation of a veteran settlement (colonia) at Camulodunum in the year 49.

The colonia would form a strategic reserve as well as setting the Britons an example of Roman urban organization and life. A provincial centre for the worship of the emperor was also established. Scapula's right flank was secured by the treaty relationship that had been established with Cartimandua, queen of the Brigantes. Hers was the largest kingdom in Britain, occupying the whole area between Derbyshire and the Tyne; unfortunately it lacked stability, nor was it united behind its queen, who lost popularity when she surrendered the British resistance leader, Caratacus, to the Romans. Nevertheless, with occasional Roman military support, Cartimandua was maintained in power until 69 against the opposition led by her husband, Venutius, and this enabled Roman governors to concentrate on Wales.

By ad 60 much had been achieved; Suetonius Paulinus, governor from 59 to 61, was invading the island of Anglesey, the last stronghold of independence, when a serious setback occurred: this was the rebellion of Boudicca, queen of the Iceni. Under its king Prasutagus the tribe of the Iceni had enjoyed a position of alliance and independence; but on his death (60) the territory was forcibly annexed and outrages occurred. Boudicca was able to rally other tribes to her assistance; chief of these were the Trinovantes of Essex, who had many grievances against the settlers of Camulodunum for their arrogant seizure of lands. Roman forces were distant and scattered; and, before peace could be restored, the rebels had sacked Camulodunum, Verulamium (St. Albans), and London, the three chief centres of Romanized life in Britain. Paulinus acted harshly after his victory, but the procurator of the province, Julius Classicianus, with the revenues in mind and perhaps also because, as a Gaul by birth, he possessed a truer vision of provincial partnership with Rome, brought about his recall.

In the first 20 years of occupation some progress had been made in spreading Roman civilization. Towns had been founded, the imperial cult had been established, and merchants were busily introducing the Britons to material benefits. It was not, however, until the Flavian period, ad 69–96, that real advances were made in this field. With the occupation of Wales by Julius Frontinus (governor from 74 to 78) and the advance into northern Scotland by Gnaeus Julius Agricola (78–84), troops were removed from southern Britain, and self-governing civitates, administrative areas based for the most part on the indigenous tribes, took over local administration.

This involved a large program of urbanization and also of education, which continued into the 2nd century; Tacitus, in his biography of Agricola, emphasizes the encouragement given to it. Roman conquest of Wales was complete by 78, but Agricola's invasion of Scotland failed because shortage of manpower prevented him from completing the occupation of the whole island. Moreover, when the British garrison was reduced (c. ad 90) by a legion because of continental needs, it became evident that a frontier would have to be maintained in the north. After several experiments, the Solway–Tyne isthmus was chosen, and there the emperor Hadrian built his stone wall (c. 122–130).

Condition of the province

There was a marked contrast in attitude toward the Roman occupation between the lowland Britons and the inhabitants of Wales and the hill country of the north. The economy of the former was that of settled agriculture, and they were largely of Belgic stock; they soon accepted and appreciated the Roman way of life. The economy of the hill dwellers was pastoral, and the urban civilization of Rome threatened their freedom of life. Although resistance in Wales was stamped out by the end of the 1st century ad, Roman influences were nonetheless weak except in the Vale of Glamorgan. In the Pennines until the beginning of the 3rd century there were repeated rebellions, the more dangerous because of the threat of assistance from free Scotland.

Army and frontier

After the emperor Domitian had reduced the garrison in about the year 90, three legions remained; their permanent bases were established at York, Chester, and Caerleon. The legions formed the foundation of Roman military power, but they were supplemented in garrison duty by numerous smaller auxiliary regiments both of cavalry and infantry, either 1,000 or 500 strong. These latter garrisoned the wall and were stationed in a network of other forts established for police work in Wales and northern England. With 15,000 legionaries and about 40,000 auxiliaries, the army of Britain was very powerful; its presence had economic as well as political results. Hadrian's Wall was the most impressive frontier work in the Roman Empire. Despite a period in the following two reigns when another frontier was laid out on the Glasgow–Edinburgh line the Antonine Wall, built of turf the wall of Hadrian came to be the permanent frontier of Roman Britain.

The northern tribes only twice succeeded in passing it, and then at moments when the garrison was fighting elsewhere. In the late Roman period, when sea raiding became prevalent, the wall lost its preeminence as a defense for the province, but it was continuously held until the end of the 4th century. But although they withdrew to Hadrian's line not later than the year 180, the Romans never abandoned interest in southern Scotland. In the 2nd century their solution was military occupation. In the 3rd, after active campaigning (208–211) by the emperor Septimius Severus and his sons during which permanent bases were built on the east coast of Scotland, the solution adopted by the emperor Caracalla was regulation of relationship by treaties. These, perhaps supported by subsidies, were enforced by supervision of the whole Lowlands by patrols based on forts beyond the wall. During the 4th century more and more reliance was placed on friendly native states, and patrols were withdrawn.

Administration

Britain was an imperial province. The governor represented the emperor, exercising supreme military as well as civil jurisdiction. As commander of three legions he was a senior general of consular rank. From the late 1st century he was assisted on the legal side by a legatus juridicus. The finances were in the hands of the provincial procurator, an independent official of equestrian status whose staff supervised imperial domains and the revenues of mines in addition to normal taxation. In the early 3rd century Britain was divided into two provinces in order to reduce the power of its governor to rebel, as Albinus had done in 196: Britannia Superior had its capital at London and a consular governor in control of two legions and a few auxiliaries; Britannia Inferior, with its capital at York, was under a praetorian governor with one legion but many more auxiliaries.

Local administration was of varied character. First came the chartered towns. By the year 98 Lincoln and Gloucester had joined Camulodunum as coloniae, and by 237 York had become a fourth.

Coloniae of Roman citizens enjoyed autonomy with a constitution based on that of republican Rome, and Roman citizens had various privileges before the law. It is likely that Verulamium was chartered as a Latin municipium (free town); in such a town the annual magistrates were rewarded with Roman citizenship. The remainder of the provincials ranked as peregrini (subjects). In military districts control was in the hands of fort prefects responsible to legionary commanders; but by the late 1st century local self-government, as already stated, was granted to civitates peregrinae, whose number tended to increase with time. These also had republican constitutions, being controlled by elected councils and annual magistrates and having responsibility for raising taxes and administering local justice. In the 1st century there were also client kingdoms whose rulers were allied to Rome; Cogidubnus, Verica's successor, who had his capital at Chichester, is the best known. But Rome regarded these as temporary expedients, and none outlasted the Flavian Period (69–96).

Roman society

Pre-Roman Celtic tribes had been ruled by kings and aristocracies; the Roman civitates remained in the hands of the rich because of the heavy expense of office. But since trade and industry now yielded increasing profits and the old aristocracies no longer derived wealth from war but only from large estates, it is likely that new men rose to power. Roman citizenship was now an avenue of social advancement, and it could be obtained by 25 years' service in the auxiliary forces as well as (more rarely) by direct grants. Soldiers and traders from other parts of the empire significantly enhanced the cosmopolitan character of the population, as did the large number of legionaries, who were already citizens and many of whom must have settled locally. The population of Roman Britain at its peak amounted perhaps to about two million.

Economy

Even before the conquest, according to the Greek geographer Strabo, Britain exported gold, silver, iron, hides, slaves, and hounds in addition to grain. A Roman gold mine is known in Wales, but its yield was not outstanding. Iron was worked in many places but only for local needs; silver, obtained from lead, was of more significance. But the basis of the economy was agriculture, and the conquest greatly stimulated production because of the requirements of the army. According to Tacitus, grain to feed the troops was levied as a tax; correspondingly more had to be grown before a profit could be made.

The pastoralists in Wales and the north probably had to supply leather, which the Roman army needed in quantity for tents, boots, uniforms, and shields. A military tannery is known at Catterick. A profit could, nonetheless, be won from the land because of the increasing demand from the towns. At the same time the development of a system of large estates (villas) relieved the ancient Celtic farming system of the necessity of shouldering the whole burden. Small peasant farmers tended to till the lighter, less-productive, more easily worked soils. Villa estates were established on heavier, richer soils, sometimes on land recently won by forest clearance, itself a result of the enormous new demand for building timber from the army and the new towns and for fuel for domestic heating and for public baths.

The villa owners had access to the precepts of classical farming manuals and also to the improved equipment made available by Roman technology. Their growing prosperity is vouched for by excavation: there are few villas that did not increase in size and luxury as corridors and wings were added or mosaics and bath blocks provided. At least by the 3rd century some landowners were finding great profit in wool; Diocletian's price edict (ad 301) shows that at least two British cloth products had won an empire-wide reputation.

Archaeological evidence indicates that the Cotswold district was one of the centres of this industry.

Trade in imported luxury goods ranging from wine to tableware and bronze trinkets vastly increased as traders swarmed in behind the army to exploit new markets. The profits of developing industries went similarly at first to foreign capitalists. This is clearly seen in the exploitation of silver-lead ore and even in the pottery industry. The Mendip lead field was being worked under military control as early as the year 49, but under Nero (54–68) both there and in Flintshire, and not much later also in the Derbyshire lead field, freedmen the representatives of Roman capital were at work. By Vespasian's reign (69–79) organized companies (societates) of prospectors are attested. Roman citizens, who must in the context be freedmen, are also found organizing the pottery industry in the late 1st century.

Large profits were made by continental businessmen in the first two centuries not only from such sources but also by the import on a vast scale of high-class pottery from Gaul and the Rhineland and on a lesser scale of glass vessels, luxury metalware, and Spanish oil and wine. A large market existed among the military, and the Britons themselves provided a second. Eventually this adverse trade balance was rectified by the gradual capture of the market by British products. Much of the exceptional prosperity of 4th-century Britain must have been due to its success in retaining available profits at home.

A final important point is the role of the Roman army in the economic development of the frontier regions. The presence as consumers of large forces in northern Britain created a revolution in previous patterns of trade and civilized settlement. Cereal production was encouraged in regions where it had been rare, and large settlements grew up in which many of the inhabitants must have been retired soldiers with an interest in the land as well as in trade and industry.

Towns

Belgic Britain had large centres of population but not towns in the Roman sense of having not merely streets and public buildings but also the amenities and local autonomy of a city. In Britain these had therefore to be provided if Roman civilization and normal methods of provincial administration were to be introduced. Thus a policy of urbanization existed in which the legions, as the nearest convenient source of architects and craftsmen, played an organizing role. The earlier towns consisted of half-timbered buildings; before ad 100 only public buildings seem to have been of stone. The administrative capitals had regular street grids, a forum with basilica (public hall), public baths, and temples; a few had theatres and amphitheatres, too. With few exceptions they were undefended.

In the 3rd century, town walls were provided, not so much as a precaution in unsettled times but as a means of keeping operational the earthwork defenses already provided during a crisis at the end of the 2nd century. These towns grew in size to about 100–130 acres with populations of about 5,000; a few were twice this size. The majority of towns in Roman Britain seem to have developed out of traders' settlements in the vicinity of early garrison-forts: those that were not selected as administrative centres remained dependent for their existence on economic factors, serving either as centres of trade or manufacture or else as markets for the agricultural peasantry. They varied considerably in size. In the north, where garrisons were permanently established, quite large trading settlements grew up in their vicinity, and at least some of these would rank as towns.

Villas

Apart from the exceptional establishment at Fishbourne, in West Sussex, whose Italian style and luxurious fittings show that it was the palace of King Cogidubnus, the houses of Romano-British villas had simple beginnings and were of a provincial type. A few owners were prosperous enough in the 2nd century to afford mosaics; but the great period of villa prosperity lay in the 4th century, when many villas grew to impressive size. Their importance was economic and has already been described. Much remains to be learned from full excavation of their subsidiary work buildings. Larger questions of tenure and organization are probably insoluble in the absence of documentary evidence, for it is dangerous to draw analogies from classical sources since conditions in Celtic Britain were very different from those of the Mediterranean world.

Religion and culture

A great variety of religious cults were to be found. In addition to numerous Celtic deities of local or wider significance, the gods of the classical pantheon were introduced and were often identified with their Celtic counterparts. In official circles the worship of the state gods of Rome and of the imperial cult was duly observed. In addition merchants and soldiers introduced oriental cults, among them Christianity. The latter, however, made little headway until the late 4th century, though the frescoes at Lullingstone in Kent and the mosaics at Hinton St. Mary in Dorset attest its presence among villa owners. Although classical temples are sometimes found in towns, the normal temple was of the Romano-Celtic type consisting of a small square shrine and surrounding portico; temples of this type are found in town and country alike.

Romanization was strongest in the towns and among the upper classes, as would be expected; there is evidence that in the countryside Celtic continued to be spoken, though it was not written. Many people were bilingual: graffiti prove that even artisans wrote Latin. Evidence of the classical education of the villa owners is provided by their mosaics, which prove an acquaintance with classical mythology and even with the Aeneid of Virgil. Sculpture and wall painting were both novelties in Roman Britain. Statues or busts in bronze or marble were imported from Gaulish or Mediterranean workshops, but British sculptors soon learned their trade and at their best produced attractive works in a provincial idiom, often for votive purposes.

Many cruder works were also executed whose interest lies in the proof they afford that the conventions of the classical world had penetrated even to the lower classes. Mosaic floors, found in towns and villas, were at first, as at Fishbourne, laid by imported craftsmen. But there is evidence that by the middle of the 2nd century a local firm was at work at Colchester and Verulamium, and in the 4th century a number of local mosaic workshops can be recognized by their styles. One of the most skilled of these was based in Cirencester.

Roman civilization thus took root in Britain; its growth was more obvious in urban circles than among the peasants and weakest in the resistant highland zone. It was a provincial version of Roman culture, but one with recognizably British traits.

The decline of Roman rule

The reforms of Diocletian ended the chaos of the 3rd century and ushered in the late imperial period. Britain, however, for a short time became a separate empire through the rebellion (286/287) of Carausius. This man had been in command against the Saxon pirates in the Channel and by his naval power was able to maintain his independence. His main achievement was to complete the new system of Saxon Shore forts around the southeastern coasts. At first he sought recognition as coemperor, but this was refused. In 293 the fall of Boulogne to Roman forces led to his murder and the accession of Allectus, who, however, fell in his turn when Constantius I invaded Britain in 296.

Allectus had withdrawn troops from the north to oppose the landing, and Hadrian's Wall seems to have been attacked, for Constantius had to restore the frontier as well as reform the administration. He divided Britain into four provinces, and in the same period the civil power was separated from the military. Late Roman sources show three separate commands respectively under the dux Britanniarum (commander of the Britains), the comes litoris Saxonici (count of the Saxon Shore), and the comes Britanniarum, though the dates of their establishment are unknown and may not have been identical.

The 4th century was a period of great prosperity in towns and countryside alike. Britain had escaped the barbarian invasions of the 3rd century and may have seemed a safe refuge for wealthy continentals. Its weakness lay in the fact that its defense was ultimately controlled by distant rather than local rulers. The garrison was perhaps weakened by withdrawals for the civil war of Magnentius (350–351); at any rate in 367 a military disaster occurred due to concerted seaborne attacks from the Picts of Scotland and the Scots of Ireland. But, though the frontier and forts behind it suffered severely, there is little trace of damage to towns or villas. Count Theodosius in 369 restored order and strengthened the defenses of the towns with external towers designed to mount artillery.

Prosperity continued, but the withdrawals of troops by Magnus Maximus in 383 and again at the end of the century by Stilicho weakened security. Thus, when Constantine III, who was declared emperor by the army in Britain in 407, took further troops to Gaul, the forces remaining in the island were insufficient to provide protection against increasing Pictish and Saxon raids. The Britons appealed to the legitimate emperor, Honorius, who was unable to send assistance but authorized the cities to provide for their own defense (410). This marks the end of Roman Britain, for the central government never reestablished control, but for a generation there was little other outward change.

Power fell gradually into the hands of tyrants. Chief of these was Vortigern (c. 425), who, unlike earlier usurpers, made no attempt to become Roman emperor but was content with power in Britain. Independence was producing separate interests. By this date Christianity had made considerable headway in the island, but the leaders followed the heretical teaching of Pelagius, himself a Briton, who had emphasized the importance of the human will over divine grace in the achievement of salvation.

It has been held that the self-reliance shown in the maintenance of national independence was inspired by this philosophy. Yet there was also a powerful Roman Catholic party anxious to reforge the links with Rome, in support of whom St. Germanus of Auxerre visited Britain in 429. It may have been partly to thwart the plans of this party that Vortigern made the mistake (c. 430; the date given by the Anglo-Saxon Benedictine scholar Bede [d. 735] is between 446 and 454) of inviting Saxons to settle and garrison strategic areas of the east coast, though he certainly also had in mind the need to ward off seaborne raids by Picts, which at this time were troublesome.

Planned settlement of this sort is the best explanation for the earliest Saxon settlements found around the mouths of the east-coast estuaries and also in the central southeast region around Oxford. For a time the system worked successfully, but, when in 442 these Saxon foederati (allies) rebelled and called in others of their race to help them, it was found that they had been given a stranglehold on Britain. A long period of warfare and chaos was inaugurated, which was economically disastrous. It was probably this period that saw the disintegration of the majority of the villa estates; with the breakdown of markets and the escape of slaves, villas ceased to be viable and must have gradually fallen into ruin, though the land itself did not cease to be cultivated. A few villas met a violent end.

The towns, under the protection of their strong defenses, at first provided refuge at any rate for the rich who could leave their lands; but by degrees decay set in as trade declined and finally even the supply of food was threatened. About 446 the British made a vain appeal for help to the Roman general Aetius (the "Groans of the Britons" mentioned in the De excidio et conquestu Britanniae of the British writer Gildas). For several decades they suffered reverses; many emigrated to Brittany. In the second half of the 5th century Ambrosius Aurelianus and the shadowy figure of Arthur began to turn the tide by the use of cavalry against the ill-armed Saxon infantry. A great victory was won at Mons Badonicus (a site not identifiable) toward 500: now it was Saxons who emigrated, and the British lived in peace all through the first half of the 6th century, as Gildas records. But in the second half the situation slowly worsened.

Anglo-Saxon England

The invaders and their early settlements

Although Germanic foederati, allies of Roman and post-Roman authorities, had settled in England in the 4th century ad, tribal migrations into Britain began about the middle of the 5th century. The first arrivals, according to the 6th-century British writer Gildas, were invited by a British king to defend his kingdom against the Picts and Scots. A tradition reached Bede that the first mercenaries were from three tribes the Angles, Saxons, and Jutes which he locates on the Cimbric Peninsula, and by implication the coastlands of northwestern Germany. Archaeology, however, suggests a more complex picture showing many tribal elements, Frankish leadership in the first waves, and Frisian contacts. Revolt by these mercenaries against their British employers in the southeast of England led to large-scale Germanic settlements near the coasts and along the river valleys. Their advance was halted for a generation by native resistance, which tradition associates with the names of Ambrosius Aurelianus and Arthur, culminating in victory about 500 by the Britons at the Battle of Mons Badonicus at an unidentified location. But a new Germanic drive began about 550, and before the century had ended, the Britons had been driven west to the borders of Dumnonia (Cornwall and Devon) and to the Welsh Marches, while invaders were advancing west of the Pennines and northward into Lothian.

The fate of the native British population is difficult to determine. The case against its large-scale survival rests largely on linguistic evidence, such as the scarcity of Romano-British words continuing into English and the use of English even by Northumbrian peasants. The case against wholesale extermination also rests on linguistic evidence, such as place-names and personal names, as well as on evidence provided by urban and rural archaeology. Certainly few Britons in England were above servile condition. By the end of the 7th century people regarded themselves as belonging to "the nation of the English," though divided into several kingdoms. This sense of unity was strengthened during long periods when all kingdoms south of the Humber acknowledged the overlordship (called by Bede an imperium) of a single ruler, known as a bretwalda, a word first recorded in the 9th century.

The first such overlord was Aelle of Sussex, in the late 5th century; the second was Ceawlin of Wessex, who died in 593. The third overlord, Aethelberht of Kent, held this power in 597 when the monk Augustine led a mission from Rome to Kent; Kent was the first English kingdom to be converted to Christianity. The Christian church provided another unifying influence, overriding political divisions, although it was not until 669 that the church in England acknowledged a single head.

The social system

Aethelberht set down in writing a code of laws; although it reflects Christian influence, the system underlying the laws was already old, brought over from the Continent in its main lines. The strongest social bond of this system was that of kinship; every freeman depended on his kindred for protection, and the social classes were distinguished by the amount of their wergild (the sum that the kindred could accept in place of vengeance if a man were killed). The normal freeman was the ceorl, an independent peasant landowner; below him in Kent were persons with lower wergilds, who were either freedmen or, as were similar persons in Wessex, members of a subject population; above the ceorls were the nobles some perhaps noble by birth but more often men who had risen by service as companions of the king with a wergild three times that of a ceorl in Kent, six times that of a ceorl elsewhere. The tie that bound a man to his lord was as strong as that of the kindred. Both nobles and ceorls might possess slaves, who had no wergild and were regarded as chattels.

Early traditions, embodied in king lists, imply that all Anglo-Saxon kingdoms except Sussex were established by rulers deemed to have descended from the gods. No invading chieftain is described by the Anglo-Saxon Chronicle as "king" although the title was soon used and chieftainship, as before the conquest, remained central to Germanic tribal society. The sacral character of kingship later increased and changed in meaning as the Christian ruler was set apart by coronation and anointment. In the established English kingdoms the king had special rights compensations for offenses committed in his presence or his home or against anyone under his protection; rights to hospitality, which later became a food rent charged on all land; and rights to various services.

He rewarded his followers with grants of land, probably at first for their lifetime only, but the need to provide permanent endowment for the church brought into being a type of land that was free from most royal dues and that did not revert to the king. From the latter part of the 7th century such land was sometimes conferred by charter. It became common to make similar grants by charter to laymen, with power to bequeath; but three services the building of forts and bridges and service in the army were almost invariably excepted from the immunity. The king received fines for various crimes; but a man's guilt was established in an assembly of freemen, where the accused tried to establish his innocence by his oath supported by oath helpers and, if this failed, by ordeal. On matters of importance the king normally consulted his witan (wise men).

There were local variations in the law, and over a period of time the law developed to meet changed circumstances. As kingdoms grew larger, for example, an official called an ealderman was needed to administer part of the area, and later a sheriff was needed to look after the royal rights in each shire. The acceptance of Christianity made it necessary to fit the clergy into the scale of compensations and assign a value to their oaths and to fix penalties for offenses such as sacrilege, heathen practices, and breaches of the marriage law. But the basic principles were little changed.

The Anglo-Saxons left England a land of villages, but the continuity of village development is uncertain. In the 7th–8th centuries, in what is called the "Middle Saxon shuffle," many early villages were abandoned, and others, from which later medieval villages descended, were founded. The oldest villages are not, as previously thought, those with names ending in -ingas but rather those ending in -ham and -ingham. English trading towns, whose names often end in -wich, from the Latin vicus ("village"), developed in the Middle Saxon period, and other urban settlements grew out of and date from the Alfredian and later defenses against Viking attack.

The conversion to Christianity

Place-names containing the names of gods or other heathen elements are plentiful enough to prove the vitality of heathenism and to account for the slow progress of conversion in some areas. In Kent, the first kingdom to accept Christianity, King Wihtred's laws in 695 contained clauses against heathen worship. The conversion renewed relations with Rome and the Continent; but the full benefit of this was delayed because much of England was converted by the Celtic church, which had lost contact with Rome.

Augustine's mission in 597 converted Kent; but it had only temporary success in Essex, which reverted to heathenism in 616. A mission sent under Bishop Paulinus from Kent to Northumbria in 627 converted King Edwin and many of his subjects in Northumbria and Lindsey. It received a setback in 632 when Edwin was killed and Paulinus withdrew to Kent. About 630 Archbishop Honorius of Canterbury sent a Burgundian, Felix, to convert East Anglia, and the East Anglian church thenceforth remained faithful to Canterbury. Soon after, the West Saxons were converted by Birinus, who came from Rome. Meanwhile, King Oswald began to restore Christianity in Northumbria, bringing Celtic missionaries from Iona. And it was the Celtic church that began in 653 to spread the faith among the Middle Angles, the Mercians, and the peoples of the Severn valley; it also won back Essex.

At first there was little friction between the Roman and Celtic missions. Oswald of Northumbria joined with Cynegils of Wessex in giving Dorchester-on-Thames as seat for Birinus' bishopric; the Irishmen Maildubh in Wessex and Fursey in East Anglia worked in areas converted by the Roman church; and James the Deacon continued Paulinus' work in Northumbria. Later, however, differences in usage especially in the calculation of the date of Easter caused controversy, which was settled in favour of the Roman party at the Synod of Whitby in 664. The adherents of Celtic usage either conformed or withdrew, and advocates of Roman practice became active in the north, the Midlands, and Essex.

Theodore of Tarsus (arrived 669), the first Roman archbishop to be acknowledged all over England, was active in establishing a proper diocesan system, whereas in the Celtic church bishops tended to move freely without fixed sees and settled boundaries; he held the first synod of the English church at Hertford in 672, and this forbade a bishop to interfere in another's diocese or any priest to move into another diocese without his bishop's permission. Sussex and the Isle of Wight the last outposts of heathenism were converted by Bishop Wilfrid and his followers from 681 to 687 and thenceforth followed Roman usages.

The Anglo-Saxons attributed their conversion to Pope Gregory I, "the Apostle of the English," who had sent Augustine. This may seem less than fair to the Celtic mission. The Celtic church made a great impression by its asceticism, fervour, and simplicity, and it had a lasting influence on scholarship. Yet the period of Celtic dominance was only 30 years. The decision at Whitby made possible a form of organization better fitted for permanent needs than the looser system of the Celtic church.

The golden age of Bede

Within a century of Augustine's landing, England was in the forefront of scholarship. This high standard arose from a combination of influences: that from Ireland, which had escaped the decay caused elsewhere by the barbarian invasions, and that from the Mediterranean, which reached England mainly through Archbishop Theodore and his companion, the abbot Adrian. Under Theodore and Adrian, Canterbury became a famous school, and men trained there took their learning to other parts of England. One of these men was Aldhelm, who had been a pupil of Maildubh (the Irish founder of Malmesbury); under Aldhelm, Malmesbury became an influential centre of learning. Aldhelm's own works, in Latin verse and prose, reveal a familiarity with many Latin authors; his writings became popular among admirers of the ornate and artificial style he had learned from his Celtic teachers. Before long a liberal education could be had at such other West Saxon monasteries as Nursling and Wimborne.

The finest centre of scholarship was Northumbria. There Celtic and classical influences met: missionaries brought books from Ireland, and many Englishmen went to Ireland to study. Other Northumbrians went abroad, especially to Rome; among them was Benedict Biscop. Benedict returned from Rome with Theodore (668–669), spent some time in Canterbury, and then brought the learning acquired there to Northumbria. He founded the monasteries at Wearmouth (674) and Jarrow (682), where Bede spent his life. Benedict and Ceolfrith, abbot of Jarrow, brought books from the Continent and assembled the fine library that was available to Bede.

Bede (c. 672–735) is remembered as a great historian whose work never lost its value; but he was also a theologian regarded throughout the Middle Ages as second only to the Church Fathers. Nonetheless, even though he was outstanding, he did not work in isolation. Other Northumbrian houses Lindisfarne, Whitby, and Ripon produced saints' lives, and Bede was in touch with many learned men, not only in Northumbria; there are also signs of scholarly activity in London and in East Anglia.

Moreover, in this period religious poetry was composed in the diction and technique of the older secular poetry in the vernacular. Beowulf, considered the greatest Old English poem, is sometimes assigned to this age, but the dating is uncertain. Art flourished, with a combination of native elements and influences from Ireland and the Mediterranean. The Hiberno-Saxon (or Anglo-Irish) style of manuscript illumination was evolved, its greatest example the Lindisfarne Gospels also showing classical influence. Masons from Gaul and Rome built stone churches. In Northumbria stone monuments with figure sculpture and vine-scroll patterns were set up.

Churches were equipped with precious objects some from abroad, some of native manufacture (even in heathen times the English had been skilled metalworkers). Manuscripts and works of art were taken abroad to churches founded by the English missions, and these churches, in turn, became centres of production. The great Sutton Hoo ship burial, discovered in 1939 at the burial site of the East Anglian royal house and perhaps the cenotaph of the bretwalda Raedwald (d. c. 625), is further evidence of influences from abroad, revealing important Anglo-Saxon contacts with Scandinavia, Byzantium, France, and the Mediterranean.

The heptarchy

The supremacy of Northumbria and the rise of Mercia

When Northumbria became eminent in scholarship, its age of political importance was over. This political dominance had begun when Aethelfrith, ruling over the united Northumbrian kingdoms of Bernicia and Deira, defeated the Dalriadic Scots at Degsastan in 603 and the Welsh at Chester in 613–616. Aethelfrith was himself defeated and killed in 616 by Edwin, the exiled heir to Deira, with the help of Raedwald of East Anglia, then overlord of the southern peoples.

Edwin continued to defeat the Welsh and became the acknowledged overlord of all England except Kent: he annexed the British kingdom of Elmet, invaded North Wales, and captured Anglesey and the Isle of Man. But he fell at Hatfield in 632 before the forces of Cadwallon, king of Gwynedd, and of Penda, a Mercian chieftain. A year later Aethelfrith's son Oswald destroyed Cadwallon and restored the kingdom of Northumbria, and he became overlord of all the lands south of the River Humber. But Mercia was becoming a serious rival; originally a small kingdom in the northwest Midlands, it had absorbed the peoples of the Severn valley, including the Hwicce, a West Saxon people annexed in 628 after a victory by Penda at Cirencester.

Penda threw off Northumbrian control when he defeated and killed Oswald in 641. He drove out Cenwalh of Wessex, who took refuge in East Anglia from 645 to 648. Penda's control of Middle Anglia, where he made his son subking in 653, brought him to the East Anglian frontier; he invaded this kingdom three times, killing three of its kings. He was able to draw an army from a wide area, including East Anglia, when he invaded Northumbria in 654; nevertheless, he was defeated and killed by Oswiu, Oswald's successor.

For a short time Oswiu was overlord of southern England, but a Mercian revolt put Penda's son Wulfhere on the throne in 657, and he greatly extended Mercian power to the southeast and south. Wulfhere became overlord of Essex, with London, and of Surrey. He also held the West Saxon lands along the middle Thames and blocked any eastward advance of the West Saxons by capturing the Isle of Wight and the mainland opposite and giving them to his godson, Aethelwalh of Sussex. Yet Wulfhere's reign ended in disaster; the Kentish monk Aedde, in his Life of St. Wilfrid, said Wulfhere roused all the southern peoples in an attack on Ecgfrith of Northumbria in 674 but was defeated and died soon after.

Ecgfrith took possession of Lindsey, a section of modern Lincolnshire, but he lost it to Aethelred of Mercia after the Battle of the Trent in 678. Thenceforward Northumbria was no threat to Mercian dominance because it was occupied in fighting the Picts in the north. After Ecgfrith was slain by them in 685, his successors took little part in external affairs.

Yet Mercian power was threatened from the south. Caedwalla had added Surrey, Sussex, and the Isle of Wight to the West Saxon kingdom and thus came near to uniting all lands south of the Thames into a single kingdom that might have held its own against Mercia. But this kingdom was short-lived. Kent became free from foreign interference in 694, two years after the accession of Wihtred, who reestablished the Kentish royal line. Sussex appears again as an independent kingdom; and Caedwalla's successor, Ine, was mainly occupied in extending his territory to the west. After Wihtred's death in 725 and Ine's abdication in 726, both Kent and Wessex had internal troubles and could not resist the Mercian kings Aethelbald and Offa.

The great age of Mercia

Adult Caucasian woman with hand on her face as if in pain. lockjaw, toothache, healthcare and medicine, human jaw bone, female Viruses, Bacteria, and Diseases

Aethelbald succeeded in 716 to the rule of all the Midlands and to the control of Essex and London. By 731 all provinces south of the Humber were subject to him. Some of his charters use a regnal style suited to this dignity, such as "king not only of the Mercians but also of all provinces... of the South English" and rex Britanniae (a Latinization of bretwalda). Aethelbald held this position, with only occasional warfare, until his death, in 757 far longer than any previous holder of the imperium. St. Boniface praised the good order he maintained in his kingdom, though complaining of his immoral life and his encroachment on church privileges. Aethelbald was murdered by his own household.

Offa did not at once attain the powerful position that later caused Charles the Great (Charlemagne) to treat with him on equal terms; Cynewulf of Wessex recovered West Saxon lands by the middle Thames and did not submit until 779. Offa was overlord in Kent by 764, in Sussex and the district of Hastings by 771; he apparently lost his authority in Kent after the Battle of Otford in 776 but recovered it in 785. His use of an East Anglian mint shows him supreme there. He claimed greater powers than earlier overlords subkings among the Hwicce and in Sussex dropped their royal titles and appeared as ealdermen, and he referred to a Kentish king as his thegn.

The English scholar Alcuin spoke of the blood shed by Offa to secure the succession of his son, and fugitives from his kingdom sought asylum with Charles the Great. Charles treated Offa as if he were sole king of England, at least of the region south of the Humber; the only other king he acknowledged was the Northumbrian ruler. Offa seemed not to have claimed authority beyond the Humber but instead allied himself with King Aethelred of Northumbria by giving him his daughter in 794.

Offa appears on the continental scene more than had any previous English king. Charles wrote to him as "his dearest brother" and wished for a marriage between his own son Charles and Offa's daughter. Offa's refusal, unless Charles let one of his daughters marry Offa's son Ecgfrith, led to a three-year quarrel in which Charles closed his ports to traders from England. This and a letter about regulating trade, written when the quarrel was over, provide evidence for the importance of cross-Channel trade, which was one reason for Offa's reform of the coinage.

Imitating the action of Pippin III in 755, Offa took responsibility for the coinage, and thenceforward the king's name normally appeared on coins. But the excellent quality in design and workmanship of his coins, especially those with his portrait, served an additional purpose: they had a propaganda value in bringing home the preeminence of the Mercian king not only to his English subjects but also to people on the Continent. Pope Adrian I regarded Offa with awe and respect.

Because Offa's laws are lost, little is known of his internal government, though Alcuin praises it. Offa was able to draw on immense resources to build a dike to demarcate his frontier against Wales. In the greatness of its conception and the skill of its construction, the dike forms a fitting memorial to him. It probably belongs to his later years, and it secured Mercia from sudden incursions.

The church and scholarship in Offa's time

Northumbria was still preeminent in scholarship, and the fame of the school of York, founded by Bede's pupil Archbishop Egbert, attracted students from the Continent and from Ireland. Eventually it supplied Alcuin to take charge of the revival of learning inaugurated by Charles the Great; Alcuin's writings exercised great influence on theological, biblical, and liturgical studies, and his pupils carried on his work well into the 9th century.

Learning was not confined to Northumbria; one Latin work was produced in East Anglia, and recent attribution of manuscripts to Lichfield suggests that Mercian scholarship has been underestimated. Offa himself took an interest in education, and men from all areas corresponded with the missionaries. The Mercian schools that supplied Alfred with scholars in the 9th century may go back to this period. Vernacular poetry was composed, perhaps including Beowulf and the poems of Cynewulf.

A steady advance was made in the creation of parishes, and monasticism flourished and received support from Offa. A great event in ecclesiastical history was the arrival of a papal legation in 787, the first since the conversion. It drew up reforming statutes, which were accepted by the two ecclesiastical provinces, meeting separately under the presidency of Offa and Aelfwald of Northumbria. Offa used the visit to secure the consecration of his son the first recorded coronation ceremony in England and also to have Mercia made into a metropolitan province with its see at Lichfield. The latter seemed desirable partly because he disliked the Kentish archbishop of Canterbury, Jaenberht, but also because it would seem fitting to him that the leading kingdom should be free from external interference in ecclesiastical affairs. This move was unpopular with the church, and in 802, when relations with Canterbury had improved, the archbishopric of Lichfield was abolished.

The decline of Mercia and the rise of Wessex

Offa died in 796, and his son died a few weeks later. Cenwulf, their successor, suppressed revolts in Kent and East Anglia, but he never attained Offa's position. Cenwulf allowed Charles to intervene in Northumbria in 808 and restore Eardwulf (who had been driven from his kingdom) to the throne a unique incident in Anglo-Saxon history. Mercian influence in Wessex was ended when Egbert became king there in 802, though there is no recorded warfare between the kingdoms for many years, during which Egbert conquered Cornwall and Cenwulf fought in Wales.

But in 825 Egbert defeated Beornwulf of Mercia and then sent an army into Kent, with the result that he was accepted as king of Kent, Surrey, Sussex, and Essex. In that same year the East Angles threw off the Mercian yoke, killing Beornwulf. In 829 Egbert became ruler of Mercia and all regions south of the Humber, which caused the chronicler to add his name to Bede's list of kings who held the imperium, calling him bretwalda. The Northumbrians accepted Egbert without fighting. Yet he held this proud position only one year; then Wiglaf recovered the Mercian throne and ruled without subjection to Egbert.

By this time Danish Viking raids were a grave menace, and Aethelwulf, who succeeded his father Egbert in 839, had the wisdom to see that Mercia and Wessex must combine against the Vikings. Friendly relations between them were established by marriage alliances and by a peaceful settlement of boundaries; this paved the way for the acceptance in 886 of Alfred, king of Wessex, as lord of all the English who had not fallen under Danish rule.

The period of the Scandinavian invasions

Viking invasions and settlements

Small scattered Viking raids began in the last years of the 8th century; in the 9th century large-scale plundering incursions were made in Britain and in the Frankish empire as well. Though Egbert defeated a large Viking force in 838 that had combined with the Britons of Cornwall and Aethelwulf won a great victory in 851 over a Viking army that had stormed Canterbury and London and put the Mercian king to flight, it was difficult to deal with an enemy that could attack anywhere on a long and undefended coastline. Destructive raids are recorded for Northumbria, East Anglia, Kent, and Wessex.

A large Danish army came to East Anglia in the autumn of 865, apparently intent on conquest. By 871, when it first attacked Wessex, it had already captured York, been bought off by Mercia, and had taken possession of East Anglia. Many battles were fought in Wessex, including one that led to a Danish defeat at Ashdown in 871. Alfred the Great, a son of Aethelwulf, succeeded to the throne in the course of the year and made peace; this gave him a respite until 876. Meanwhile the Danes drove out Burgred of Mercia, putting a puppet king in his place, and one of their divisions made a permanent settlement in Northumbria.

Alfred was able to force the Danes to leave Wessex in 877, and they settled northeastern Mercia; but a Viking attack in the winter of 878 came near to conquering Wessex. That it did not succeed is to be attributed to Alfred's tenacity. He retired to the Somerset marshes, and in the spring he secretly assembled an army that routed the Danes at Edington. Their king, Guthrum, accepted Christianity and took his forces to East Anglia, where they settled.

The importance of Alfred's victory cannot be exaggerated. It prevented the Danes from becoming masters of the whole of England. Wessex was never again in danger of falling under Danish control, and in the next century the Danish areas were reconquered from Wessex. Alfred's capture of London in 886 and the resultant acceptance of him by all the English outside the Danish areas was a preliminary to this reconquest. That Wessex stood when the other kingdoms had fallen must be put down to Alfred's courage and wisdom, to his defensive measures in reorganizing his army, to his building fortresses and ships, and to his diplomacy, which made the Welsh kings his allies. Renewed attacks by Viking hosts in 892–896, supported by the Danes resident in England, caused widespread damage but had no lasting success.

Alfred's government and his revival of learning

Good internal government contributed to Alfred's successful resistance to the Danes. He reorganized his finances and the services due from thegns, issued an important code of laws, and scrutinized carefully the exercise of justice. Alfred saw the Viking invasions as a punishment from God, especially because of a neglect of learning, without which men could not know and follow the will of God. He deplored the decay of Latin and enjoined its study by those destined for the church, but he also wished all young freemen of adequate means to learn to read English, and he aimed at supplying men with "the books most necessary for all men to know," in their own language.

Alfred had acquired an education despite great difficulties, and he translated some books himself with the help of scholars from Mercia, the Continent, and Wales. Among them they made available works of Bede and Orosius, Gregory and Augustine, and the De consolatione philosophiae of Boethius. Compilation of the Anglo-Saxon Chronicle began in his reign. The effects of Alfred's educational reforms can be glimpsed in succeeding reigns, and his works continued to be copied. Only in his attempt to revive monasticism did he achieve little, for the monastic idea had lost its appeal in England as well as on the Continent during the Viking Age.

The achievement of political unity

The reconquest of the Danelaw

When Alfred died in 899, his son Edward succeeded him. A large-scale incursion by the Danes of Northumbria ended in their crushing defeat at Tettenhall in 910. Edward completed his father's plan of building a ring of fortresses around Wessex, and his sister Aethelflaed took similar measures in Mercia. In 912 Edward was ready to begin the series of campaigns by which he relentlessly advanced into the Danelaw (Danish territory in England), securing each advance by a fortress, until he won back Essex, East Anglia, and the east-Midland Danish areas. Aethelflaed moved similarly against the Danish territory of the Five Boroughs (Derby, Leicester, Nottingham, Lincoln, and Stamford). She obtained Derby and Leicester and gained a promise of submission from the Northumbrian Danes before she died in 918. Edward had by then reached Stamford, but he broke off his advance to secure his acceptance by the Mercians at Tamworth and to prevent their setting up an independent kingdom. Then he took Nottingham, and all the Danes in Mercia submitted to him.

Meanwhile another danger had arisen: Norsemen from Ireland had been settling for some time west of the Pennines, and Northumbria was threatened by Raegnald, a Norse leader from Dublin, who made himself king at York in 919. Edward built fortresses at Thelwall and Manchester, and in 920 he received Raegnald's submission, along with that of the Scots, the Strathclyde Welsh, and all the Northumbrians. Yet Norse kings reigned at York intermittently until 954.

The kingdom of England

Athelstan succeeded his father Edward in 924. He made terms with Raegnald's successor Sihtric and gave him his sister in marriage. When Sihtric died in 927, Athelstan took possession of Northumbria, thus becoming the first king to have direct rule of all England. He received the submission of the kings of Wales and Scotland and of the English ruler of Northumbria beyond the Tyne.

Athelstan was proud of his position, calling himself "king of all Britain" on some of his coins and using in his charters flamboyant rhetoric carrying the same message; he held great courts attended by dignitaries from all over England and by Welsh kings; he subjected the Welsh to tribute and quelled a revolt of the Britons of Cornwall. His sisters were married to continental princes Charles the Simple, king of the Franks; Otto, son of Henry the Fowler; and Hugh, duke of the Franks. Among those brought up at his court were Louis, Charles's son; Alan of Brittany, Athelstan's godson; and Haakon, son of Harald Fairhair of Norway; they all returned to win their respective inheritances with his support. He was a generous donor to continental and English churches. But Athelstan is remembered chiefly as the victor at Brunanburh, against a combine of Olaf Guthfrithson, king of Dublin; Owain of Strathclyde; and Constantine, king of the Scots, whom Athelstan had defeated in 934. They invaded England in 937, and their defeat is celebrated by a poem in the Anglo-Saxon Chronicle.

Immediately after Athelstan's death in 939 Olaf seized not only Northumbria but also the Five Boroughs. By 944 Athelstan's successor, his younger brother Edmund, had regained control, and in 945 Edmund conquered Strathclyde and gave it to Malcolm of Scotland. But Edmund's successor, Eadred, lost control of Northumbria for part of his reign to the Norse kings Erik Bloodax (son of Harald Fairhair) and Olaf Sihtricson. When Erik was killed in 954, Northumbria became a permanent part of the kingdom of England.

By becoming rulers of all England, the West Saxon kings had to administer regions with variant customs, governed under West Saxon, Mercian, or Danish law. In some parts of the area of Danish occupation, especially in northern England and the district of the Five

Boroughs, the evidence of place-names, personal names, and dialect seems to indicate dense Danish settlement, but this has been seriously questioned; many "Danish" features are also found in Anglo-Saxon areas, and Danish names do not always prove Danish institutions. Moreover, the older Anglo-Saxon regions, such as Mercia, which often cut across both Danish and English areas, were politically more significant.

Money, however, was calculated in marks and ores instead of shillings in Danish areas, and arable land was divided into plowlands and oxgangs instead of hides and virgates in the northern and northeastern parts of the Danelaw. Most important was the presence in some areas of a number of small landholders with a much greater degree of independence than their counterparts elsewhere; many ceorls had so suffered under the Danish ravages that they had bought a lord's support by sacrificing some of their independence. Excavations (1976–81) have shown 10th-century Jorvik (York), a Danish settlement, to have been a centre of international trade, economic specialization, and town planning; it was on its way to becoming by 1086 (in the Domesday survey) one of Europe's largest cities, numbering at least 2,000 households.

The kings did not try to eradicate the local peculiarities. King Edgar (reigned 959–975) expressly granted local autonomy to the Danes. But from Athelstan's time it was decreed that there was to be one coinage for all the king's dominion, and a measure of uniformity in administrative divisions was gradually achieved. Mercia became divided into shires on the pattern of those of Wessex. It is uncertain how early the smaller divisions of the shires were called "hundreds," but they now became universal (except in the northern Danelaw, where an area called a wapentake carried on its fiscal and jurisdictional functions). An ordinance of the mid-10th century laid down that the court in each hundred (called "hundred courts") must meet every four weeks to handle local legal matters, and Edgar enjoined that the shire courts must meet twice a year and the borough courts three times. This pattern of local government survived the Norman Conquest.

The church and the monastic revival

To those who judged the church solely by the state of its monasteries, the first half of the 10th century seemed a period of inertia. In fact, the great tasks of converting the heathen settlers, restoring ecclesiastical organization in Danish areas, and repairing the damages of the invasions elsewhere must have absorbed much energy. Even so, learning and book production were not at so low an ebb as monastic reformers claimed. Moreover, new monasteries were founded and benefactions were made to older ones, even though, by post-revival standards, none of these monasteries was enforcing a strict monastic rule and several benefactions were held by secular priests. Alfred had failed to arouse much enthusiasm for monasticism.

The movement for reform began in England about 940 and soon came under the influence of reforms in Fleury and Lorraine. King Edgar, an enthusiastic supporter, promoted the three chief reformers to important positions Dunstan to Canterbury, Aethelwold to Winchester, and Oswald to Worcester and later to York. The secular clergy were violently ejected from Winchester and some other places; Oswald gradually replaced them with monks at Worcester. All three reformers founded new houses, including the great monasteries in the Fenlands, where older houses had perished in the Danish invasion; but Oswald had no success in Northumbria. The reformers, however, were concerned with more than monasticism they paid great attention to other needs of their dioceses; the scholars Abbot Aelfric and Archbishop Wulfstan, trained by the reformers, directed much of their writings to improving the education and morals of the parish clergy and, through them, of the people.

The monastic revival resulted in a great revival of both vernacular and Latin literature, of manuscript production and illumination, and of other forms of art. It reached its zenith in the troubled years of King Ethelred II (reigned 978–1016), after a brief, though violent, reaction to monasticism following Edgar's death. In the 11th century monasteries continued to be productive and new houses were founded; there was also a movement to impose a communal life on bodies of secular priests and to found houses of secular canons.

The Anglo-Danish state

The Danish conquest and the reigns of the Danish kings

Ethelred succeeded as a child in 978, after the murder of his stepbrother Edward. He took the throne in an atmosphere of insecurity and distrust, which partly accounts for the incompetence and treachery rife in his reign. Viking raids began in 980 and steadily increased in intensity. They were led by formidable leaders: from 991 to 994 by Olaf Tryggvason, later king of Norway, and frequently from 994 by Sweyn, king of Denmark. Ethelred's massacre of the Danes in England on St. Brice's Day, 1002, called for vengeance by Sweyn and, from 1009 to 1012, by a famous Viking, Thorkell the Tall. In 1013 the English, worn out by continuous warfare and heavy tributes to buy off the invaders, accepted Sweyn as king. Ethelred, his wife Emma, and his younger sons sought asylum with Richard, duke of Normandy, brother of Emma. Ethelred was recalled to England after Sweyn's death in 1014; but Sweyn's son Canute (Cnut) renewed the invasions and, in spite of valiant resistance by Ethelred's son and successor, Edmund, obtained half of England after a victory at Ashingdon in October 1016 and the rest after Edmund's death that November.

Canute rewarded some of his followers with English lands and ruthlessly got rid of some prominent Englishmen, among them Edmund's brother Edwy. (Edmund's infant sons, however, were carried away to safety in Hungary.) Yet Canute's rule was not tyrannical, and his reign was remembered as a time of good order. The Danish element in his entourage diminished; and the Englishmen Leofric, Earl of Mercia, and Godwine, Earl of Wessex, became the most powerful magnates. Canute married Ethelred's widow, Emma, thus removing the danger of Norman support for her sons by Ethelred. Canute fought a successful campaign in Scotland in 1031, and Englishmen were drawn into his wars in Scandinavia, which made him lord of Norway. But at home there was peace.

Probably under the influence of Archbishop Wulfstan he became a stout supporter of the church, which in his reign had the vitality to engage in missionary work in Scandinavia. Religious as well as political motives may have caused his pilgrimage to Rome in 1027 to attend the coronation of the emperor Conrad; from the pope, the emperor, and the princes whom he met he obtained concessions for English pilgrims and traders going to Rome. Canute's laws, drafted by Archbishop Wulfstan, are mainly based on those of earlier kings, especially Edgar.

Already in 1018 the English and Danes had come to an agreement "according to Edgar's law." No important changes were made in the machinery of government except that small earldoms were combined to make great earldoms, a change that placed much power in the hands of their holders. No attempt was made to restore the English line when Canute died in 1035; he was followed by his sons Harold and Hardecanute, whose reigns were unpopular. Denmark passed to Sweyn, son of Canute's sister Estrith, in 1043. Meanwhile the Norwegians in 1035 had driven out another Sweyn, the son whom Canute had set to rule over them with his mother, Aelfgifu, and had elected Magnus.

The close links with Scandinavia had benefited English trade, but they left one awkward heritage: Hardecanute and Magnus made an agreement that if either died without a son, the survivor was to succeed to both kingdoms. Hardecanute died without a son in 1042, but he was succeeded by Ethelred's son Edward, who was known as the Confessor or the Saint because of his reputation for chastity. Magnus was prevented by trouble with Denmark from invading England as he intended in 1046; but Harold Hardraada inherited Magnus' claim to the English throne, and he came to enforce it in 1066.

The reign of Edward the Confessor and the Norman Conquest

It is easy to regard the years of Edward's rule simply as a prelude to the catastrophe of 1066, yet there are other aspects of his reign. Harrying caused by political disturbances or by incursions of the Scots or Welsh was only occasional and localized; friendly relations were usually maintained with Malcolm of Scotland, whom Earl Siward of Northumbria had supported against Macbeth in 1054; and in 1063 the victories of Harold, Earl of Wessex, and his brother Tostig ended the trouble from Wales. The normal course of administration was maintained, with efficient mints, writing office, taxation system, and courts of justice. Trade was prosperous. The church contained several good and competent leaders, and bad appointments like those of the Normans, Ulf to Dorchester and Robert to London and Canterbury, and of Stigand to Winchester were the exception. Scholarship was not in decline, and manuscripts were produced in great number. English illumination and other forms of art were admired abroad.

The troubles of the reign came from the excessive power concentrated in the hands of the rival houses of Leofric of Mercia and Godwine of Wessex and from resentment caused by the king's introduction of Norman friends, though their influence has sometimes been exaggerated. A crisis arose in 1051 when Godwine defied the king's order to punish the men of Dover, who had resisted an attempt by Eustace of Boulogne to quarter his men on them by force. The support of Earl Leofric and Earl Siward enabled Edward to secure the outlawry of Godwine and his sons; and William of Normandy paid Edward a visit during which Edward may have promised William succession to the English throne, although this Norman claim may have been mere propaganda. Godwine and his sons came back the following year with a strong force, and the magnates were not prepared to engage them in civil war but forced the king to make terms. Some unpopular Normans were driven out, including Archbishop Robert, whose archbishopric was given to Stigand; this act supplied one excuse for the papal support of William's cause.

Harold succeeded his father Godwine as earl of Wessex in 1053; Tostig was made earl of Northumbria in 1055; and their younger brothers were also provided with earldoms. To settle the question of succession, negotiations were begun in 1054 to bring Edward, Edmund's son (nephew of Edward the Confessor), from Hungary; but Edward died in 1057, leaving a son, Edgar Aetheling, then a child, who was passed over in 1066. In about 1064 Harold of Wessex, when visiting Normandy, swore to support William's claim. Only Norman versions of the incident survive and the true circumstances cannot be ascertained, but William used Harold's broken oath to help secure papal support later. In 1065 Harold acquiesced in the appointment of Morcar, brother of Edwin, Earl of Mercia, to replace Tostig when the Northumbrians revolted against him, and thus Harold turned his brother into an enemy. King Edward, when dying, named Harold to succeed him, and, after overcoming Northumbrian reluctance with the help of Bishop Wulfstan of Worcester, Harold was universally accepted.

Harold might have proved an effective ruler, but the forces against him were too strong. The papacy, without hearing the defense in favour of Harold's succession, gave its blessing to an invasion of a people who had always been distinguished for their loyalty to Rome, and this papal support helped William to collect his army widely. The threat from Harold III Hardraade, who was joined by Tostig, prevented Harold from concentrating his forces in the south and took him north at a critical moment. He fought at Hastings only 24 days after the armies of Mercia and Northumbria had been put out of action by enormous losses at Fulford and only 19 days after he had defeated and killed Harold III Hardraade and Tostig at Stamford Bridge. Harold was slain at Hastings, and on Christmas Day, 1066, William of Normandy was crowned king of England. Although the Anglo-Saxon fighting force was perhaps the best in Europe and the defeat at Hastings due largely to a series of historical accidents, it is not difficult to understand the English chronicler's view that God was angry with the English people.

The Normans (1066–1154)

William I (1066–87)

The Norman Conquest has long been argued about. The question has been whether William I introduced fundamental changes in England or based his rule solidly on Anglo-Saxon foundations. A particularly controversial issue has been the introduction of feudalism. On balance, the debate has favoured dramatic change while also granting that in some respects the Normans learned much from the English past. Yet William replaced his initial policy of trying to govern through Englishmen with an increasingly thoroughgoing Normanization.

Resistance and rebellion

The Conquest was not achieved at a single stroke. In 1068 Exeter rose against the Normans, and a major rising began in the north. A savage campaign in 1069–70, the so-called harrying of the north, emphasized William's military supremacy and his brutality. A further English rising in the Fens achieved nothing. In 1075 William put down rebellion by the earls of Hereford, Norfolk, and Northumbria. The latter, the last surviving English earl, was executed for treason.

The introduction of feudalism

The Conquest resulted in the subordination of England to a Norman aristocracy. William probably distributed estates to his followers on a piecemeal basis as lands came into his hands. He granted lands directly to fewer than 180 men, making them his tenants in chief. Their estates were often well distributed, consisting of manors scattered through a number of shires. In vulnerable regions, however, compact blocks of land were formed, clustered around castles. The tenants in chief owed homage and fealty to the king and held their land in return for military service. They were under obligation to supply a certain number of knights for the royal feudal host a number that was not necessarily related to the quantity or quality of land held.

Early in the reign many tenants in chief provided knights from their own households to meet demands for service, but they soon began to grant some of their own lands to knights who would serve them just as they in turn served the king. They could not, however, use their knights for private warfare, which, in contrast to Normandy, was forbidden in England. In addition to drawing on the forces provided by feudal means, William made extensive use of mercenary troops to secure the military strength he needed. Castles, which were virtually unknown in pre-Conquest England and could only be built with royal permission, provided bases for administration and military organization. They were an essential element in the Norman settlement of England.

Government and justice

William hoped to be able to rule England in much the same way as his Anglo-Saxon predecessors had done, though in many respects the old institutions and practices had to be changed in response to the problems of ruling a conquered land. The Anglo-Saxon witan, or council, became the king's curia regis, a meeting of the royal tenants in chief, both lay and ecclesiastical. William was said by chroniclers to have held full courts three times a year, at Christmas, Easter, and Whitsuntide, to which all the great men of the realm were summoned and at which he wore his crown. These were similar to the great courts he held in Normandy. Inevitably there were many disputes over land, and the curia regis was where justice was done to the great tenants in chief. William himself is said to have sat one Sunday "from morn till eve" to hear a plea between William de Braose and the abbot of Fécamp.

William at first did little to change Anglo-Saxon administrative organization. The royal household was at the centre of royal government, and the system, such as it was, under Edward the Confessor had probably been quite similar to that which existed in Normandy at the same period, although the actual titles of the officers were not the same. Initially under William there also was little change in personnel. But, by the end of his reign, all important administrative officials were Norman, and their titles corresponded to those in use in Normandy. There were a steward, a butler, a chamberlain, a constable, a marshal, and a head of the royal scriptorium, or chancellor. This scriptorium was the source from which all writs (i.e., written royal commands) were issued. At the start of William's reign the writs were in English, and by the end of it, in Latin.

In local government the Anglo-Saxon shire and hundred courts continued to function as units of administration and justice, but with important changes. Bishops and earls ceased to preside over the shire courts. Bishops now had their own ecclesiastical courts, while earls had their feudal courts. But although earls no longer presided over shire courts, they were entitled to take a third of the proceeds coming from them. The old Anglo-Saxon office of sheriff was transformed into a position resembling that of the Norman vicomte, as native sheriffs were replaced by Norman nobles. They controlled the shire and hundred courts, were responsible for collecting royal revenue, and controlled the royal castles that had been built both to subdue and protect the country.

William made the most of the financial system he had inherited. In addition to customary dues, such as revenues from justice and income from royal lands, his predecessors had been able to levy a geld, or tax, assessed on the value of land and originally intended to provide funds to buy off Danish invaders. The Confessor had abandoned this tax, but the Conqueror collected it at least four times. Profits from the ample royal estates must have been significant, along with those from royal mints and towns.

The Conqueror greatly strengthened the administration of justice in his new land. He occasionally appointed justiciars to preside over local cases and at times named commissioners to act as his deputies in the localities. There were a number of great trials during the reign. The most famous of them was the trial at Pinnenden Heath of a case between Lanfranc, archbishop of Canterbury, and the king's half brother, Odo, bishop of Bayeux and earl of Kent. Not only all the Normans of the shire but also many Englishmen, especially those learned in the customary law, attended. On occasion jurors were summoned to give a collective verdict under oath. Historians have debated as to whether juries were introduced as a result of the Viking conquests or were a Norman innovation, derived from Carolingian practice in France. Whichever argument is correct, it is evident that, under the Normans, juries came into more frequent use. William introduced one measure to protect his followers: he made the local community of the hundred responsible for the murder of any Norman.

Church–state relations

The upper ranks of the clergy were Normanized and feudalized, following the pattern of lay society. Bishops received their lands and the symbols of their spiritual office from the king. They owed knight service and were under firm royal control. Sees were reorganized, and most came to be held by continental clergy. In 1070 Lanfranc replaced Stigand as archbishop of Canterbury. An ecclesiastical lawyer, teacher, and church statesman, Lanfranc, a native of Italy, had been a monk at Bec and an abbot of Saint Stephen's at Caen. Lanfranc and William understood each other and worked together to introduce discipline and order into the English church.

The see of York was subordinated to Canterbury, and efforts were made to bring the ecclesiastical affairs of Ireland and Scotland under Lanfranc's control. Several church councils were held in England to legislate for the English church, as similar councils did in Normandy. William denied that he owed homage or fealty to the pope for his English lands, although he acknowledged papal support in winning the new realm. William and Lanfranc resisted Pope Gregory VII's claim to papal supremacy: the king decreed that without his consent no pope was to be recognized in England, no papal letter was to be received, no church council was to legislate, and no baron or royal official was to be excommunicated. During William's reign the controversy over the right of lay rulers to invest ecclesiastics with the symbols of their office did not affect England, in contrast to other parts of Latin Christendom.

William's accomplishments

At Christmas 1085 William had "deep speech" with his council and as a result ordered a general survey of the land to be made. Historians have debated the purpose of this "Domesday" survey, some seeing it as primarily a tax assessment, others emphasizing its importance as a basis for assignment of feudal rights and duties. Its form owed much to Anglo-Saxon precedent, but within each county section it was organized on a feudal basis. It was probably a multipurpose document with the main emphasis on resources for taxation. It was incomplete, for the far north of England, London, and Winchester were not included, while the returns for Essex, Norfolk, and Suffolk were not condensed into the same form as was used for the rest of the country. Domesday is a unique record and offers rich materials for research.

One policy that caused deep resentment under William I, and even hatred under his successor William II, was the taking over of vast tracts of land for the king's forest. In some areas whole villages were destroyed and the people driven out; elsewhere, people living in forest areas, though not necessarily removed, were subjected to a severe system of law with drastic penalties for poaching.

William the Conqueror is presented in contemporary chronicles as a ruthless tyrant who rigorously put down rebellion and devastated vast areas, especially in his pacification of the north in 1069–70. He was, however, an able administrator. Perhaps one of his greatest contributions to England's future was the linking up of England with continental affairs. If the country had been conquered again by the Danes, as seemed possible, it might have remained in a backwater of European development. In the event, England was linked, economically and culturally, to France and continental Europe. The aristocracy spoke French, while Latin was the language of the church and the administration.

The sons of William I

William II Rufus (1087–1100)

Under William I's two sons William II Rufus and Henry I, strong, centralized government continued, and England's link with Normandy was strengthened. Rebellion by Norman barons, led by the king's half uncles, Odo of Bayeux and Robert of Mortain, was soon put down by

William II, who made promises of good government and relief from taxation and the severity of the forest laws. Odo of Bayeux was banished, and William of St. Calais, bishop of Durham, tried for treason. As an ecclesiastic he rejected the jurisdiction of the king's court. But Lanfranc pointed out that it was not as a churchman but as lord of his temporal fiefs that he was being tried. He was finally allowed to leave the country, in return for surrender of his fiefs.

William II's main preoccupation was to win Normandy from his elder brother Robert. After some initial skirmishing, William's plans were furthered by Robert's decision to go on crusade in 1096. Robert mortgaged his lands to William for 10,000 marks, which was raised in England by drastic and unpopular means. In his last years William campaigned successfully in Maine and the French Vexin so as to extend the borders of Normandy. His death was the result of an "accident" possibly engineered by his younger brother Henry: he was shot with an arrow in the New Forest. Henry, who was conveniently with the hunting party, rode posthaste to Winchester, seized the treasury, and was chosen king the next day.

Henry I (1100–35)

A good politician and administrator, Henry I was the ablest of the Conqueror's sons. At his coronation on Aug. 5, 1100, he issued a charter intended to win the support of the nation. This propaganda document, in which Henry promised to give up many practices of the past, demonstrates how oppressive Norman government had become. Henry promised not to exploit church vacancies, as his brother had done, and guaranteed that reliefs, sums paid by feudal vassals when they took over their fathers' estates, would be "just and legitimate." He also promised to return to the laws of Edward the Confessor, though this cannot have been intended literally.

Following the suppression of rebellion in England, the conquest of Normandy was an important priority for Henry. By 1105 he took the offensive, and in September 1106 he won a decisive battle at Tinchebray that gave him control of the whole of Normandy. Robert was captured and was to spend the rest of his 80 years in castle dungeons. His son, William Clito, escaped and remained until his death in 1128 a thorn in Henry's flesh. Success in Normandy was followed by wars against Louis VI of France, but by 1120 Henry was everywhere successful in both diplomacy and war. He had arranged a marriage for his only legitimate son, William, to Matilda, daughter of Fulk of Anjou, and had received Fulk's homage for Maine. Pope Calixtus II, his cousin, gave him full support for his control of Normandy on condition that his son William should do homage to the French king.

Relations with the church had not always been easy. Henry had inherited from William II a quarrel with the church that became part of the Europe-wide Investiture Controversy. After Lanfranc's death William had delayed appointing a successor, presumably for the privilege of exploiting the resources of the archbishopric. After four years, during a bout of illness, he appointed Anselm of Bec, one of the great scholars of his time (1093). Anselm did homage for his temporalities, but whether or not he was ever invested with the symbols of spiritual office by the king is not clear. Papal confirmation was complicated by the fact that there were two claimants to the papal throne. Anselm refused to accept a decision made by the king's supporters and insisted on receiving his pallium from Urban II, a reform pope in the tradition of Gregory VII, rather than from the imperial nominee, Clement III. Conflict between king and archbishop flared up again in 1097 over what William considered to be an inadequate Canterbury contingent for his Welsh war. The upshot was that Anselm went into exile until William's death. At Rome he heard new papal decrees against lay investiture.

Anselm supported Henry's bid for the throne and returned from exile in 1100. Almost immediately he quarreled with Henry when the king asked him to do homage and to receive his archbishopric from his hands. After various ineffective appeals to Rome, Anselm again went into exile. A compromise was finally arranged in 1107, when it was agreed that the king would surrender investiture with the symbols of spiritual office in return for an agreement that he should supervise the election of the archbishop and take homage for the temporalities before investiture with the spiritual symbols took place. It was said that the concession cost the king "a little, perhaps, of his royal dignity, but nothing of his power to enthrone anyone he pleased."

Henry continued and extended the administrative work of his father. His frequent absences from England prompted the development of a system that could operate effectively in his absence, under the guidance of such men as Roger, bishop of Salisbury. The exchequer was developed as a department of government dealing with royal revenues, and the first record of the sheriffs' regular accounting at the exchequer, or Pipe Roll, to survive is that of 1129–30. Justices with wide-ranging commissions were sent out into the shires to reinforce local administration and to inquire into crown pleas, royal revenues, and other matters of interest and profit for the king. Henry's government was highly efficient, but it was also harsh and demanding.

During the last 15 years of his reign the succession was a major issue. William, Henry's only legitimate son, was drowned in 1120, leaving Henry's daughter Matilda, wife of the German emperor Henry V, as heir. When Henry V died in 1125, Matilda returned to England. Henry I persuaded his barons to swear an oath in her support but did not consult them over her second marriage to Geoffrey of Anjou, who at 14 was 11 years her junior. Within a year Geoffrey repudiated Matilda, but during a temporary reconciliation, Matilda and Geoffrey had three children.

Henry was a skilled politician, adept at using the levers of patronage. Men such as Geoffrey de Clinton, the royal chamberlain, owed much to the favours they received from the king, and they served him well in return. There was tension between the established nobility and the "new men" raised to high office by the king, but Henry maintained control with great effect and distributed favours evenhandedly. In England his rule, particularly when seen in retrospect, was characterized by peace, order, and justice. He died, probably of a heart attack, on Dec. 1, 1135.

The period of anarchy (1135–54)

Matilda and Stephen

Henry I's death precipitated a 20-year crisis whose immediate cause was a succession dispute. But there has been much debate among historians as to whether the problems of these years were the result of some deeper malaise.

No one was enthusiastic about accepting Matilda as queen, especially as her husband, Geoffrey of Anjou, was actually at war with Henry at the time of his death. Robert, Earl of Gloucester, one of Henry's many illegitimate sons, was an impressive candidate for the throne, as were Henry's nephews, Theobald and Stephen of Blois. The outcome of the struggle in 1135 was unexpected: while Theobald, the elder brother, was receiving the homage of continental vassals for Normandy, Stephen took ship for England and claimed the throne. Having secured the treasury at Winchester, he was crowned on December 22.

Stephen had been quick and resolute in securing the crown. But after the first flush of victory he made concessions that, instead of winning him support, served to expose his weakness. One such concession was to King David of Scotland, who was also the Earl of Huntingdon in England. When David learned of Stephen's succession, he crossed the border by force. He was effectively bought off by Stephen's agreeing that David's son Henry should receive Carlisle, Doncaster, and the honour of Huntingdon. Stephen obtained the support of Robert of Gloucester by a lavish charter. He also granted a charter to the church forbidding simony and confirmed the rights of church courts to all jurisdiction over clerics. Stephen's lavish appointment of new earls (19 in the course of the reign) was intended in part as a way of undermining the power of the sheriffs and constituted a shift of power away from the centre. Expenditure in Stephen's early years was heavy and achievements few.

Stephen soon alienated the church. Much power in central government had been concentrated in the hands of Roger, bishop of Salisbury, and his family. One of Roger's nephews was bishop of Ely, and another was bishop of Lincoln. This was resented by the Beaumont family, headed by the Earl of Leicester, and their allies, who formed a powerful court faction. They planned the downfall of the bishops, and, when a council meeting was held at Oxford in June 1139, they seized on the opportunity provided by a brawl in which some of Roger's men were involved. Rumours of treason were spread, and Stephen demanded that the bishops should make satisfaction. When they did not do so, he ordered their arrest. Thenceforth Stephen was in disfavour with the clergy; he had already forfeited the support of his brother Henry of Blois, bishop of Winchester, by failing to make him archbishop of Canterbury in 1137. As papal legate, Henry was to be the most influential member of the clergy in the realm.

Civil war

Matilda did not land in England until 1139. She and her half brother Robert of Gloucester established themselves in the southwest; Stephen's main strength lay in the east. In 1141 Stephen was defeated and taken prisoner at the battle of Lincoln, but Matilda alienated the Londoners and lost support. When Stephen was exchanged for Robert of Gloucester, who was captured at Winchester, Matilda's fortunes waned. The Angevin cause, however, prospered in Normandy. Although Matilda's son, Henry, mounted an unsuccessful invasion from Normandy in 1147, in 1153 he carried out a vigorous and effective campaign. Stephen, saddened by the death of his elder son Eustace, agreed to a compromise peace. He was to remain king, but he recognized Henry as his heir.

One chronicler said, "In this king's time there was nothing but disturbance and wickedness and robbery." Though this was an exaggeration, it is clear that disorder was widespread, with a great many adulterine castles built (that is, unlicensed castles). It was possible for the earls of Chester and Leicester to make a treaty without any reference to royal authority. Stephen's government lost control of much of England, and power was fragmented and decentralized.

There has been much debate as to why men fought in the civil war. It was much more than a simple succession dispute and can be seen as a natural reaction both to the strong, centralized government of Henry I and to the weak rule of Stephen. The aim of many magnates was to recover lands and offices to which they considered they had hereditary rights: much land had changed hands under Henry I. Men such as Ranulf de Gernons, 4th Earl of Chester, and Geoffrey de Mandeville, 1st Earl of Essex, changed sides frequently, obtaining fresh grants each time. Essex wanted to recover the lands and positions his grandfather had held. Most men, however, probably did not want to demolish royal government but rather wished to control and profit from it. The institutions of government did not disappear altogether. The period of the "anarchy" strengthened feudal principles of succession to land, but such offices as those of sheriff and castellan did not become hereditary.

England in the Norman period

Despite, or perhaps in part because of, the political strains of this period, these were constructive years. The economy, for which Domesday Book is a magnificent source, was essentially agrarian, the main unit being the manor, where the lord's land (or demesne) was worked by unfree peasants who held their land in return for performing labour services. Towns, notably London, flourished, and many received new privileges based on continental practice. The church benefited from closer connections with the Continent in many ways. One such benefit was the arrival of new religious orders: the first Cluniac house was established at Lewes in 1077, and the Cistercians came to England in 1129. A great many Augustinian houses were founded in the first part of the 12th century. Imposing buildings such as Durham Cathedral and the Tower of London give eloquent testimony to the architectural achievement of the Normans, while the illuminated Winchester Bible and Psalter, made for Henry of Blois, bear witness to the artistic excellence of the age.

The early Plantagenets

Henry II (1154–89)

Matilda's son Henry Plantagenet, the first and greatest of three Angevin kings of England, succeeded Stephen in 1154. Aged 21, he already possessed a reputation for restless energy and decisive action. He was to inherit vast lands. As heir to his mother and to Stephen he held England and Normandy; as heir to his father he held Anjou (hence Angevin), Maine, and Touraine; as heir to his brother Geoffrey he obtained Brittany; as husband of Eleanor, the divorced wife of Louis VII of France, he held Aquitaine, the major part of southwestern France. Altogether his holdings in France were far larger than those of the French king. They have become known as the Angevin empire, although Henry never in fact claimed any imperial rights or used the title of emperor. From the beginning Henry showed himself determined to assert and maintain his rights in all his lands. In England this meant reasserting the centralized power of his grandfather, Henry I. His success in these aims is the measure of his greatness.

Government of England

In the first decade of his reign Henry was largely concerned with continental affairs, though he made sure that the adulterine castles in England were destroyed. Many of the earldoms created in the anarchy of Stephen's reign were allowed to lapse. Major change in England began in the mid-1160s. The Assize of Clarendon of 1166, and that of Northampton 10 years later, promoted public order. Juries were used to provide evidence of what crimes had been committed and to bring accusations. New forms of legal action were introduced, notably the so-called possessory assizes, which determined who had the right to immediate possession of land, not who had the best fundamental right.

That could be decided by the grand assize, by means of which a jury of 12 knights would decide the case. The use of standardized forms of writ greatly simplified judicial administration. "Returnable" writs, which had to be sent back by the sheriffs to the central administration, enabled the crown to check that its instructions were obeyed. An increasing number of cases came before royal courts rather than private feudal courts. Henry I's practice of sending out itinerant justices was extended and systematized. In 1170 a major inquiry into local administration, the Inquest of Sheriffs, was held, and many sheriffs were dismissed.

There were important changes to the military system. In 1166 the tenants in chief were commanded to disclose the number of knights enfeoffed on their lands so that Henry could take proper financial advantage of changes that had taken place since his grandfather's day. Scutage (money payment in lieu of military service) was an important source of funds, and Henry preferred scutage to service because mercenaries were more efficient than feudal contingents. In the Assize of Arms of 1181 Henry determined the arms and equipment appropriate to every free man, based on his income from land. This measure, which could be seen as a revival of the principles of the Anglo-Saxon fyrd, was intended to provide for a local militia, which could be used against invasion, rebellion, or for peacekeeping.

Struggle with Thomas Becket

Henry attempted to restore the close relationship between church and state that had existed under the Norman kings. His first move was the appointment in 1162 of Thomas Becket as archbishop of Canterbury. Henry assumed that Becket, who had served efficiently as chancellor since 1155 and been a close companion to him, would continue to do so as archbishop. Becket, however, disappointed him. Once appointed archbishop, he became a militant defender of the church against royal encroachment and a champion of the papal ideology of ecclesiastical supremacy over the lay world. The struggle between Henry and Becket reached a crisis at the Council of Clarendon in 1164. In the Constitutions of Clarendon Henry tried to set down in writing the ancient customs of the land. The most controversial issue proved to be that of jurisdiction over "criminous clerks" (clerics who had committed crimes); the king demanded that such men should, after trial in church courts, be sent for punishment in royal courts.

Becket initially accepted the Constitutions but would not set his seal to them. Shortly thereafter, however, he suspended himself from office for the sin of yielding to the royal will in the matter. Although he failed to obtain full papal support at this stage, Alexander III ultimately came to his aid over the Constitutions. Later in 1164 Becket was charged with peculation of royal funds when chancellor. After Becket had taken flight for France, the king confiscated the revenues of his province, exiled his friends, and confiscated their revenues.

In 1170 Henry had his eldest son crowned king by the archbishop of York, not Canterbury, as was traditional. Becket, in exile, appealed to Rome and excommunicated the clergy who had taken part in the ceremony. A reconciliation between Becket and Henry at the end of the same year settled none of the points at issue. When Becket returned to England, he took further measures against the clergy who had taken part in the coronation. In Normandy the enraged king, hearing the news, burst out with the fateful words that incited four of his knights to take ship for England and murder the archbishop in Canterbury Cathedral.

Almost overnight the martyred Thomas became a saint in the eyes of the people. Henry repudiated responsibility for the murder and reconciled himself with the church. But despite various royal promises to abolish customs injurious to the church, royal control of the church was little affected. Henceforth criminous clerks were to be tried in church courts, save for offenses against the forest laws. Disputes over ecclesiastical patronage and church lands that were held on the same terms as lay estates were, however, to come under royal jurisdiction. Finally Henry did penance at Canterbury, allowing the monks to scourge him. But with Becket out of the way, it proved possible to negotiate most of the points at issue between church and state. The martyred archbishop, however, was to prove a potent example for future prelates.

Rebellion of Henry's sons and Eleanor of Aquitaine

Henry's sons, urged on by their mother and by a coalition of his enemies, raised a rebellion throughout his domains in 1173. King William I the Lion of Scotland joined the rebel coalition and invaded the north of England. Lack of cooperation among the rebels, however, enabled Henry to defeat them one at a time with a mercenary army.

The Scottish king was taken prisoner at Alnwick. Queen Eleanor was retired to polite imprisonment for the rest of Henry's life. The king's sons and the baronial rebels were treated with leniency, but many baronial castles were destroyed following the rising. A brief period of amity between Henry and Louis of France followed, and the years between 1175 and 1182 marked the zenith of Henry's prestige and power. In 1183 the younger Henry again tried to organize opposition to his father, but he died in June of that year. Henry spent the last years of his life locked in combat with the new French king, Philip II Augustus, with whom his son Richard had entered into an alliance. Even his youngest son, John, deserted him at the end.

Richard I (1189–99)

Henry II died in 1189, an embittered old man. He was succeeded by his son Richard I, nicknamed the Lionheart. Richard, a renowned and skillful warrior, was mainly interested in the Crusade to recover Jerusalem and in the struggle to maintain his French holdings against Philip Augustus. He spent only about six months of his 10-year reign in England. During his frequent absences he left a committee in charge of the realm. The chancellor, William Longchamp, bishop of Ely, dominated the early part of the reign until forced into exile by baronial rebellion in 1191. Walter of Coutances, archbishop of Rouen, succeeded Longchamp, but the most important and able of Richard's ministers was Hubert Walter, archbishop of Canterbury, justiciar from 1193 to 1198, and chancellor from 1199 to 1205. With the king's mother, Eleanor, he put down a revolt by Richard's brother John in 1193 with strong and effective measures. But when Richard returned from abroad, he forgave John and promised him the succession.

This reign saw some important innovations in taxation and military organization. Warfare was expensive, and in addition Richard was captured on his return from the Crusade by Leopold V of Austria and held for a high ransom of 150,000 marks. Various methods of raising money were tried: an aid, or scutage; a carucage, or tax on plow lands; a general tax of a fourth of revenues and chattels (this was a development of the so-called Saladin Tithe raised earlier for the Crusade); and a seizure of the wool crop of Cistercian and Gilbertine houses. The ransom, although never paid in full, caused Richard's government to become highly unpopular. Richard also faced some unwillingness on the part of his English subjects to serve in France. A plan to raise a force of 300 knights who would serve for a whole year met with opposition led by the bishops of Lincoln and Salisbury. Richard was, however, remarkably successful in mustering the resources, financial and human, of his kingdom in support of his wars. It can also be argued that his demands on England weakened the realm unduly and that Richard left his successor a very difficult legacy.

John (1199–1216)

Richard, mortally wounded at a siege in France in 1199, was succeeded by his brother John, one of the most detested of English kings. John's reign was characterized by failure. Yet while he must bear a heavy responsibility for his misfortunes, it is only fair to recognize that he inherited the resentment that had built up against his brother and father. Also, while his reign ended in disaster, some of his financial and military measures anticipated positive developments in Edward I's reign.

Loss of French possessions

John had nothing like the military ability or reputation of his brother. He could win a battle in a fit of energy, only to lose his advantage in a spell of indolence. After repudiating his first wife, Isabella of Gloucester, John married the fiancée of Hugh IX the Brown of the Lusignan family, one of his vassals in Poitou. For this offense he was summoned to answer to Philip II, his feudal overlord for his holdings in France. When John refused to attend, his lands in France were declared forfeit. In the subsequent war he succeeded in capturing his nephew Arthur of Brittany, whom many in Anjou and elsewhere regarded as Richard I's rightful heir. Arthur died in mysterious and suspicious circumstances. But once the great castle of Château Gaillard, Richard I's pride and joy, had fallen in March 1204, the collapse of Normandy followed swiftly. By 1206 all that was left of the inheritance of the Norman kings was the Channel Islands. John, however, was determined to recover his losses.

Struggle with the papacy

Upon his return to England John became involved in a conflict with Pope Innocent III over the choice of an archbishop. At Hubert Walter's death in 1205 the monks at Canterbury had secretly elected their subprior and sent him to Rome to receive the pallium from the pope. The secret got out, however, and John forced the election of one of his confidants, John de Grey, bishop of Norwich, who then was also sent to Rome. Innocent III was not a man to miss such a good opportunity to demonstrate the plenitude of papal power. He quashed both elections and engineered the election of the learned and talented cardinal Stephen Langton. John, however, refused to receive Stephen and seized the revenues of Canterbury. Since John had already quarreled with his half brother the archbishop of York, who had fled abroad, England was without either archbishop. In 1208 Innocent imposed an interdict on England, forbidding the administration of the sacraments and certain church rites. In the following year he excommunicated John. The bishops of Winchester and Norwich remained the sole support of John's power in the church. John made the most of the opportunity to collect the revenues of the sees vacated by bishops who had gone into exile.

In theory John's excommunication freed his vassals from their oaths of fealty to him, but there was no immediate rebellion. John was able to conduct highly successful expeditions to Scotland, Wales, and Ireland,

and it was not until 1212 that a plot, involving Robert Fitzwalter and Eustace de Vesci, was first hatched against the king. John's brilliant solution to the problem of multiple threats was to effect a reconciliation with the papacy. He agreed to accept Stephen Langton as archbishop, to reinstate the exiled clergy, and to compensate the church for his exactions. In addition he surrendered his kingdom to the pope, receiving it back as a fief from the pope. He now had an able ally at no great cost in terms of concessions on his part.

Revolt of the barons and Magna Carta

Ever since the loss of Normandy John had been building up a coalition of rulers in Germany and the Low Countries to assist him against the French king. His chief ally was Otto IV, king of Germany and Holy Roman emperor. Plans for a campaign in Poitou proved very unpopular in England, especially with the northern barons. In 1214 John's allies were defeated at Bouvines, and the king's own campaign in Poitou disintegrated. John had to withdraw and return home to face his disgruntled barons.

John's efforts had been very costly, and measures such as the tax of a 13th in 1207 (which raised about £60,000) were highly unpopular. In addition John levied massive reliefs (inheritance duties) on some barons: Nicholas de Stuteville, for example, was charged 10,000 marks (about £6,666) to inherit his brother's lands in 1205. The fact alone that John, unlike his predecessors on the throne, spent most of his time in England made his rule more oppressive. Resistance sprang chiefly from the northern barons who had opposed service in Poitou, but by the spring of 1215 many others had joined them in protest against John's abuse or disregard of law and custom.

On June 15, 1215, the rebellious barons met John at Runnymede on the Thames. The king was presented with a document known as the Articles of the Barons, on the basis of which Magna Carta was drawn up. For a document hallowed in history during more than 750 years and frequently cited as a forerunner of the Declaration of Independence and the Declaration of the Rights of Man and of the Citizen, Magna Carta is a singularly undramatic document. It is thorny with problems of feudal law and custom that are largely untranslatable into modern idiom. Still, it was remarkable in many ways, not least because it was not written in a purely baronial interest but aimed to provide protection for all freemen. It was an attempt to provide guarantees against the sort of arbitrary disregard of feudal right that the three Angevin kings had made familiar.

The level of reliefs, for example, was set at £100 for a barony. Some clauses derived from concessions already offered by the king in efforts to divide opposition. The celebrated clause 39, which promised judgment by peers or by the law of the land to all freemen, had its origins in a letter sent by Innocent III to the king. The barons, however, were not attempting to dismantle royal government; in fact, many of the legal reforms of Henry II's day were reinforced. Nor did they seek to legitimate rebellion but rather they tried to ensure that the king was beneath rather than above the law. In immediate terms Magna Carta was a failure, for it was no more than a stage in ineffective negotiations to prevent civil war. John was released by the pope from his obligations under it. The document was, however, reissued with some changes under John's son, with papal approval, and so it became, in its 1225 version, a part of the permanent law of the land. John himself died in October 1216, with the civil war still at an inconclusive stage.

Economy and society

From about 1180 the pace of economic change quickened, with a shift to what is known as "high farming." The direct management of estates began to replace a rentier system. There was a marked price and wage inflation. Daily wages for a knight rose from eight pence a day early in

Henry II's day to two shillings under John. Landlords who relied upon fixed rents found times difficult, but most responded by taking manors into their own hands and by profiting from direct sales of demesne produce at market. A new class of professional estate managers, or stewards, began to appear. Towns continued to prosper, and many bought privileges of self-government from Richard I and John. The weaving industry was important, and England was noted as a producer of very high quality woolen cloth.

England, notably under Henry II, participated in the cosmopolitan movement that has come to be called the "12th-century Renaissance." Scholars frequented the court, and works on law and administration, especially the Dialogue of the Exchequer and the law book attributed to Ranulf de Glanville, show how modern ideas were being applied to the arts of government. In ecclesiastical architecture new methods of vaulting gave builders greater freedom, as may be seen, for example, in the construction of the choir at Canterbury, rebuilt after a fire in 1174 by William of Sens. In military architecture, the traditional rectangular plan was abandoned in keeps such as those at Orford and Conisborough. It was a self-confident, innovative, and assertive age.

The 13th century

The 13th century saw England develop a much clearer identity. The loss of continental possessions under King John focused the attention of the monarchy on England in a way that had not happened since 1066. Not only did the concept of the community of the realm develop used both by the crown and its opponents but the period was also notable in constitutional terms, seeing the beginning of Parliament.

The notion that the realm was a community and that it should be governed by representatives of that community perhaps found its first practical expression in the period following the issue of Magna Carta in which a council of regency ruled on behalf of a child king not yet able to govern in his own right. The phrase "community of the land" initially meant little more than the totality of the baronage. But the need to obtain a wider degree of consent to taxation, and perhaps also the impact of new ideas derived from Roman law, led to change. In addition the county communities exerted some pressure. Knights were being asked to play an increasingly important part in local government, and soon they made their voice heard at a national level. In the conflict that broke out between Henry III and the barons in the latter part of that king's reign, political terms acquired some sophistication, and under Edward I the concept of representation was further developed.

Henry III (1216–72)

Minority

The years until his death in 1219 were dominated by William Marshal, 1st Earl of Pembroke. As regent in all but name he achieved success in the civil war and, assisted by the papal legate Guala, did much to restore royal government in its aftermath. After Marshal's death there was a struggle for political power between Hubert de Burgh, the justiciar, and Peter des Roches, bishop of Winchester. Despite factional disputes, by the time Henry III declared himself to be of age in 1227, the minority government had achieved much. To have retained control of royal castles was a notable achievement, while the seizure of Bedford Castle from Fawkes de Breauté, a former protégé of King John, was a spectacular triumph.

Early reign

Henry came under increasing foreign dominance. His marriage in 1236 to Eleanor of Provence was followed by an influx of her Savoyard relations, while the other significant group of foreigners was headed by the king's half brothers, the Lusignans (children of his mother, Isabella, by her second marriage). Attempts to recover the lost lands in

France with expeditions in 1230 and 1242 were unsuccessful. Only in Wales did he achieve limited military success. In the 1250s plans, backed by the papacy, were made to place Henry's second son Edmund on the Sicilian throne; by 1258 these plans had involved the crown in an impossibly heavy financial commitment of 135,000 marks. A lenient policy toward the magnates did not yield much support for the king, and after 1237 it proved impossible to negotiate the grant of direct taxes with unwilling subjects.

Henry, moreover, faced a series of political crises. A baronial revolt in 1233, led by Richard, son of William Marshal, ended in tragedy. Richard was killed in Ireland, to the king's great grief: there were allegations that the king had been tricked into agreeing to the earl's destruction. Further political crises in 1238 and 1244 did nothing to resolve tensions. In 1238 the king's brother, Richard, Earl of Cornwall, rebelled, and leading advisers such as William of Savoy left the royal council. In 1244 Henry III faced opposition in Parliament from both lay and ecclesiastical magnates. A draft proposal suggested a complex system for adding four men to the council, who were to be "conservators of liberties" as well as overseers of royal finance. The king was able, however, to exploit the differences between his opponents, and their campaign achieved little. Henry was naive; he was, on the one hand, overly trustful and, on the other, bitter against those who betrayed his trust. There was growing discontent at a local level with the conduct of royal government.

The county communities

The society of the period should not be seen solely in terms of the feudal hierarchy. There are indications that the community of the county, dominated by local knights and the stewards of the magnates, was of growing importance in this period. Although the crown could and did rely extensively on the knights in local government and administration, the knights were resentful of any intrusion of royal officers from outside and determined to defend local rights and privileges. Incidents such as that in Lincolnshire in 1226, when the county community protested against innovations in the holding of the county court and appealed to Magna Carta, show a new political awareness at a local level. The localities resented the increased burdens placed on them by Henry III's government, and tension between court and country was evident.

Simon de Montfort and the Barons' War

The main crisis of the reign came in 1258 and was brought on by a cluster of causes. The Savoyard and Lusignan court factions were divided; there were reverses in Wales; the costs of the Sicilian affair were mounting; and there was perceived to be a crisis in local government. In May 1258 the king was compelled to agree to a meeting of Parliament and to the appointment of a joint committee of dissident barons and his own supporters, 12 from each side, which was to recommend measures for the reform of the kingdom. In the Provisions of Oxford, drawn up in June, a scheme was set out for the creation of a council of 15 to supervise royal government. Parliament was to be held three times a year, at which the 15 would meet with 12 barons representing "the community" (le commun in the original French).

The office of justiciar was to be revived, and he, with the chancellor and treasurer, was to account annually before the council. The new justiciar was to hear complaints throughout the country against royal officials. Sheriffs were to be local men, appointed for one year. The households of the king and queen were to be reformed. The drafting of further measures took time. In October 1259 a group calling itself the Community of Bachelors, which seems to have claimed to represent the lesser vassals and knights, petitioned for the fulfillment of the promises of the magnates and king to remedy its grievances. As a result the Provisions of Westminster were duly published, comprising detailed legal measures that in many cases were in the interests of the knightly class.

The Provisions of Oxford led to two years in which the king was under tutelage; he was less even than the first among equals because he was not free to choose his own councillors. The Oxford settlement, however, began to break down in 1260. There were divisions among the king's opponents, notably between the Earl of Gloucester and the ambitious Simon de Montfort, Earl of Leicester, Henry's brother-in-law. The king's eldest son, Edward, at first backed the unpopular Lusignans, whose exile had been demanded, but then came to an agreement with Simon de Montfort before being reconciled to his father. In 1261, when a papal bull released Henry from his oath to support the Provisions of Oxford, he dismissed the baronial sheriffs, castellans, and other officials imposed on him. Simon de Montfort, by now the undisputed leader of the opposition, raised rebellion, but an agreement was reached to submit the dispute to the arbitration of Louis IX of France. The verdict of the Mise of Amiens in 1264, however, was so favourable to Henry III that Simon de Montfort could not accept it.

Civil war was inevitable. In May 1264 Simon won a resounding victory at Lewes, and a new form of government was set up. Representatives of the boroughs were summoned to Parliament for the first time early in 1265, along with knights of the shire. Simon's motive for summoning Parliament was undoubtedly political: he needed support from many elements of society. In May 1265 the young Edward, held hostage since 1264 to ensure fulfillment of the terms of the peace of Lewes, escaped and rallied the royalist forces, notably the Welsh marcher lords who played a decisive part throughout these conflicts. In August, Simon was defeated and slain at Evesham.

Later reign

Henry spent the remainder of his reign settling the problems created by the rebellion. He deprived Simon's supporters of their lands, but "the Disinherited" fought back from redoubts in forests or fens. The garrison of Kenilworth Castle carried on a notable resistance. Terms were set in 1266 for former rebels to buy back their lands, and with the issue of the Statute of Marlborough, which renewed some of the reform measures of the Provisions of Westminster, the process of reconstruction began. By 1270 the country was sufficiently settled for Edward to be able to set off on crusade, from which he did not return until two years after his father's death. By then the community of the realm was ready to begin working with, not against, the crown.

Edward I (1272–1307)

Edward was in many ways the ideal medieval king. He went through a difficult apprenticeship, was a good fighter, and was a man who enjoyed both war and statecraft. His crusading reputation gave him prestige, and his chivalric qualities were admired. Although he had a gift for leadership, he lacked sympathy for others and had an obstinacy that led to inflexibility.

Law and government

In the 13th century the development of law became a dominant concern, as is shown by the great treatise On the Laws and Customs of England, attributed to the royal judge Bracton but probably put together in the 1220s and '30s under one of his predecessors on the King's Bench. Soon after Edward's return to England in 1274, a major inquiry into government in the localities took place that yielded the so-called Hundred Rolls, a heterogeneous group of records, and brought home the need for changes in the law. In 1275 the First Statute of Westminster was issued. A succession of other statutes followed in later years, providing a kind of supplement to the common law. Some measures protected the king's rights; others remedied the grievances of his subjects. In the quo warranto proceedings set up under the Statute of Gloucester of 1278 the magnates were asked by what warrant they claimed rights of jurisdiction and other franchises. This created much argument, which was resolved in the Statute of Quo Warranto of 1290. By the Statute of Mortmain of 1279 it was provided that no more land was to be given to the church without royal license. The Statute of Quia Emptores of 1290 had the effect of preventing further subinfeudation of land. In the first and second statutes of Westminster, of 1275 and 1285, many deficiencies in the law were corrected, such as those concerning the relationship between lords and tenants and the way in which the system of distraint was operated. Merchants benefited from the Statute of Acton Burnell of 1283 and the Statute of Merchants of 1285, which facilitated debt collection. Problems of law and order were tackled in the Statute of Winchester of 1285.

Finance

Edward began his reign with heavy debts incurred on crusade, and his various wars also were costly. In 1275 Edward gained a secure financial basis when he negotiated a grant of export duties on wool, woolfells, and hides that brought in an average of £10,000 a year. He borrowed extensively from Italian bankers on the security of these customs revenues. The system of levying taxes on an assessment of the value of movable goods was also of great value. Successive profitable taxes were granted, mostly in Parliament. It was partly in return for one such tax, in 1290, that Edward expelled the Jews from England. Their moneylending activities had made them unpopular, and royal exploitation had so impoverished the Jews that there was no longer an advantage for Edward in keeping them in England.

The growth of Parliament

Edward fostered the concept of the community of the realm and the practice of calling representative knights of the shire and burgesses from the towns to Parliament. Representatives were needed to give consent to taxation, as well as to enhance communication between the king and his subjects. The process of petitioning the king and his council in Parliament was greatly encouraged. Historians have argued much about the nature of Edward's Parliament, some seeing the dispensation of justice as the central element, others emphasizing the multifaceted character of an increasingly complex institution. Some see Edward as responding to the dictates of Roman law, while others interpret the development of Parliament in terms of the practical solution of financial and political problems.

Historians used to refer to the 1295 assembly as the Model Parliament because it contained all the elements later associated with the word parliament, but in fact these can all be found earlier. The writs to the sheriffs asking them to call knights and burgesses did, however, reach a more or less final form in 1295. They were to be summoned "with full and sufficient authority on behalf of themselves and the community . . . to do whatever shall be ordained by common counsel." Representatives of the lower clergy were also summoned. This Parliament was fully representative of local communities and of the whole community of the realm, but many Parliaments were attended solely by the magnates with no representatives present.

Edward's wars

In the first half of his reign Edward was thoroughly successful in Wales. Llywelyn ap Gruffudd, prince of Gwynedd, had taken advantage of the Barons' War to try to expand his authority throughout Wales. He refused to do homage to Edward, and in 1277 the English king conducted a short and methodical campaign against him. Using a partly feudal, partly paid army, the core of which was provided by the royal household knights, and a fleet from the Cinque Ports, Edward won a quick victory and exacted from Llywelyn the Treaty of Conway. Llywelyn agreed to perform fealty and homage, to pay a large indemnity (from which he was soon excused), and to surrender certain districts of North Wales. There was considerable Welsh resentment after 1277 at the manner in which Edward imposed his jurisdiction in Wales.

David, Llywelyn's younger brother, was responsible for a renewal of war in 1282. He was soon joined by Llywelyn, who was killed in battle late in the year. David was captured and executed as a traitor in 1283. This second Welsh war proved much longer, more costly, and more difficult for the English than the first. In the succeeding peace North Wales was organized into counties, and law was revised along English lines. Major castles, notably Flint and Rhuddlan, had been built after the first Welsh war; now Conway, Caernarvon, and Harlech were started, designed by a Savoyard expert, Master James of St. George. Merchant settlements, colonized with English craftsmen and merchants, were founded. Archbishop Pecham reorganized the Welsh church and brought it more fully under the sway of Canterbury. A brief revolt in 1287 was soon quelled, but Edward faced a major rebellion in 1294–95, after which he founded the last of his Welsh castles, Beaumaris in Anglesey.

Edward devoted much attention to Gascony, the land he held in southwestern France. He went there prior to returning to England at the start of the reign and spent the period 1286–89 there. In 1294 he had to undertake a costly defense of his French lands, when war began with Philip IV, king of France. Open hostilities lasted until 1297. In this case the French were the aggressors. Following private naval warfare between Gascon and Norman sailors, Philip summoned Edward (who, as Duke of Aquitaine, was his vassal) to his court and, having deceived English negotiators, decreed Gascony confiscate. Edward built up a grand alliance against the French, but the war proved costly and inconclusive.

Edward intervened in Scotland in 1291, when he claimed jurisdiction over a complex succession dispute. King Alexander III had been killed when his horse fell one stormy night in 1286. His heiress was his three-year-old granddaughter, Margaret, the Maid of Norway. Arrangements were made for her to marry Edward's son Edward, but these plans were thwarted by Margaret's death in 1290. There were 13 claimants to the Scottish throne, the two main candidates being John de Balliol and Robert de Bruce, both descendants of David, 8th Earl of Huntingdon, brother of William I the Lion. Balliol was the grandson of David's eldest daughter, and Bruce was the son of his second daughter. A court of 104 auditors, of whom 40 were chosen by Balliol and 40 by Bruce, was set up. Balliol was designated king and performed fealty and homage to Edward.

Edward did all he could to emphasize his own claims to feudal suzerainty over Scotland, and his efforts to put these into effect provoked Scottish resistance. In 1295 the Scots, having imposed a baronial council on Balliol, made a treaty with the French. War was inevitable, and in a swift and successful campaign Edward defeated Balliol in 1296, forcing him to abdicate. The victory, however, had been too easy. Revolt against the inept officials Edward had appointed to rule in Scotland came in 1297, headed by William Wallace and Andrew Moray. Victory for Edward at the battle of Falkirk in 1298, however, did not win the war. A lengthy series of costly campaigns appeared to have brought success by 1304, and in the next year Edward set up a scheme for governing Scotland, by now termed by the English a land, not a kingdom. But in 1306 Robert de Bruce, grandson of the earlier claimant to the throne, a man who had fought on both sides in the war, seized the Scottish throne and reopened the conflict, which continued into the reign of Edward II, who succeeded his father in 1307.

It has been claimed that during his wars Edward I transformed the traditional feudal host into an efficient, paid army. In fact, feudal summonses continued throughout his reign, though only providing a proportion of the army. The paid forces of the royal household were a very important element, but it is clear that the magnates also provided substantial unpaid forces for campaigns of which they approved. The scale of infantry recruitment increased notably, enabling Edward to muster armies up to 30,000 strong. The king's military successes were primarily due to the skill of his government in mobilizing resources, in terms of men, money, and supplies, on an unprecedented scale.

Domestic difficulties

The wars in the 1290s against the Welsh, French, and Scots imposed an immense burden on England. The character of the king's rule changed as the preoccupation with war put an end to further reform of government and law. Edward's subjects resented the heavy taxation, large-scale recruitment, and seizures of food supplies and wool crops. Pope Boniface VIII forbade the clergy to pay taxes to the king. A political crisis ensued in 1297, which was only partly resolved by the reissue of Magna Carta and some additional concessions. Argument continued for much of the rest of the reign, while the king's debts mounted. The Riccardi, Edward's bankers in the first part of the reign, were effectively bankrupted in 1294, and their eventual successors, the Frescobaldi, were unable to give the king the same level of support as their predecessors.

Social, economic, and cultural change

The population expanded rapidly in the 13th century, reaching a level of about five million. Great landlords prospered with the system of high farming, but the average size of small peasant holdings fell, with no compensating rise in productivity. There has been debate about the fate of the knightly class: some historians have argued that lesser landowners suffered a decline in wealth and numbers, while others have pointed to their increased political importance as evidence of their prosperity. Although there were probably both gainers and losers, the overall number of knights in England almost certainly fell to less than 2,000. Ties between magnates and their feudal tenants slackened as the relationship became increasingly a legal rather than a personal one. Lords began to adopt new methods of recruiting their retinues, using contracts demanding service either for life or for a short term, in exchange for fees, robes, and wages. Towns continued to grow, with many new ones being founded, but the weaving industry suffered a decline, in part because of competition from rural areas and in part as a result of restrictive guild practices. In trade, England became increasingly dependent on exports of raw wool.

The advent of the friars introduced a new element to the church. The universities of Oxford and Cambridge were developing rapidly, and in Robert Grosseteste and Roger Bacon, England produced two major, if somewhat eccentric, intellectual figures. Ecclesiastical architecture flourished, showing a strong French influence: Henry III's patronage of the new Westminster Abbey was particularly notable. Edward I's castles in North Wales rank high among the finest examples of medieval military architecture.

The 14th century

The 14th century, despite some gains, was a bleak age. At its beginning and close were kings whose reigns ended in failure. In between, however, came the 50-year reign of the popular and successful Edward III. During the century the importance of the Commons in Parliament continued to grow. But dominant factors of the age were war and plague. The increased scale, cost, and frequency of wars from the 1290s onward imposed heavy burdens on state and society. Conflicts between England and France continued intermittently throughout the century, those from 1337 onward being called the Hundred Years' War. The Black Death struck in 1348–49; it became endemic, recurring several times in the second half of the century, and brought with it profound economic and social change.

Edward II (1307–27)

Edward II's reign was an almost unmitigated disaster. He inherited some of his problems from his father, the most significant being a treasury deficit of some £200,000, and the Scottish war. He inherited none of his father's strengths. He was a good horseman but did not enjoy swordplay or tournaments, preferring swimming, ditch digging, thatching, and theatricals. Although surrounded by a ruling class strongly tied to his family by blood and service, Edward rejected the company of his peers, preferring that of Piers Gaveston, son of a Gascon knight, with whom he probably had a homosexual relationship. Edward's father had exiled Gaveston in an attempt to quash the friendship. Edward the son recalled him and conferred on him the highest honours he had to bestow: the earldom of Cornwall and marriage to his niece Margaret de Clare, sister of the Earl of Gloucester. Edward also recalled Archbishop Winchelsey and Bishop Bek of Durham, both of whom had gone into exile under Edward I. He dismissed and put on trial one of his father's most trusted servants, the treasurer, Walter Langton.

Historians used to emphasize the constitutional struggle that took place in this reign, seeing a conflict between a baronial ideal of government conducted with the advice of the magnates and based on the great offices of state, the Chancery and the Exchequer, on the one hand, and a royal policy of reliance upon the departments of the royal household, notably the wardrobe and chamber, on the other. More recent interpretations have shifted the emphasis to personal rivalries and ambitions.

Opposition to Edward began to build as early as January 1308. At the coronation in February a new clause was added to the king's oath that obligated him to promise that he would keep such laws "as the community of the realm shall have chosen." In April the barons came armed to Parliament and warned the king that "homage and the oath of allegiance are stronger and bind more by reason of the crown than by reason of the person of the king." The first phase of the reign culminated in the production of the Ordinances in 1311. They were in part directed against Gaveston who was again to be exiled and other royal favourites, but much of the document looked back to the grievances of Edward I's later years, echoing concessions made by the king in 1300. Hostility was expressed to the practice of prise (compulsory purchase of foodstuffs for royal armies). Baronial consent was required for foreign war (possibly in remembrance of Edward I's Flanders campaign of 1297).

The privy seal was not to be used to interfere in justice. A long list of officials were to be chosen with the advice and consent of the barons in Parliament. All revenues were to be paid into the Exchequer. The king's bankers, the Frescobaldi, who had also served Edward I, were to be expelled from the realm. Royal grants of land made since the appointment of the Ordainers in 1310 were annulled. It is noteworthy that the first clear statement that consent should be given in Parliament is to be found in the Ordinances. No explicit role, however, was given to the Commons, the representative element in Parliament.

The middle years of Edward's reign were dominated by the enigmatic figure of Thomas, 2nd Earl of Lancaster, the king's cousin and chief opponent, whose surly inactivity for long periods blocked effective political initiatives. His political program never amounted to much more than enforcement of the Ordinances. He supervised the capture and execution of Gaveston in 1312 and came to dominance after the disastrous defeat of a royal army at the hands of the Scottish pikemen and bowmen at Bannockburn in 1314. At the Lincoln Parliament of 1316 he was named chief councillor, but he soon withdrew from active government.

A conciliar regime was set up with the Treaty of Leake of 1318. This was once thought to have been the work of a "middle party," but the political alliances of this period cannot be categorized in such a manner. New royal favourites emerged, and in 1321 the peace was broken when the Welsh marcher lords moved against two of them, a father and son, both called Hugh Despenser. When Parliament met, the two were exiled, but they soon returned. In this brief civil war, which ended in 1322, Edward was victorious. He had Lancaster executed for treason after his ignominious defeat at Boroughbridge in 1322. In death Lancaster attracted a popular sympathy he had rarely received in life, with many rumours of miracles at his tomb. Edward had many of Lancaster's followers executed in a horrific bloodbath. In the same year the Ordinances were repealed in Parliament at York, and in the Statute of York the intention of returning to the constitutional practices of the past was announced.

But in specifying that the "consent of the prelates, earls, and barons, and of the community of the realm" was required for legislation, the Statute of York provided much scope for historical argument; some historians have made claims for a narrow baronial interpretation of what is meant by "community of the realm," while others have seen the terminology as giving the representative element in Parliament a new role. A tract written in this period, the Modus tenendi parliamentum, certainly placed a new emphasis on the representatives of shire, borough, and lower clergy. In terms of practical politics, however, the Statute of York permitted the fullest resumption of royal authority.

The final period of the reign saw the Despensers restored to power. They carried out various administrative reforms, ably assisted by the treasurer, Walter Stapledon. For the first time in many years, a substantial treasury of about £60,000 was built up. At the same time, crude blackmail and blatant corruption characterized this regime. A brief war against the French was unsuccessful. The reign ended with the invasion of Edward's estranged queen, Isabella, assisted by Roger Mortimer, soon to be Earl of March. With the support above all of the Londoners, the government was overthrown, the Despensers executed, and the king imprisoned. Parliament was called in his name, and he was simultaneously deposed and persuaded to abdicate in favour of his son, Edward III. After two conspiracies to release him, he was almost certainly killed in Berkeley Castle.

Edward III (1327–77)

The Hundred Years' War, to 1360

Edward III achieved personal power when he overthrew his mother's and Mortimer's dominance in 1330 at the age of 17. Their regime had been just as corrupt as that of the Despensers but less constructive. The young king had been sadly disappointed by an unsuccessful campaign against the Scots in 1327; in 1333 the tide turned when he achieved victory at Halidon Hill. Edward gave his support to Edward Balliol as claimant to the Scottish throne, rather than to Robert I's son David II. But as long as the Scots had the support of the French king Philip VI, final success proved impossible, and this was one of the causes for the outbreak of the French war in 1337. Another was the long-standing friction over Gascony, chronic since 1294 and stemming ultimately from the Treaty of Paris of 1259.

By establishing that the kings of England owed homage to the kings of France for Gascony the treaty had created an awkward relationship. The building of bastides (fortified towns) by each side contributed to friction, as did piracy by English and French sailors. The English resented any appeals to the French court by Gascons. English-French rivalry also extended into the Netherlands, which was dependent on English wool for industrial prosperity but some of whose states, including Flanders, were subject to French claims of suzerainty. Finally, there was the matter of the French throne itself. Edward, through his mother, was closer in blood to the last ruler of the Capetian dynasty than was the Valois Philip VI. The claim was of great propaganda value to Edward, for it meant that he did not appear as simply a rebellious vassal of the French king. His allies could fight for him without dishonour.

The initial phase of the war was inconclusive. Edward won a naval victory at Sluys in 1340, but he lacked the resources to follow it up. Although intervention in a succession dispute in Brittany saw the English register successes, stalemate came in 1343. The first great triumph came with the invasion of Normandy in 1346. As Edward was retreating northward, he defeated the French at Crécy and then settled to the siege of Calais, which fell in 1347. The French allies, the Scots, were also defeated in 1346 at Neville's Cross, where their king, David II, was taken prisoner. The focus of the war moved south in 1355, when the king's son, the Black Prince, was sent to Gascony. He launched a successful raid in 1355 and another in 1356, and at Poitiers he defeated and captured the French king John, for whom a heavy ransom was charged. As at Crécy, English archery proved decisive. A major campaign in 1359–60, planned as the decisive blow, proved unsatisfactory to the English. Rheims did not open its gates to Edward as he had hoped, and a storm caused severe damage to the army and its baggage in April 1360. Negotiations led to a truce at Brétigny, and in the subsequent negotiations Edward agreed to drop his claim to the French throne. In return, English possessions in France would be held in full sovereignty. The terms, particularly those involving the exchange of territory, were not carried out in full, but neither side wished to reopen the war immediately. War was costly, and Edward III's armies were no longer recruited by feudal means. Most were formed by contract, and all who fought received wages as well as a share of the profits of campaigning. These could be substantial if wealthy nobles were captured and ransomed.

Domestic achievements

The war, and the need to finance it, dominated domestic affairs under Edward III. The king faced a crisis in 1340–41 because he found himself disastrously indebted by 1339, even though he had received generous grants from Parliament since 1336. It was estimated that he owed £300,000. He had seized wool exports and had borrowed recklessly from Italian, English, and Flemish bankers and merchants. A grant in 1340 of a ninth of all produce failed to yield the expected financial return. In the autumn of 1340 Edward returned from abroad and charged John Stratford, archbishop of Canterbury, the man who had been in charge in his absence, with working against him. He also engaged in a widespread purge of royal ministers.

Stratford whipped up opposition to the king, and in Parliament in 1341 statutes were passed that were reminiscent of the kind of restraints put on earlier and less popular kings. Officers of state and of the king's household were to be appointed and sworn in Parliament. Commissioners were to be sworn in Parliament to audit the royal accounts. Peers were to be entitled to trial before their peers in Parliament. Breaches of the Charters were to be reported in Parliament. Charges were brought against Stratford, only to be dropped. But in 1343 Edward III was able to repudiate the statutes. The crisis had little permanent effect, though it did demonstrate the king's dependence on Parliament, and within it on the Commons, for supply.

In the following years the country was well governed, with William Edington and John Thoresby serving the king loyally and well. Edward's compliance toward the requests of the Commons made it relatively easy for him to obtain the grants he needed. Discontent in 1346–47 was overcome by the good news from France. Much of the legislation passed at this time was in the popular interest. In 1352 the king agreed that no one should be bound to find soldiers for the war save by common consent in Parliament, and demands for purveyance were moderated. The Statute of Provisors of 1351 set up statutory procedures against the unpopular papal practice of making appointments to church benefices in England, and the Statute of Praemunire two years later forbade appeals to Rome in patronage disputes.

The crown in practice had sufficient weapons available to it to deal with these matters, but Edward was ready to accept the views of his subjects, even though he did little about them later. Much attention was given to the organization of the wool trade because it was intimately bound up with the finance of war. In 1363 the Calais staple was set up, under which all English exports of raw wool were channeled through Calais. The currency was reformed very effectively with the introduction in the 1340s of a gold coinage alongside the traditional silver pennies.

Law and order

The maintenance of law and order, a prime duty for a medieval king, had reached a point of crisis by the end of Edward I's reign when special commissions, known as commissions of trailbaston, were set up to try to deal with the problem. Matters became worse under Edward II, from whose reign there is much evidence of gang warfare, often involving men of knightly status. Maintaining law and order was also an urgent issue in Edward III's reign. In the early years there was conflict between the magnates, who wanted to be given full authority in the localities, and the county knights and gentry, who favoured locally appointed keepers of the peace. A possible solution, favoured by the chief justice, Geoffrey Scrope, was to extend the jurisdiction of the king's bench into the localities.

There was a major crime wave in 1346 and 1347, intensified by the activities of soldiers returning from France. The justices reacted by greatly extending the use of accusations of treason, but the Commons protested against procedures they claimed did little to promote order and much to impoverish the people. In 1352 the crown gave way, producing in the Statute of Treason a narrow definition of great treason that made it impossible to threaten common criminals with the harsh penalties which followed conviction for treason. The concern of the Commons had been that in cases of treason goods and land forfeited by those found guilty went to the crown, not to the overlord. In 1361 the position of justice of the peace was established by statute, marking another success for the Commons.

The crises of Edward's later years

The war with France was reopened in 1369 and went badly. The king was in his dotage and, since the death of Queen Philippa in 1369, in the clutches of his unscrupulous mistress Alice Perrers. The heir to the throne, Edward the Black Prince, was ill and died in 1376. Lionel of Antwerp, Duke of Clarence, the next son, had died in 1368, and John of Gaunt, Duke of Lancaster, the third surviving son, was largely occupied with his claims to Castile, his inheritance through his second wife, Constance. Edmund of Langley, the fourth surviving son, was a nonentity, and the youngest, Thomas of Woodstock, was not yet of age.

In 1371 Parliament demanded the dismissal of William of Wykeham, the chancellor, and the appointment of laymen to state offices. The new government, dominated by men such as William Latimer, the chamberlain, proved unpopular and ineffective. When the so-called Good Parliament met in 1376, grievances had accumulated and needed to be dealt with. As in previous crises, a committee consisting of four bishops, four earls, and four barons was set up to take responsibility for the reforms. Then, under the leadership of Peter de la Mare, who may be termed the first Speaker, the Commons impeached Latimer, Alice Perrers, and a number of ministers and officials, some of whom had profited personally from the administration of the royal finances. The Commons took the role of prosecutors before the Lords in what amounted to a new procedure.

John of Gaunt, an unpopular figure at this time, had, as a result of the king's illness, presided uncomfortably over the Good Parliament. He ensured that the achievement of Peter de la Mare and his colleagues was ephemeral, taking charge of the government at the end of the reign. De la Mare was jailed in Nottingham. William of Wykeham was attacked for alleged peculation as chancellor, and Alice Perrers was restored to court. The Parliament of 1377 reversed all important acts of the Good Parliament. There were rumours in London that Gaunt aimed at the throne. But the Black Prince's widow made peace between Gaunt and the Londoners, and Wykeham's temporalities were restored. The reign ended in truce, if not peace.

Richard II (1377–99)

Richard II's reign was fraught with crises economic, social, political, and constitutional. He was 10 years old when his grandfather died, and the first problem the country faced was having to deal with his minority. A "continual council" was set up to "govern the king and his kingdom." Although John of Gaunt was still the dominant figure in the royal family, neither he nor his brothers were included.

The Peasants' Revolt (1381)

Financing the increasingly expensive and unsuccessful war with France was a major preoccupation. At the end of Edward III's reign a new device, a poll tax of four pence a head, had been introduced. A similar but graduated tax followed in 1379, and in 1380 another set at one shilling a head was granted. It proved inequitable and impractical, and, when the government tried to speed up collection in the spring of 1381, a popular rebellion the Peasants' Revolt ensued. Although the poll tax was the spark that set it off, there were also deeper causes related to changes in the economy and to political developments. The government, in particular, engendered hostility to the legal system by its policies of expanding the powers of the justices of the peace at the expense of local and manorial courts.

In addition, popular poor preachers spread subversive ideas with slogans such as: "When Adam delved and Eve span / Who was then the gentleman?" The Peasants' Revolt began in Essex and Kent. Widespread outbreaks occurred through the southeast of England, taking the form of assaults on tax collectors, attacks on landlords and their manor houses, destruction of documentary evidence of villein status, and attacks on lawyers. Attacks on religious houses, such as that at St. Albans, were particularly severe, perhaps because they had been among the most conservative of landlords in commuting labour services.

The men of Essex and Kent moved on London to attack the king's councillors. Admitted to the city by sympathizers, they attacked John of Gaunt's palace of the Savoy as well as the Fleet prison. On June 14 the young king made them various promises at Mile End; on the same day they broke into the Tower and killed Sudbury, the chancellor, Hales, the treasurer, and other officials. On the next day Richard met the rebels again at Smithfield, and their main leader, Wat Tyler, presented their demands. But during the negotiations Tyler was attacked and slain by the mayor of London. The young king rode forward and reassured the rebels, asking them to follow him to Clerkenwell. This proved to be a turning point, and the rebels, their supplies exhausted, began to make their way home. Richard went back on the promises he had made, saying, "Villeins ye are and villeins ye shall remain." In October Parliament confirmed the king's revocation of charters but demanded amnesty save for a few special offenders.

The events of the Peasants' Revolt may have given Richard an exalted idea of his own powers and prerogative as a result of his success at Smithfield, but for the rebels the gains of the rising amounted to no more than the abolition of the poll taxes. Improvements in the social position of the peasantry did occur, but not so much as a consequence of the revolt as of changes in the economy that would have occurred anyhow.

John Wycliffe

Religious unrest was another subversive factor under Richard II. England had been virtually free from heresy until John Wycliffe, a priest and an Oxford scholar, began his career as a religious reformer with two treatises in 1375–76. He argued that the exercise of lordship depended on grace and that, therefore, a sinful man had no right to authority. Priests and even the pope himself, Wycliffe went on to argue, might not necessarily be in a state of grace and thus would lack authority. Such doctrines appealed to anticlerical sentiments and brought Wycliffe into direct conflict with the church hierarchy, although he received protection from John of Gaunt. The beginning of the Great Schism in 1378 gave Wycliffe fresh opportunities to attack the papacy, and in a treatise of 1379 on the Eucharist he openly denied the doctrine of transubstantiation. He was ordered before a church court at Lambeth in 1378. In 1380 his views were condemned by a commission of theologians at Oxford, and he was forced to leave the university. At Lutterworth he continued to write voluminously until his death in 1384. The movement he inspired was known as Lollardy. Two of his followers translated the Bible into English, and others went out to spread Wycliffe's doctrines, which soon became debased and popularized. The movement continued to expand despite the death of its founder and the government's attempts to destroy it.

Political struggles and Richard's deposition

Soon after putting down the Peasants' Revolt, Richard began to build up a court party, partly in opposition to Gaunt. A crisis was precipitated in 1386 when the king asked Parliament for a grant to meet the French threat. Parliament responded by demanding the dismissal of the king's favourites, but Richard insisted that he would not dismiss so much as a scullion in his kitchen at the request of Parliament. In the end he was forced by the impeachment of the chancellor, Michael de la Pole, to agree to the appointment of a reforming commission. Richard withdrew from London and went on a "gyration" of the country. He called the judges before him at Shrewsbury and asked them to pronounce the actions of Parliament illegal. An engagement at Radcot Bridge, at which Richard's favourite, Robert de Vere, 9th Earl of Oxford, was defeated, settled the matter of ascendancy. In the Merciless Parliament of 1388 five lords accused the king's friends of treason under an expansive definition of the crime.

Richard was chastened, but he began to recover his authority as early as the autumn of 1388 at the Cambridge Parliament. Declaring himself to be of age in 1389, Richard announced that he was taking over the government. He pardoned the Lords Appellant and ruled with some moderation until 1394, when his queen, Anne of Bohemia, died. After putting down a rebellion in Ireland, he was, for a time, almost popular. He began to implement his personal policy once more and rebuilt a royal party with the help of a group of young nobles. He made a 28-year truce with France and married the French king's seven-year-old daughter. He built up a household of faithful servants, including the notorious Sir John Bushy, Sir William Bagot, and Sir Henry Green. He enlisted household troops and built a wide network of "king's knights" in the counties, distributing to them his personal badge, the White Hart.

The first sign of renewed crisis emerged in January 1397, when complaints were put forward in Parliament and their author, Thomas Haxey, was adjudged a traitor. Richard's rule, based on fear rather than consent, became increasingly tyrannical. Three of the Lords Appellant of 1388 were arrested in July and tried in Parliament. The Earl of Arundel was executed and Warwick exiled. Gloucester, whose death was reported to Parliament, had probably been murdered. The acts of the 1388 Parliament were repealed. Richard was granted the customs revenues for life, and the powers of Parliament were delegated to a committee after the assembly was dissolved. Richard also built up a power base in Cheshire.

Events leading to Richard's downfall followed quickly. The Duke of Norfolk and Henry Bolingbroke, John of Gaunt's son, accused each other of treason and were banished, the former for life, the latter for 10 years. When Gaunt himself died early in 1399, Richard confiscated his estates instead of allowing his son to claim them. Richard, seemingly secure, went off to Ireland. Henry, however, landed at Ravenspur in Yorkshire to claim, as he said, his father's estates and the hereditary stewardship. The Percys, the chief lords in the north, welcomed him. Popular support was widespread, and when Richard returned from Ireland his cause was lost.

The precise course of events is hard to reconstruct, in view of subsequent alterations to the records. A Parliament was called in Richard's name, but before it was fully assembled at the end of September, its members were presented with Richard's alleged abdication and Henry's claim to the throne as legitimate descendant of Henry III as well as by right of conquest. Thirty-three articles of deposition were set forth against Richard, and his abdication and deposition were duly accepted. Richard died at Pontefract Castle, either of self-starvation or by smothering. Thus ended the last attempt of a medieval king to exercise arbitrary power. Whether or not Richard had been motivated by new theories about the nature of monarchy, as some have claimed, he had failed in the practical measures necessary to sustain his power. He had tried to rule through fear and mistrust in his final years, but he had neither gained sufficient support among the magnates by means of patronage nor created a popular basis of support in the shires.

Economic crisis and cultural change

Although the outbreak of the Black Death in 1348 dominated the economy of the 14th century, a number of adversities had already occurred in the preceding decades. Severe rains in 1315 and 1316 caused famine, which led to the spread of disease. Animal epidemics in succeeding years added to the problems, as did an increasing shortage of currency in the 1330s. Economic expansion, which had been characteristic of the 13th century, had slowed to a halt. The Black Death, possibly a combination of bubonic and pneumonic plagues, carried off from one-third to one-half of the population. In some respects it took time for its effects to become detrimental to the economy, but with subsequent outbreaks, as in 1361 and 1369, the population declined further, causing a severe labour shortage. By the 1370s wages had risen dramatically and prices of foodstuffs fallen. Hired labourers, being fewer, asked for higher wages and better food, and peasant tenants, also fewer, asked for better conditions of tenure when they took up land.

Some landlords responded by trying to reassert labour services where they had been commuted. The Ordinance (1349) and Statute (1351) of Labourers tried to set maximum wages at the levels of the pre-Black Death years, but strict enforcement proved impossible. The Peasants' Revolt of 1381 was one result of the social tension caused by the adjustments needed after the epidemic. Great landlords saw their revenues fall as a result of the Black Death, although probably by only about 10 percent, whereas for the lower orders of society real wages rose sharply by the last quarter of the 14th century because of low grain prices and high wages.

Edward III ruined the major Italian banking companies in England by failing to repay loans early in the Hundred Years' War. This provided openings for English merchants, who were given monopolies of wool exports by the crown in return for their support. The most notable was William de la Pole of Hull, whose family rose to noble status. Heavy taxation of wool exports was one reason for the growth of the cloth industry and cloth exports in the 14th century. The wine trade from Gascony was also important. In contrast to the 13th century, no new towns were founded, but London in particular continued to prosper despite the ravages of plague.

In cultural terms, a striking change in the 14th century was the increasing use of English. Although an attempt to make the use of English mandatory in the law courts failed because lawyers claimed that they could not plead accurately in the language, the vernacular began to creep into public documents and records. Henry of Lancaster even used English when he claimed the throne in 1399. Chaucer wrote in both French and English, but his important poetry is in the latter. The early 14th century was an impressive age for manuscript illumination in England, with the so-called East Anglian school, of which the celebrated Luttrell Psalter represents a late example. In ecclesiastical architecture the development of the Perpendicular style, largely in the second half of the 14th century, was particularly notable.

Lancaster and York

Recent scholarship has done much to transform the view that the 15th century was a period dominated by a factious nobility, when constructive achievements were few. In particular, the character of the nobility has been reconceived, and the century has emerged in a more positive light. It appears that even in politics and administration much was done that anticipated the achievements of the Tudors, while in the economy the foundations for future growth and prosperity were laid.

Henry IV (1399–1413)

Henry of Lancaster gave promise of being able to develop a better rapport with his people than his predecessor, Richard II. He was a warrior of great renown who had traveled to Jerusalem and had fought in Prussia against infidels. He also had a reputation for affability and for statesmanlike self-control, and he had won his crown with the support of "the estates of the realm." It did not matter much whether that meant Parliament or something more vague and symbolic. Henry, however, intended to rule as a true king, with the prerogatives of the crown unimpaired, whereas his Parliaments, from the first, expected him to govern with the advice and consent of his council, and to listen to Parliament regarding requests for money. Thus although Archbishop Arundel stressed in 1399 that Henry wished to be properly advised and that he intended to be governed by common advice and counsel, some argument and conflict was inevitable.

The rebellions

Henry's immediate task after his accession was to put down a rebellion threatening to restore Richard. The earls of Rutland, Kent, and Huntingdon, supported by the bishop of Carlisle, conspired against the king. The rising was unexpected, but Henry won support in London and defeated the rebels near Cirencester. More significant was the revolt of Owain Glyn Dwr that broke out in 1399 and became serious in 1402. Glyn Dwr sought a French alliance and captured Edmund Mortimer, uncle of the Earl of March, Richard II's legitimate heir. Mortimer was persuaded to join the rebellion, which now aimed to make March king. In 1403 the Welsh rebels joined the Percys of Northumberland in a powerful coalition. The younger Percy, "Hotspur," was killed at Shrewsbury in 1403. The elder was pardoned, only to rebel once more in 1405, again in conjunction with Glyn Dwr. Henry broke the alliance with a victory at Shipton Moor. Percy was finally killed in 1408, but Glyn Dwr, driven into the mountains of North Wales, was never captured.

Henry and Parliament

Henry's relations with his Parliaments were uneasy. The main problem, of course, was money. Henry, as Duke of Lancaster, was a wealthy man, but as king he had forfeited some of his income by repudiating Richard II's tactics, though he also avoided Richard's extravagance. His needs were still great, threatened as he was by rebellion in England and war in France. A central issue was Parliament's demand, as in 1404, that the king take back all royal land that had been granted and leased out since 1366. This was so that he might "live of his own." The king could hardly adopt a measure that would cause much upheaval. Arguments in 1406 were so protracted that the Parliament met for 159 days, becoming the longest Parliament of the medieval period. On several occasions the Commons insisted on taxes being spent in the way that they wished, primarily on the defense of the realm.

The later Parliaments of Henry's reign brought no new problems, but the king became less active in government as he was more and more incapacitated by illness. From 1408 to 1411 the government was dominated first by Archbishop Arundel and then by the king's son Henry, who, with the support of the Beaufort brothers, sons of John of Gaunt by Katherine Swynford, attempted to win control over the council. There was much argument over the best political strategy to adopt in France, where civil war was raging; young Henry wanted to resume the war in France, but the king favoured peace. In 1411 the king recovered his authority, and the Prince of Wales was dismissed from the council. Uneasy relations between the prince and his father lasted until Henry IV's death in 1413.

Henry V (1413–22)

Henry V's brief reign is important mainly for the glorious victories in France, which visited on his infant son the enormous and not-so-glorious burden of governing both France and England. Two rebellions undermined the security of the realm in the first two years of the reign. The first was organized by Sir John Oldcastle, a Lollard and former confidant of the king. Though Oldcastle was not arrested until 1417, little came of his rising. Another plot gathered around Richard, 5th Earl of Cambridge, a younger brother of the Duke of York. The aim was to place the Earl of March on the throne, but March himself gave the plot away, and the leading conspirators were tried and executed on the eve of the king's departure for France.

The French war

Henry invaded France in 1415 with a small army of some 9,000 men. The siege of Harfleur was followed by a march toward Calais. At Agincourt the English were forced to fight because their route onward was blocked; they won an astonishing victory. Between 1417 and 1419 Henry followed up this success with the conquest of Normandy and the grant of Norman lands to English nobles and lesser men. This was a new strategy for the English to adopt, replacing the plundering raids of the past. In 1420 in the Treaty of Troyes it was agreed that Henry would marry Catherine, Charles VI's daughter. He was to be heir to the French throne, and that throne was to descend to his heirs in perpetuity. But Charles VI's son, the Dauphin, was not a party to the treaty, and so the war continued. Henry, still wanting money but reluctant to ask for subsidies at a time when he needed all the support he could get for the treaty, obtained forced loans. There were increasing indications of unease in England. In 1422 Henry contracted dysentery and died at the siege of Meaux in August, leaving as his heir a son less than a year old.

Domestic affairs

England was competently governed under Henry V. Problems of law and order were dealt with by reviving the use of the King's Bench as a traveling court; central and local administration operated smoothly. Henry proved adept at persuading men to serve him energetically for limited rewards. Parliament, well-satisfied with the course of events in France, gave the king all the support he needed. War finance was efficiently managed, and although Henry died in debt, the level was a manageable one. His was a most successful reign.

Henry VI (1422–61 and 1470–71)

Henry VI was a pious and generous man, but he lacked the attributes needed for effective kingship. Above all he lacked political sense and was no judge of men. Until 1437 he was a child, under the regency of a council of nobles dominated by his uncles and his Beaufort kin. When he was declared of age, the Beauforts were the real rulers of England. In 1445, through the initiative of the Earl (later Duke) of Suffolk, he married Margaret of Anjou, who with Suffolk dominated the king. Finally, in the period from 1450 to 1461 he suffered two bouts of mental illness. During these crises Richard, 3rd Duke of York, ruled the kingdom as protector.

Domestic rivalries and the loss of France

In the first period of the reign John, Duke of Bedford, proved to be as able a commander in the French war as had his brother Henry V. But in 1429 Joan of Arc stepped forth and rallied French resistance. Bedford died in 1435, and the Congress of Arras, an effort at a general peace settlement, failed. When Philip of Burgundy deserted the English alliance and came to terms with Charles VII, the conflict became a war of attrition. By 1453 the English had lost all their overseas possessions save Calais.

Despite the factional nature of politics, there was no breakdown at home. The country was ruled by a magnate council with the increasingly reluctant financial support of Parliament. Humphrey, Duke of Gloucester, and Henry Beaufort, bishop of Winchester (cardinal from 1426), were the dominant figures. The main problem was financing the war. The bishop had great wealth, which he increased by lending to the crown, receiving repayment out of the customs. Divisions in the council became more acute after 1435, with Gloucester advocating an aggressive war policy. He was, however, discredited when his wife was accused of witchcraft in 1441.

In 1447 both Cardinal Beaufort and Gloucester died, the latter in suspicious circumstances. The Duke of Suffolk was in the ascendant; he had negotiated a peace with France in 1444 and arranged the king's marriage to Margaret of Anjou in 1445. When war was renewed in 1446, the English position in Normandy collapsed. Becoming the scapegoat for the English failure, Suffolk was impeached in the Parliament of March 1450. As he was fleeing into exile, he was slain by English sailors from a ship called the Nicholas of the Tower. Edmund Beaufort, 2nd Duke of Somerset, succeeded him as leader of the court party.

Cade's rebellion

Less than three months later Jack Cade, a man of obscure origins, led a popular rebellion in southeastern England. In contrast to the rising of 1381, this was not a peasant movement; Cade's followers included many gentry, whose complaints were mainly about lack of government rather than economic repression. Thus the remedies they proposed were political, such as the resumption of royal estates that had been granted out, the removal of corrupt councillors, and improved methods of collecting taxes. The rebels demanded that the king accept the counsel of Henry's rival, the Duke of York. They executed Lord Saye and Sele, the treasurer, and the sheriff of Kent, but the rising was soon put down.

The beginning of the Wars of the Roses

The so-called Wars of the Roses was the struggle between the Yorkist and Lancastrian descendants of Edward III for control of the throne and of local government. The origins of the conflict have been the subject of much debate. It can be seen as brought about as a result of Henry VI's inadequacy and the opposition of his dynastic rival Richard, Duke of York, but local feuds between magnates added a further dimension. Because of the crown's failure to control these disputes, they acquired national significance. Attempts have been made to link these civil conflicts to what is known as "bastard feudalism," the system that allowed magnates to retain men in their service by granting them fees and livery and made possible the recruiting of private armies. Yet this system can be seen as promoting stability in periods of strong rule as well as undermining weak rule such as that of Henry VI. Many nobles sought good government, rather than being factious, and were only forced into war by the king's incompetence. The outbreak of civil war in England was indirectly linked to the failure in France, for Henry VI's government had suffered a disastrous loss of prestige and, with it, authority.

The Duke of York had a claim to the throne in two lines of descent. One was through his mother, great-granddaughter of Lionel of Antwerp, Duke of Clarence, second surviving son of Edward III, and the other was through his father, son of Edmund of Langley, 1st Duke of York, fourth surviving son of Edward III. According to feudal principles he had a better hereditary right than anyone of the Lancastrian line. He had been sent as royal lieutenant to Ireland in 1446, but he returned from there with 4,000 men in 1450 to reassert his right to participate in the king's council and to counter Somerset's machinations. In 1454 York was made protector of the king, who had become insane in 1453, even though the queen and court party had tried to disguise the king's illness. Early in 1455 Henry recovered his wits. During his spell of insanity his queen had a son, Edward, which changed the balance of politics. York was no longer the heir apparent, and the country was faced with the prospect, should the king die, of another lengthy minority.

In 1455 York gathered forces in the north, alleging that he could not safely attend a council called to meet at Leicester without the support of his troops. He met the king at St. Albans. Negotiations were unsuccessful, and in the ensuing battle York's forces, larger than the king's, won a decisive victory. Somerset was slain and the king captured. A Yorkist regime was set up, with York as constable and the Earl of Warwick, emerging as the strong support of the Yorkist cause, as captain of Calais. The king fell ill again in the autumn of 1455, and York was again protector for a brief period; the king, however, recovered early in 1456.

Hostilities were renewed in 1459. The Yorkists fled without fighting before a royal force at Ludford Bridge, but the Lancastrians failed to make the most of the opportunity. Demands for money, purveyances, and commissions of array increased the burdens but not the benefits of Lancastrian rule. The earls of Warwick and Salisbury, with York's son Edward, used Calais as a base from which to invade England, landing at Sandwich in 1460. A brief battle at Northampton in July went overwhelmingly for the Yorkists, and the king was captured. At Parliament the Duke of York claimed the throne as heir to Richard II. The Commons and judges refused to consider a matter so high, leaving it to the Lords' decision. During the fortnight of debate the Lancastrians regrouped, and when Richard met them at Wakefield, he was defeated and killed. Warwick, somewhat later, was defeated at St. Albans.

The Yorkist cause would have been lost if it had not been for Richard's son, Edward, Earl of March, who defeated the Lancastrians first at Mortimer's Cross and then at Towton Moor early in 1461. He was crowned king on June 28, but dated his reign from March 4, the day the London citizens and soldiers recognized his right as king.

Edward IV (1461–70 and 1471–83)

During the early years of his reign, from 1461 to 1470, Edward was chiefly concerned with putting down opposition to his rule. Lancastrian resistance in the northeast and in Wales caused problems. France and Burgundy were also of concern because Margaret of Anjou's chief hope of recovering Lancastrian fortunes lay in French support; but Louis XI was miserly in his aid. Edward's main internal problem lay in his relations with Warwick, who had been his chief supporter in 1461. Richard Neville, 16th Earl of Warwick, called "the Kingmaker," was cousin to the king and related to much of the English nobility. Edward, however, refused to be dominated by him, particularly with respect to his marriage. When the crucial moment came in Warwick's negotiations for the king to marry the French king's sister-in-law, Edward disclosed his secret marriage in 1464 to a commoner, Elizabeth Woodville.

The marriage of the king's sister to Charles the Bold of Burgundy was a success for the Woodvilles, for Warwick was not involved in the negotiations. Warwick allied himself to Edward's younger brother George, Duke of Clarence, and ultimately, through the machinations of Louis XI, joined forces with Margaret of Anjou, deposed Edward in 1470, and brought back Henry VI. The old king, dressed in worn and unregal clothing, was from time to time exhibited to the London citizens, while Warwick conducted the government. Edward IV went into brief exile in the Netherlands. But with the help of his brother-in-law, Charles the Bold, he recovered his throne in the spring of 1471 after a rapid campaign with successes at Barnet and Tewkesbury.

Henry VI was put to death in the Tower, and his son was killed in battle.

The second half of Edward's reign, 1471–83, was a period of relative order, peace, and security. The one event reminiscent of the politics of the early reign was the trial of the Duke of Clarence, who was attainted in Parliament in 1478 and put to death, reputedly by drowning in a butt of Malmsey wine. But Edward was popular. Because his personal resources from the duchy of York were considerable and because he agreed early in his reign to acts of resumption whereby former royal estates were taken back into royal hands, Edward had a large personal income and was less in need of parliamentary grants than his predecessors had been. Thus he levied few subsidies and called Parliament only six times. Among the few subsidies Edward did levy were benevolences, supposedly voluntary gifts, from his subjects primarily to defray the expenses of war. In 1475 Edward took an army to France but accepted a pension from the French king for not fighting, thereby increasing his financial independence still further. Councils were set up to govern in the Marches of Wales and in the north, where Edward's brother Richard presided efficiently. Edward's rule was characterized by the use of his household, its servants, and its departments, such as the chamber. He was a pragmatic ruler, whose greatest achievement was to restore the prestige of the monarchy. Where he failed was to make proper provision for the succession after his death.

Edward died in 1483, at age 40, worn out, it was said, by sexual excesses and by debauchery. He left two sons, Edward and Richard, to the protection of his brother Richard, Duke of Gloucester. After skirmishes with the queen's party Richard placed both of the boys in the Tower of London, then a royal residence as well as a prison. He proceeded to eliminate those who opposed his function as protector and defender of the realm and guardian to the young Edward V. Even Lord Hastings, who had sent word to Richard of Edward IV's death and who had warned him against the queen's party, was accused of treachery and was executed. On the day after the date originally set for Edward V's coronation the Lords and Commons summoned to Parliament unanimously adopted a petition requesting Richard to take over the throne. He accepted and was duly crowned king on July 6, taking the oath in English.

Richard III (1483–85)

Richard was readily accepted no doubt because of his reputed ability and because people feared the insecurity of a long minority. The tide began to turn against him in October 1483, when it began to be rumoured that he had murdered or connived at the murder of his nephews. Whether this was true or not matters less than the fact that it was thought to be true and that it obscured the king's able government during his brief reign. Legislation against benevolences and protection for English merchants and craftsmen did little to counteract his reputation as a treacherous friend and a wicked uncle. Rebellion failed in 1483. But in the summer of 1485, when Henry Tudor, sole male claimant to Lancastrian ancestry and the throne, landed at Milford Haven, Richard's supporters widely deserted him, and he was defeated and killed at the Battle of Bosworth Field.

Central to all social change in the 15th century was change in the economy. Although plague remained endemic in England, there was little change in the level of population. Villein labour service largely disappeared, to be replaced by copyhold tenure (tenure by copy of the record of the manorial court). The period has been considered a golden age for the English labourer, but individual prosperity varied widely. There was a well-developed land market among peasants, some of whom managed to rise above their neighbours and began to constitute a class called yeomen. Large landlords entirely abandoned direct management of their estates in favour of a leasehold system. In many cases they faced growing arrears of rent and found it difficult to maintain their income levels. Because many landholders solved the problem of labour shortage by converting their holdings to sheep pasture, much land enclosure took place. As a result a great many villages were abandoned by their inhabitants.

Though England remained a predominantly agrarian society, significant development and change occurred in the towns. London continued to grow, dominating the southeast. Elsewhere the development of the woolen industry brought major changes. Halifax and Leeds grew at the expense of York, and the West Riding at the expense of the eastern part of Yorkshire. Suffolk and the Cotswold region became important in the national economy. As the cloth trade grew in importance, so did the association of the Merchant Adventurers. The merchants of the Staple, who had a monopoly on the export of raw wool, did less well. Italian merchants prospered in 15th-century England, and important privileges were accorded to the German Hanseatic merchants by Edward IV.

Culturally the 15th century was a period of sterility. Monastic chronicles came to an end, and the writing of history declined. Thomas Walsingham (d. c. 1422) was the last of a distinguished line of St. Albans chroniclers. Although there were some chronicles written by citizens of London as well as two lives of Henry V, distinguished works of history did not come until later. Neither were there any superior works of philosophy or theology. Reginald Pecock, an arid Scholastic philosopher, wrote an English treatise against the Lollards and various other works emphasizing the rational element in the Christian faith; he was judged guilty of heresy for his pains. No noteworthy poets succeeded Chaucer, though a considerable quantity of English poetry was written in this period. John Lydgate produced much verse in the Lancastrian interest. The printer William Caxton set up his press in 1476 to publish English works for the growing reading public. The first great collections of family correspondence, those of the Pastons, Stonors, and Celys, survive from this period.

The 15th century, however, was an important age in the foundation of schools and colleges. Some schools were set up as adjuncts to chantries, some by guilds, and some by collegiate churches. Henry VI founded Eton College in 1440 and King's College, Cambridge, in 1441. Other colleges at Oxford and Cambridge were also founded in this period. The Inns of Court expanded their membership and systematized their teaching of law. Many gentlemen's sons became members of the Inns, though not necessarily lawyers: they needed the rudiments of law to be able to defend and extend their estates. The influence of the Italian Renaissance in learning and culture was very limited before 1485, although there were some notable patrons, such as Humphrey, Duke of Gloucester, who collected books and supported scholars interested in the new learning.

Only in architecture did England show great originality. Large churches were built in English Perpendicular style, especially in regions made rich by the woolen industry. The tomb of Richard Beauchamp at Warwick and King's College Chapel in Cambridge show the quality of English architecture and sculpture in the period.

England under the Tudors

Henry VII (1485–1509)

When Henry Tudor, earl of Richmond, seized the throne on August 22, 1485, leaving the Yorkist Richard III dead upon the field of battle, few Englishmen would have predicted that 118 years of Tudor rule had begun. Six sovereigns had come and gone, and at least 15 major battles had been fought between rival contenders to the throne since that moment in 1399 when the divinity that "doth hedge a king" was violated and Richard II was forced to abdicate. Simple arithmetic forecast that Henry VII would last no more than a decade and that the Battle of Bosworth Field was nothing more than another of the erratic swings of the military pendulum in the struggle between the house of

York and the house of Lancaster. What gave Henry Tudor victory in 1485 was not so much personal charisma as the fact that key noblemen deserted Richard III at the moment of his greatest need, that Thomas Stanley (2nd Baron Stanley) and his brother Sir William stood aside during most of the battle in order to be on the winning team, and that Louis XI of France supplied the Lancastrian forces with 1,000 mercenary troops.

The desperateness of the new monarch's gamble was equalled only by the doubtfulness of his claim. Henry VII's Lancastrian blood was tainted by illegitimacy twice over. He was descended on his mother's side from the Beaufort family, the offspring of John of Gaunt and his mistress Katherine Swynford, and, though their children had been legitimized by act of Parliament, they had been specifically barred from the succession. His father's genealogy was equally suspect: Edmund Tudor, earl of Richmond, was born to Catherine of Valois, widowed queen of Henry V, by her clerk of the wardrobe, Owen Tudor, and the precise marital status of their relationship has never been established. Had quality of Plantagenet blood, not military conquest, been the essential condition of monarchy, Edward, earl of Warwick, the 10-year-old nephew of Edward IV, would have sat upon the throne.

Might, not soiled right, had won out on the high ground at Bosworth Field, and Henry VII claimed his title by conquest. The new king wisely sought to fortify his doubtful genealogical pretension, however, first by parliamentary acclamation and then by royal marriage. The Parliament of November 1485 did not confer regal power on the first Tudor monarch victory in war had already done that but it did acknowledge Henry as "our new sovereign lord." Then, on January 18, 1486, Henry VII married Elizabeth of York, the eldest daughter of Edward IV, thereby uniting "the white rose and the red" and launching England upon a century of "smooth-fac'd peace with smiling plenty."

"God's fair ordinance," which Shakespeare and later generations so clearly observed in the events of 1485–86, was not limited to military victory, parliamentary sanction, and a fruitful marriage; the hidden hand of economic, social, and intellectual change was also on Henry's side. The day was coming when the successful prince would be more praised than the heroic monarch and the solvent sovereign more admired than the pious one. Henry Tudor was probably no better or worse than the first Lancastrian, Henry IV; they both worked diligently at their royal craft and had to fight hard to keep their crowns, but the seventh Henry achieved what the fourth had not a secure and permanent dynasty because England in 1485 was moving into a period of unprecedented economic growth and social change.

Economy and society

By 1485 the kingdom had begun to recover from the demographic catastrophe of the Black Death and the agricultural depression of the late 14th century. As the 15th century came to a close, the rate of population growth began to increase and continued to rise throughout the following century. The population, which in 1400 may have dropped as low as 2.5 million, had by 1600 grown to about 4 million. More people meant more mouths to feed, more backs to cover, and more vanity to satisfy. In response, yeoman farmers, gentleman sheep growers, urban cloth manufacturers, and merchant adventurers produced a social and economic revolution. With extraordinary speed, the export of raw wool gave way to the export of woolen cloth manufactured at home, and the wool clothier or entrepreneur was soon buying fleece from sheep raisers, transporting the wool to cottagers for spinning and weaving, paying the farmer's wife and children by the piece, and collecting the finished article for shipment to Bristol, London, and eventually Europe. By the time Henry VII seized the throne, the Merchant Adventurers, an association of London cloth exporters, were controlling the London-Antwerp market. By 1496 they were a chartered organization with a legal monopoly of the woolen cloth trade, and, largely as a consequence of their political and international importance, Henry successfully negotiated the Intercursus Magnus, a highly favourable commercial treaty between England and the Low Countries.

As landlords increased the size of their flocks to the point that ruminants outnumbered human beings 3 to 1 and as clothiers grew rich on the wool trade, inflation injected new life into the economy. England was caught up in a vast European spiral of rising prices, declining real wages, and cheap money. Between 1500 and 1540, prices in England doubled, and they doubled again in the next generation. In 1450 the cost of wheat was what it had been in 1300; by 1550 it had tripled. Contemporaries blamed inflation on human greed and only slowly began to perceive that rising prices were the result of inflationary pressures brought on by the increase in population, international war, and the flood of gold and silver arriving from the New World.

Inflation and the wool trade together created an economic and social upheaval. A surfeit of land, a labour shortage, low rents, and high wages, which had prevailed throughout the early 15th century as a consequence of economic depression and reduced population, were replaced by a land shortage, a labour surplus, high rents, and declining wages. The landlord, who a century before could find neither tenants nor labourers for his land and had left his fields fallow, could now convert his meadows into sheep runs. His rents and profits soared; his need for labour declined, for one shepherd and his dog could do the work of half a dozen men who had previously tilled the same field. Slowly the medieval system of land tenure and communal farming broke down. The common land of the manor was divided up and fenced in, and the peasant farmer who held his tenure either by copy (a document recorded in the manor court) or by unwritten custom was evicted.

The total extent of enclosure and eviction is difficult to assess, but, between 1455 and 1607, in 34 counties more than 500,000 acres (200,000 hectares), or about 2.75 percent of the total, were enclosed, and some 50,000 persons were forced off the land. Statistics, however, are deceptive regarding both the emotional impact and the extent of change. The most disturbing aspect of the land revolution was not the emergence of a vagrant and unemployable labour force for whom society felt no social responsibility but an unprecedented increase in what men feared most change. Farming techniques were transformed, the gap between rich and poor increased, the timeless quality of village life was upset, and, on all levels of society, old families were being replaced by new.

The beneficiaries of change, as always, were the most grasping, the most ruthless, and the best educated segments of the population: the landed country gentlemen and their socially inferior cousins, the merchants and lawyers. By 1500 the essential economic basis for the landed country gentleman's future political and social ascendancy was being formed: the 15th-century knight of the shire was changing from a desperate and irresponsible land proprietor, ready to support the baronial feuding of the Wars of the Roses, into a respectable landowner desiring strong, practical government and the rule of law. The gentry did not care whether Henry VII's royal pedigree could bear close inspection; their own lineage was not above suspicion, and they were willing to serve the prince "in parliament, in council, in commission and other offices of the commonwealth."

Dynastic threats

It is no longer fashionable to call Henry VII a "new monarch," and, indeed, if the first Tudor had a model for reconstructing the monarchy, it was the example of the great medieval kings. Newness, however, should not be totally denied Henry Tudor; his royal blood was very "new," and the extraordinary efficiency of his regime introduced a spirit into government that had rarely been present in the medieval past. It was, in fact, "newness" that governed the early policy of the reign, for the Tudor dynasty had to be secured and all those with a better or older claim to the throne liquidated. Elizabeth of York was deftly handled by marriage; the sons of Edward IV had already been removed from the list, presumably murdered by their uncle Richard III; and Richard's nephew Edward Plantagenet, the young earl of Warwick, was promptly imprisoned. But the descendants of Edward IV's sister and daughters remained a threat to the new government. Equally dangerous was the persistent myth that the younger of the two princes murdered in the Tower of London had escaped his assassin and that the earl of Warwick had escaped his jailers.

The existence of pretenders acted as a catalyst for further baronial discontent and Yorkist aspirations, and in 1487 John de la Pole, a nephew of Edward IV by his sister Elizabeth, with the support of 2,000 mercenary troops paid for with Burgundian gold, landed in England to support the pretensions of Lambert Simnel, who passed himself off as the authentic earl of Warwick. Again Henry Tudor was triumphant in war; at the Battle of Stoke, de la Pole was killed and Simnel captured and demoted to a scullery boy in the royal kitchen. Ten years later Henry had to do it all over again, this time with a handsome Flemish lad named Perkin Warbeck, who for six years was accepted in Yorkist circles in Europe as the real Richard IV, brother of the murdered Edward V. Warbeck tried to take advantage of Cornish anger against heavy royal taxation and increased government efficiency and sought to lead a Cornish army of social malcontents against the Tudor throne. It was a measure of the new vigour and popularity of the Tudor monarchy, as well as the support of the gentry, that social revolution and further dynastic war were total failures, and Warbeck found himself in the Tower along with the earl of Warwick. In the end both men proved too dangerous to live, even in captivity, and in 1499 they were executed.

The policy of dynastic extermination did not cease with the new century. Under Henry VIII, the duke of Buckingham (who was descended from the youngest son of Edward III) was killed in 1521; the earl of Warwick's sister, the countess of Salisbury, was beheaded in 1541 and her descendants harried out of the land; and in January 1547 the poet Henry Howard, earl of Surrey, the grandson of Buckingham, was put to death. By the end of Henry VIII's reign, the job had been so well done that the curse of Edward III's fecundity had been replaced by the opposite problem: the Tudor line proved to be infertile when it came to producing healthy male heirs. Henry VII sired Arthur, who died in 1502, and Henry VIII in turn produced only one legitimate son, Edward VI, who died at the age of 16, thereby ending the direct male descent.

Financial policy

It was not enough for Henry VII to secure his dynasty; he also had to reestablish the financial credit of his crown and reassert the authority of royal law. Medieval kings had traditionally lived off four sources of nonparliamentary income: rents from the royal estates, revenues from import and export taxes, fees from the administration of justice, and feudal moneys extracted on the basis of a vassal's duty to his overlord. The first Tudor was no different from his Yorkist or medieval predecessors; he was simply more ruthless and successful in demanding every penny that was owed him. Henry's first move was to confiscate all the estates of Yorkist adherents and to restore all property over which the crown had lost control since 1455 (in some cases as far back as 1377). To these essentially statutory steps he added efficiency of rent collection. In 1485 income from crown lands had totalled £29,000; by 1509 annual land revenues had risen to £42,000, and the profits from the duchy of Lancaster had jumped from

£650 to £6,500. At the same time, the Tudors profited from the growing economic prosperity of the realm, and annual customs receipts rose from more than £20,000 to an average of £40,000 by the time Henry died.

The increase in customs and land revenues was applauded, for it meant fewer parliamentary subsidies and fit the medieval formula that kings should live on their own, not parliamentary, income. But the collection of revenues from feudal and prerogative sources and from the administration of justice caused great discontent and earned Henry his reputation as a miser and extortionist. Generally, Henry demanded no more than his due as the highest feudal overlord, and, a year after he became sovereign, he established a commission to look into land tenure to discover who held property by knight's fee that is, by obligation to perform military services.

Occasionally he overstepped the bounds of feudal decency and abused his rights. In 1504, for instance, he levied a feudal aid (tax) to pay for the knighting of his son who had been knighted 15 years before and had been dead for two. Henry VIII continued his father's policy of fiscal feudalism, forcing through Parliament in 1536 the Statute of Uses to prevent any landowner from escaping "relief" and wardship (feudal inheritance taxes) by settling the ownership of his lands in a trustee for the sole benefit ("use") of himself and establishing the Court of Wards and Liveries in 1540 to handle the profits of feudal wardship. The howl of protest was so great that in 1540 Henry VIII had to compromise, and by the Statute of Wills a subject who held his property by knight's fee was permitted to bequeath two-thirds of his land without feudal obligation.

To fiscal feudalism Henry VII added rigorous administration of justice. As law became more effective, it also became more profitable, and the policy of levying heavy fines as punishment upon those who dared break the king's peace proved to be a useful whip over the mighty magnate and a welcome addition to the king's exchequer. Even war and diplomacy were sources of revenue; one of the major reasons Henry VII wanted his second son, Henry, to marry his brother's widow was that the king was reluctant to return the dowry of 200,000 crowns that Ferdinand and Isabella of Spain had given for the marriage of their daughter Catherine of Aragon. Generally, Henry believed in a good-neighbour policy apparent in his alliance with Spain by the marriage of Arthur and Catherine in 1501 and peace with Scotland by the marriage of his daughter Margaret to James IV in 1503 on the grounds that peace was cheap and trade profitable. In 1489, however, he was faced with the threat of the union of the duchy of Brittany with the French crown; and England, Spain, the empire, and Burgundy went to war to stop it.

Nevertheless, as soon as it became clear that nothing could prevent France from absorbing the duchy, Henry negotiated the unheroic but financially rewarding Treaty of Étaples in 1492, whereby he disclaimed all historic rights to French territory (except Calais) in return for an indemnity of £159,000. By fair means or foul, when the first Tudor died, his total nonparliamentary annual income had risen at least twofold and stood in the neighbourhood of £113,000 (some estimates put it as high as £142,000). From land alone the king received £42,000, while the greatest landlord in the realm had to make do with less than £5,000; economically speaking, there were no longer any overmighty magnates.

The administration of justice

Money could buy power, but respect could only be won by law enforcement. The problem for Henry VII was not to replace an old system of government with a new one no Tudor was consciously a revolutionary but to make the ancient system work tolerably well. He had to tame but not destroy the nobility, develop organs of administration directly under his control, and wipe out provincialism and privilege wherever they appeared. In the task of curbing the old nobility, the king was immeasurably helped by the high aristocratic death rate during the Wars of the Roses; but where war left off, policy took over. Commissions of Array composed of local notables were appointed by the crown for each county in order to make use of the power of the aristocracy in raising troops but to prevent them from maintaining private armies (livery) with which to intimidate justice (maintenance) or threaten the throne.

Previous monarchs had sought to enforce the laws against livery and maintenance, but the first two Tudors, though they never totally abolished such evils, built up a reasonably efficient machine for enforcing the law, based on the historic premise that the king in the midst of his council was the fountain of justice. Traditionally, the royal council had heard all sorts of cases, and its members rapidly began to specialize. The Court of Chancery had for years dealt with civil offenses, and the Court of Star Chamber evolved to handle alleged corruption of justice (intimidation of witnesses and jurors, bribing of judges, etc.), the Court of Requests poor men's suits, and the High Court of Admiralty piracy. The process by which the conciliar courts developed was largely accidental, and the Court of Star Chamber acquired its name from the star-painted ceiling of the room in which the councillors sat, not from the statute of 1487 that recognized its existence. Conciliar justice was popular because the ordinary courts where common law prevailed were slow, cumbersome, and more costly; favoured the rich and mighty; and tended to break down when asked to deal with riot, maintenance, livery, perjury, and fraud. The same search for efficiency applied to matters of finance. The traditional fiscal agency of the crown, the exchequer, was burdened with archaic procedures and restrictions, and Henry VII turned to the more intimate and flexible departments of his personal household specifically to the treasurer of the chamber, whom he could supervise directly as the central tax-raising, rent-collecting, and money-disbursing segment of government.

The Tudors sought to enforce law in every corner of their kingdom, and step by step the blurred medieval profile of a realm shattered by semiautonomous franchises, in which local law and custom were obeyed more than the king's law, was transformed into the clear outline of a single state filled with loyal subjects obeying the king's decrees. By 1500 royal government had been extended into the northern counties and Wales by the creation of the Council of the North and the Council for the Welsh Marches. The Welsh principalities had always been difficult to control, and it was not until 1536 that Henry VIII brought royal law directly into Wales and incorporated the 136 self-governing lordships into a greater England with five new shires.

If the term new monarchy was inappropriate in 1485, the same cannot be said for the year of Henry VII's death, for when he died in 1509, after 24 years of reign, he bequeathed to his son something quite new in English history: a safe throne, a solvent government, a prosperous land, and a reasonably united kingdom. Only one vital aspect of the past remained untouched, the semi-independent Roman Catholic Church, and it was left to the second Tudor to challenge its authority and plunder its wealth.

Henry VIII (1509–47)

Cardinal Wolsey

An 18-year-old prince inherited his father's throne, but the son of an Ipswich butcher carried on the first Tudor's administrative policies. While the young sovereign enjoyed his inheritance, Thomas Wolsey collected titles archbishop of York in 1514, lord chancellor and cardinal legate in 1515, and papal legate for life in 1524. He exercised a degree of power never before wielded by king or minister, for, as lord chancellor and cardinal legate, he united in his portly person the authority of church and state. He sought to tame both the lords temporal and the lords spiritual administering to the nobility the "new law of the Star Chamber," protecting the rights of the underprivileged in the poor men's Court of Requests, and teaching the abbots and bishops that they were subjects as well as ecclesiastical princes. Long before Henry assumed full power over his subjects' souls as well as their bodies, his servant had marked the way. The cardinal's administration, however, was stronger on promise than on performance, and, for all his fine qualities and many talents, he exposed himself to the accusation that he prostituted policy for pecuniary gain and personal pride.

Together, the king and cardinal plunged the kingdom into international politics and war and helped to make England one of the centres of Renaissance learning and brilliance. But the sovereign and his chief servant overestimated England's international position in the Continental struggle between Francis I of France and the Holy Roman emperor Charles V. Militarily, the kingdom was of the same magnitude as the papacy the English king had about the same revenues and could field an army about the same size and, as one contemporary noted, England, with its back door constantly exposed to Scotland and its economy dependent upon the Flanders wool trade, was a mere "morsel among those choppers" of Europe. Nevertheless, Wolsey's diplomacy was based on the expectation that England could swing the balance of power either to France or to the empire and, by holding that position, could maintain the peace of Europe. The hollowness of the cardinal's policy was revealed in 1525 when Charles disastrously defeated and captured Francis at the Battle of Pavia. Italy was overrun with the emperor's troops, the pope became an imperial chaplain, all of Europe bowed before the conqueror, and England sank from being the fulcrum of Continental diplomacy to the level of a second-rate power just at the moment when Henry had decided to rid himself of

The king's "Great Matter"

It is still a subject of debate whether Henry's decision to seek an annulment of his marriage and wed Anne Boleyn was a matter of state, of love, or of conscience; quite possibly all three operated. Catherine was fat, seven years her husband's senior, and incapable of bearing further children. Anne was everything that the queen was not pretty, vivacious, and fruitful. Catherine had produced only one child that lived past infancy, a girl, Princess Mary (later Mary I); it seemed ironic indeed that the first Tudor should have solved the question of the succession only to expose the kingdom to what was perceived as an even greater peril in the second generation: a female ruler. The need for a male heir was paramount, for the last queen of England, Matilda, in the 12th century, had been a disaster, and there was no reason to believe that another would be any better. Finally, there was the question of the king's conscience. Henry had married his brother's widow, and, though the pope had granted a dispensation, the fact of the matter remained that every male child born to Henry and Catherine had died, proof of what was clearly written in the Bible: "If a man takes his brother's wife, it is impurity; he has uncovered his brother's nakedness; they shall be childless" (Leviticus 20:21).

Unfortunately, Henry's annulment was not destined to stand or fall upon the theological issue of whether a papal dispensation could set aside such a prohibition, for Catherine was not simply the king's wife; she was also the aunt of the emperor Charles V, the most powerful sovereign in Europe. Both Henry and his cardinal knew that the annulment would never be granted unless the emperor's power in Italy could be overthrown by an Anglo-French military alliance and the pope rescued from imperial domination, and for three years Wolsey worked desperately to achieve this diplomatic and military end.

Caught between an all-powerful emperor and a truculent English king, Pope Clement VII procrastinated and offered all sorts of doubtful solutions short of annulment, including the marriage of Princess Mary and the king's illegitimate son, Henry Fitzroy, duke of Richmond; the legitimizing of all children begotten of Anne Boleyn; and the transfer of Catherine into a nunnery so that the king could be given permission to remarry. Wolsey's purpose was to have the marriage annulled and the trial held in London. But in 1529, despite the arrival of Lorenzo Cardinal Campeggio to set up the machinery for a hearing, Wolsey's plans exploded. In July the pope ordered Campeggio to move the case to Rome, where a decision against the king was a foregone conclusion, and in August Francis and the emperor made peace at the Treaty of Cambrai. Wolsey's policies were a failure, and he was dismissed from office in October 1529. He died on November 29, just in time to escape trial for treason.

The Reformation background

Henry now began groping for new means to achieve his purpose. At first he contemplated little more than blackmail to frighten the pope into submission. But slowly, reluctantly, and not realizing the full consequences of his actions, he moved step by step to open defiance and a total break with Rome. Wolsey, in his person and his policies, had represented the past. He was the last of the great ecclesiastical statesmen who had been as much at home in the cosmopolitan world of European Christendom, with its spiritual centre in Rome, as in a provincial capital such as London. By the time of Henry's matrimonial crisis, Christendom was dissolving. Not only were late medieval kingdoms assuming the character of independent nation-states, but the spiritual unity of Christ's seamless cloak was also being torn apart by heresy. Henry possibly would never have won his annulment had there not existed in England men who desired a break with Rome, not because it was dynastically expedient but because they regarded the pope as the "whore of Babylon."

The religious life of the people was especially vibrant in the early decades of the 16th century, and, although there were numerous vociferous critics of clerical standards and behaviour, the institutional church was generally in good heart. Only during the extraordinary period in the 12th and 13th centuries, when money was being poured into the creation of parishes and the building of several thousand parish churches and 19 great cathedrals, was more spent on religion than in the decades between the arrival of the Tudors and the Reformation. And now it was not just great landowners but the people in general who poured money into their churches. Perhaps one in three parish churches underwent major refurbishments in this period.

Hundreds of elaborate chantry chapels and altars were erected, money invested in parish guilds doubled (for the benefit of the living in the form of pensions and doles and for the benefit of the dead in the form of masses), and the number of those seeking ordination reached a new peak. In Bedfordshire at least charitable giving was highly selective; some religious orders were much more favoured than others. There is also some evidence that the monastic life and the endowment of monasteries were slowing down, but in essence the church was successfully meeting the spiritual needs of huge numbers of people.

Precisely because of the religiosity of the people, there was a growing volume of complaint about clerical absenteeism and pluralism in general and about the unavailability of the bishops in particular. Many prelates served as the top civil servants of the crown rather than as shepherds of Christ's flock. And as inflation began to take off, so did attempts by clerics to maximize their incomes by a rather ruthless determination to collect everything to which they were entitled such as the "best beasts" demanded as mortuary fees from grieving and impoverished parents of dead children. Spasmodic persecution had failed to eradicate the Lollard legacy of John Wycliffe in substantial pockets of southern England, and the infiltration of Lutheran books and of printed Bibles opened the eyes of some among the learned and among those who traded with the Baltic states and the Low Countries to the possibility of alternative ways of encountering God. The powerful force of the "Word" took hold of some and made the mumbling of prayers, the billowing of incense, and the selling of indulgences to rescue souls from the due penalty of their sins seem the stuff of idolatry and not of true worship. But in 1532, when Henry VIII began to contemplate a schism from Rome, embracing Protestantism was the last thing on his mind, and very few of his subjects would have wished him to do so.

The break with Rome

With Wolsey and his papal authority gone, Henry turned to the authority of the state to obtain his annulment. The so-called Reformation Parliament that first met in November 1529 was unprecedented; it lasted seven years, enacted 137 statutes (32 of which were of vital importance), and legislated in areas that no medieval Parliament had ever dreamed of entering. "King in Parliament" became the revolutionary instrument by which the medieval church was destroyed.

The first step was to intimidate the church, and in 1531 the representatives of the clergy who were gathered in Convocation were forced under threat of praemunire (a statute prohibiting the operation of the legal and financial jurisdiction of the pope without royal consent) to grant Henry a gift of £119,000 and to acknowledge him supreme head of the church "as far as the law of Christ allows." Then the government struck at the papacy, threatening to cut off its revenues; the Annates Statute of 1532 empowered Henry, if he saw fit, to abolish payment to Rome of the first year's income of all newly installed bishops. The implied threat had little effect on the pope, and time was running out, for by December 1532 Anne Boleyn was pregnant, and on January 25, 1533, she was secretly married to Henry.

If the king was to be saved from bigamy and if his child was to be born in holy wedlock, he had less than eight months to get rid of Catherine of Aragon. Archbishop William Warham had conveniently died in August 1532, and in March 1533 a demoralized and frightened pontiff sanctioned the installation of Thomas Cranmer as primate of the English church.

Cranmer was a friend of the annulment, but, before he could oblige his sovereign, the queen's right of appeal from the archbishop's court to Rome had to be destroyed; this could be done only by cutting the constitutional cords holding England to the papacy. Consequently, in April 1533 the crucial statute was enacted; the Act of Restraint of Appeals boldly decreed that "this realm of England is an empire." A month later an obliging archbishop heard the case and adjudged the king's marriage to be null and void. On June 1 Anne was crowned rightful queen of England, and three months and a week later, on September 7, 1533, the royal child was born. To "the great shame and confusion" of astrologers, it turned out to be Elizabeth Tudor (later Elizabeth I).

Henry was mortified; he had risked his soul and his crown for yet another girl. But Anne had proved her fertility, and it was hoped that a male heir would shortly follow. In the meantime it was necessary to complete the break with Rome and rebuild the Church of England. By the Act of Succession of March 1534, subjects were ordered to accept the king's marriage to Anne as "undoubted, true, sincere and perfect." A second Statute "in Restraint of Annates" severed most of the financial ties with Rome, and in November the constitutional revolution was solemnized in the Act of Supremacy, which announced that Henry Tudor was and always had been "Supreme Head of the Church of England"; not even the qualifying phrase "as far as the law of Christ allows" was retained.

The consolidation of the Reformation

The medieval tenet that church and state were separate entities with divine law standing higher than human law had been legislated out of existence; the new English church was in effect a department of the Tudor state. The destruction of the Roman Catholic Church led inevitably to the dissolution of the monasteries. As monastic religious fervour and economic resources had already begun to dry up, it was easy enough for the government to build a case that monasteries were centres of vice and corruption. In the end, however, what destroyed them was neither apathy nor abuse but the fact that they were contradictions within a national church, for religious foundations by definition were international, supranational organizations that traditionally supported papal authority.

Though the monasteries bowed to the royal supremacy, the government continued to view them with suspicion, arguing that they had obeyed only out of fear, and their destruction got under way early in 1536. In the name of fiscal reform and efficiency, foundations with endowments of under £200 a year (nearly 400 of them) were dissolved on the grounds that they were too small to do their job effectively. By late 1536 confiscation had become state policy, for the Pilgrimage of Grace, a Roman Catholic-inspired uprising in the north, which appeared to the government to have received significant support from monastic clergy, seemed to be clear evidence that all monasteries were potential nests of traitors. By 1539 the foundations, both great and small, were gone. Moreover, property constituting at least 13 percent of the land of England and Wales was nationalized and incorporated into the crown lands, thereby almost doubling the government's normal peacetime, nonparliamentary income.

Had those estates remained in the possession of the crown, English history might have been very different, for the kings of England would have been able to rule without calling upon Parliament, and the constitutional authority that evolved out of the crown's fiscal dependence on Parliament would never have developed. For better or for worse, Henry and his descendants had to sell the profits of the Reformation, and by 1603 three-fourths of the monastic loot had passed into the hands of the landed gentry. The legend of a "golden shower" is false; monastic property was never given away at bargain prices, nor was it consciously presented to the kingdom in order to win the support of the ruling elite. Instead, most though not all of the land was sold at its fair market value to pay for Henry's wars and foreign policy. The effect, however, was crucial: the most powerful elements within Tudor society now had a vested interest in protecting their property against papal Catholicism.

The marriage to Anne, the break with Rome, and even the destruction of the monasteries went through with surprisingly little opposition. It had been foreseen that the royal supremacy might have to be enacted in blood, and the Act of Supremacy (March 1534) and the Act of Treason (December 1534) were designed to root out and liquidate the dissent. The former was a loyalty test requiring subjects to take an oath swearing to accept not only the matrimonial results of the break with Rome but also the principles on which it stood; the latter extended the meaning of treason to include all those who did "maliciously wish, will or desire, by words or writing or by craft imagine" the king's death or slandered his marriage. Sir Thomas More (who had succeeded Wolsey as lord chancellor), Bishop John Fisher (who almost alone among the episcopate had defended Catherine during her trial), and a handful of monks suffered death for their refusal to accept the concept of a national church. Even the Pilgrimage of Grace of 1536–37 was a short-lived eruption.

The uprisings in Lincolnshire in October and in Yorkshire during the winter were without doubt religiously motivated, but they were also as much feudal and social rebellions as revolts in support of Rome. Peasants, landed country gentlemen, and barons with traditional values united in defense of the monasteries and the old religion, and for a moment the rebels seemed on the verge of toppling the Tudor state. The nobility were angered that they had been excluded from the king's government by men of inferior social status, and they resented the encroachment of bureaucracy into the northern shires. The gentry were concerned by rising taxes and the peasants by threatened enclosure.

But the three elements had little in common outside religion, and the uprisings fell apart from within. The rebels were soon crushed and their leaders including Robert Aske, a charismatic Yorkshire country attorney were brutally executed. The Reformation came to England piecemeal, which goes far to explain the government's success. Had the drift toward Protestantism, the royal supremacy, and the destruction of the monasteries come as a single religious revolution, it would have produced a violent reaction. As it was, the Roman Catholic opposition could always argue that each step along the way to Reformation would be the last.

The decade of Reformation led to a transformation in the operations of Tudor government. Not only were new revenue courts created to handle all the wealth of the monasteries, but problems of dynastic and national security required a much more hands-on royal control of provincial affairs. In and through the English Parliament, Henry incorporated the principality of Wales and the marcher lordships (previously independent of the crown's direct control) into the English legal and administrative system. In the process, he not only shired the whole of Wales, granted seats in the English Parliament to the Welsh shires and boroughs, and extended the jurisdiction of the common-law courts and judges to Wales, but he also insisted that legal processes be conducted in English. The palatinates of the north were similarly incorporated, and all those grants by which royal justice was franchised out to private individuals and groups were revoked. For the first time the king's writ and the king's justice were ubiquitous in England.

In 1541 the Irish Parliament, which represented only the area around Dublin known as the Pale, passed an act creating the Kingdom of Ireland and declared it a perpetual appendage of the English crown. Now, for the first time in 300 years, the king set out to make good his claim to jurisdiction over the whole island. English viceroys sought to impose English law, English inheritance customs, English social norms, and the English religious settlement upon all the people there. In an attempt to achieve this in a peaceful and piecemeal way, the Anglo-Irish lords and the heads of Gaelic clans were invited to surrender their lands and titles to the crown on the promise of their regrant on favourable terms. Thus began a century of wheedling and cajoling, of rebellion and confiscation, of accommodation and plantation, that was to be a constant drain on the English Exchequer and a constant source of tragedy for the native people of Ireland.

Henry VIII did not seek to incorporate Scotland into his imperium. Though he tried to keep his nephew James V, then king of Scotland, "on-side" during his feud with Rome and never forgot that on 23 previous occasions Scottish kings had sworn feudal obeisance to kings of England, Henry never laid claim to the Scottish throne.

Henry's last years

Henry was so securely seated upon his throne that the French ambassador announced that he was more an idol to be worshipped than a king to be obeyed. The king successfully survived four more matrimonial experiments, the enmity of every major power in Europe, and an international war. On May 19, 1536, Anne Boleyn's career was terminated by the executioner's ax. She had failed in her promise to produce further children to secure the succession. Her enemies poisoned the king's mind against her with accusations of multiple adulteries. The king's love turned to hatred, but what sealed the queen's fate was probably the death of her rival, Catherine of Aragon, on January 8, 1536. From that moment it was clear that, should Henry again marry, whoever was his wife, the children she might bear would be legitimate in the eyes of Roman Catholics and Protestants alike. How much policy, how much revulsion for Anne, and how much attraction for Jane Seymour played in the final tragedy is beyond analysis, but 11 days after Anne's execution Henry married Jane. Sixteen months later the future Edward VI was born. Jane died as a consequence, but Henry finally had what it had taken a revolution to achieve a legitimate male heir.

Henry married thrice more, once for reasons of diplomacy, once for love, and once for peace and quiet. Anne of Cleves, his fourth wife, was the product of Reformation international politics. For a time in 1539 it looked as if Charles V and Francis would come to terms and unite against the schismatic king of England, and the only allies Henry possessed were the Lutheran princes of Germany. In something close to panic he was stampeded into marriage with Anne of Cleves. But the following year, the moment the diplomatic scene changed, he dropped both his wife and the man who had engineered the marriage, his vicar-general in matters spiritual, Thomas Cromwell. Anne was divorced July 12, Cromwell was executed July 28, and Henry married Catherine Howard the same day.

The second Catherine did not do as well as her cousin, the first Anne; she lasted only 18 months. Catherine proved to be neither a virgin before her wedding nor a particularly faithful damsel after her marriage. With the execution of his fifth wife, Henry turned into a sick old man, and he took as his last spouse Catherine Parr, who was as much a nursemaid as a wife. During those final years the king's interests turned to international affairs. Henry's last wars (1543–46) were fought not to defend his church against resurgent European Catholicism but to renew much older policies of military conquest in France and Scotland. Though he enlarged the English Pale at Calais by seizing the small French port of Boulogne and though his armies crushed the Scots at the Battles of Solway Moss (1542) and Pinkie

(1547) and ravaged much of Lowland Scotland during the "Rough Wooing," the wars had no lasting diplomatic or international effects except to assure that the monastic lands would pass into the hands of the gentry.

By the time Henry died (January 28, 1547), medievalism had nearly vanished. The crown stood at the pinnacle of its power, able to demand and receive a degree of obedience from both great and small that no medieval monarch had been able to achieve. The measure of that authority was threefold: (1) the extent to which Henry had been able to thrust a very unpopular annulment and supremacy legislation down the throat of Parliament, (2) his success in raising unprecedented sums of money through taxation, and (3) his ability to establish a new church on the ashes of the old. It is difficult to say whether these feats were the work of the king or his chief minister, Thomas Cromwell. The will was probably Henry's and the parliamentary means his minister's, but, whoever was responsible, by 1547 England had come a long way on the road of Reformation. The crown had assumed the authority of the papacy without as yet fundamentally changing the old creed, but the ancient structure was severely shaken.

Throughout England men were arguing that because the pontiff had been proved false, the entire Roman Catholic creed was suspect, and the cry went up to "get rid of the poison with the author." It was not long before every aspect of Roman Catholicism was under attack the miracle of the mass whereby the bread and wine are transformed into the glorified body and blood of Christ (see transubstantiation), the doctrine of purgatory, the efficacy of saints and images, the concept of an ordained priesthood with the power to mediate grace through the sacraments, the discipline of priestly celibacy, and so on. The time had come for Parliament and the supreme head to decide what constituted the "true" faith for Englishmen.

Henry never worked out a consistent religious policy: the Ten Articles of 1536 and the Bishop's Book of the following year tended to be somewhat Lutheran in tone; the Six Articles of 1539, or the Act for Abolishing Diversity of Opinion, and the King's Book of 1543 were mildly Roman Catholic. Whatever the religious colouring, Henry's ecclesiastical via media was based on obedience to an authoritarian old king and on subjects who were expected to live "soberly, justly and devoutly." Unfortunately for the religious, social, and political peace of the kingdom, both these conditions disappeared the moment Henry died and a nine-year-old boy sat upon the throne.

Edward VI (1547–53)

Henry was succeeded by his nine-year-old son, Edward VI, but real power passed to his brother-in-law, Edward Seymour, earl of Hertford, who became duke of Somerset and lord protector shortly after the new reign began. Somerset ruled in loco parentis; the divinity of the crown resided in the boy king, but authority was exercised by an uncle who proved himself to be more merciful than tactful and more idealistic than practical. Sweet reason and tolerance were substituted for the old king's brutal laws. The treason and heresy acts were repealed or modified, and the result came close to destroying the Tudor state. The moment idle tongues

To stem religious dissent, the lord protector introduced The Book of Common Prayer in 1549 and an act of uniformity to enforce it. Written primarily by Thomas Cranmer, the first prayer book of Edward VI was a literary masterpiece but a political flop, for it failed in its purpose. It sought to bring into a single Protestant fold all varieties of middle-of-the-road religious beliefs by deliberately obscuring the central issue of the exact nature of the mass whether it was a miraculous sacrament or a commemorative service. The Book of Common Prayer succeeded only in antagonizing Protestants and Roman Catholics alike.

Somerset is best remembered for these religious reforms, but their effectiveness was much blunted by their association with greed. Henry VIII had plundered and dissolved the monasteries and had mounted a half-successful campaign to accuse the monastic communities of corruption, licentiousness, and putting obedience to a foreign power above their obedience to him. Somerset extended the state's plunder to the parish churches and to the gold and silver piously and generously given by thousands of layfolk for the adornment of the parish churches. Their descendants watched the desecration with sullen anger. The rhetoric of cleansing parish churches of idolatrous and sacrilegious images sounded hollow as wagonloads of gold and silver objects headed toward the smelter's shop in the lord protector's backyard.

All this in turn was linked to what has been called Somerset's idée fixe, the permanent solution to the problem of the Anglo-Scottish frontier. Every time Henry VIII had tried to assert his claims to French territories, kings of Scotland had taken the opportunity to invade England. On each occasion and especially in 1513 and 1542 the Scottish armies had been humiliated and a high proportion of the nobility killed or captured (James IV had been killed at the Battle of Flodden, and, when James V heard of the massacre of his nobility and men at Solway Moss, "he turned his face to the wall and died").

In 1543 the captured nobles agreed to a marriage treaty that was intended to see the marriage of Henry's son and heir, Edward VI, to the infant Mary (Mary, Queen of Scots), with the aim of uniting the thrones of England and Scotland. But the Scots broke their promise and shipped Mary off to France with the intention of marrying her to the heir of the French throne. Foreseeing the permanent annexation of Scotland to France in the same way that the Netherlands had been annexed to Spain, Somerset determined to conquer the Scottish Lowlands and to establish permanent castles and strongholds as a buffer between the kingdoms. It cost him most of the country's remaining treasure and much of his popularity, and the whole policy proved a failure.

Somerset was no more successful in solving the economic and social difficulties of the reign. Rising prices, debasement of the currency, and the cost of war had produced an inflationary crisis in which prices doubled between 1547 and 1549. A false prosperity ensued in which the wool trade boomed, but so also did enclosures with all their explosive potential. The result was social revolution. Whether Somerset deserved his title of "the good duke" is a matter of opinion. Certainly, the peasants thought that he favoured the element in the House of Commons that was anxious to tax sheep raisers and to curb enclosures and that section of the clergy that was lashing out at economic inequality. In the summer of 1549, the peasantry in Cornwall and Devonshire revolted against the Prayer Book in the name of the good old religious days under Henry VIII, and, almost simultaneously, the humble folk in Norfolk rose up against the economic and social injustices of the century. At the same time that domestic rebellion was stirring, the protector had to face a political and international crisis, and he proved himself to be neither a farsighted statesman nor a shrewd politician. He embroiled the country in a war with Scotland that soon involved France and ended in an inconclusive defeat, and he earned the enmity and disrespect of the members of his own council. In the eyes of the ruling elite, Somerset was responsible for governmental ineptitude and social and religious revolution. The result was inevitable: a palace revolution ensued in October 1549, in which he was arrested and deprived of office, and two and a half years later he was executed on trumped-up charges of treason.

The protector's successor and the man largely responsible for his fall was John Dudley, earl of Warwick, who became duke of Northumberland. The duke was a man of action who represented most of the acquisitive aspects of the landed elements in society and who allied himself with the extreme section of the Protestant reformers. Under Northumberland, England pulled out of Scotland and in 1550 returned Boulogne to France; social order was ruthlessly reestablished in the countryside, the more conservative of the Henrician bishops were imprisoned, the wealth of the parish churches was systematically looted, and uncompromising Protestantism was officially sanctioned. The Ordinal of 1550 transformed the divinely ordained priest into a preacher and teacher, The Second Prayer Book of Edward VI (1552) was avowedly Protestant, altars were turned into tables, clerical vestments gave way to plain surplices, and religious orthodoxy was enforced by a new and more stringent Act of Uniformity.

How long a kingdom still attached to the outward trappings of Roman Catholicism would have tolerated doctrinal radicalism and the plundering of chantry lands and episcopal revenues under Somerset and Northumberland is difficult to say, but in 1553 the ground upon which Northumberland had built his power crumbled: Edward was dying of consumption. To save the kingdom from Roman Catholicism and himself from Roman Catholic Mary, who was Edward's successor under the terms of a statute of Henry VIII as well as that king's will, Northumberland with the support, perhaps even the encouragement, of the dying king tried his hand at kingmaking. Together they devised a new order of succession in which Mary and Elizabeth were declared illegitimate and the crown passed to Lady Jane Grey, the granddaughter of Henry VIII's sister (Mary, duchess of Suffolk) and, incidentally, Northumberland's daughter-in-law. The gamble failed, for when Edward died on July 6, 1553, the kingdom rallied to the daughter of Catherine of Aragon. Whatever their religious inclinations, Englishmen preferred a Tudor on the throne. In nine days the interlude was over, and Northumberland and his daughter-in-law were in the Tower of London.

Mary I (1553–58)

Roman Catholicism was not a lost cause when Mary came to the throne. If she had lived as long as her sister Elizabeth was to live (the womb cancer from which Mary died in 1558 not only brought her Catholic restoration to an end but rendered her childless and heirless), England would probably have been an irrevocably Catholic country. Mary was indeed determined to restore Catholicism, but she was also determined to act in accordance with the law. She worked with and through successive Parliaments to reverse all the statutes that excluded papal jurisdiction from England and to revoke her half-brother's doctrinal and liturgical reforms; however, she persuaded Rome to allow her to confirm the dissolution of the monasteries and the secularization of church properties. New monasteries were to be created, but the vast wealth of the dissolved ones remained in lay hands. She also gave the married Protestant clergy a straight choice: to remain with their wives and surrender their livings or to surrender their wives and resume their priestly ministry. Her resolute Catholicism was laced with realism. With her principal adviser, Reginald Cardinal Pole, she planned for a long-term improvement in the education and training of the clergy and the sumptuous refurbishment of parish churches. She took her inspiration from the Erasmian humanist reforms long championed by Pole in his Italian exile.

But this liberal Catholicism was in the process of being repudiated by the Council of Trent, with its uncompromising policies. Pole was recalled to Rome by a hard-line pope and accused of heresy for his previous attempts to achieve an accommodation with Protestantism. Mary's plans were torpedoed as much by the internal struggle for control of the Roman church as by the strength of Protestant opposition in England. Most potential leaders of a resistance movement had been encouraged by Mary to emigrate and had done so, but there were scores of underground Protestant cells during her reign. In thousands of parish churches, the restored liturgy and worship were welcomed.

Mary's decision to marry Prince Philip of Spain (later Philip II), her Habsburg cousin and the son of Charles V, the man who had defended her mother's marital rights, proved to be unwise. Given her age she was 32 when she came to the throne a quick marriage was essential to childbearing, but this one proved to be a failure. Her marriage was without love or children, and, by associating Roman Catholicism in the popular mind with Spanish arrogance, it triggered a rebellion that almost overthrew the Tudor throne. In January 1554, under the leadership of Sir Thomas Wyatt the Younger, the peasants of Kent rose up against the queen's Roman Catholic and Spanish policies, and 3,000 men marched on London. The rebellion was crushed, but it revealed to Mary and her chief minister, Cardinal Pole, that the kingdom was filled with disloyal hearts who placed Protestantism and nationalism higher than their obedience to the throne.

The tragedy of Mary's reign was the belief not only that the old church of her mother's day could be restored but also that it could be best served by fire and blood. At least 282 men and women were martyred in the Smithfield Fires during the last three years of her reign; compared with events on the Continent, the numbers were not large, but the emotional impact was great. Among the first half-dozen martyrs were the Protestant leaders Cranmer, Nicholas Ridley, Hugh Latimer, and John Hooper, who were burned to strike terror into the hearts of lesser men. Their deaths, however, had the opposite effect; their bravery encouraged others to withstand the flames, and the Smithfield Fires continued to burn because nobody could think of what to do with heretics except put them to death. The law required it, the prisons were overflowing, and the martyrs themselves offered the government no way out except to enforce the grisly laws.

Mary's reign was a study in failure. Her husband, who was 10 years her junior, remained in England as short a time as possible; the war between France and the Habsburg empire, into which her Spanish marriage had dragged the kingdom, was a disaster and resulted in the loss of England's last Continental outpost, Calais; her subjects came to call her "Bloody Mary" and greeted the news of her death and the succession of her sister, Elizabeth, on November 17, 1558, with ringing bells and bonfires.

Elizabeth I (1558–1603)

No one in 1558, any more than in 1485, would have predicted that despite the social discord, political floundering, and international humiliation of the past decade the kingdom again stood on the threshold of an extraordinary reign. To make matters worse, the new monarch was the wrong sex. Englishmen knew that it was unholy and unnatural that "a woman should reign and have empire above men." At age 25, however, Elizabeth I was better prepared than most women to have empire over men. She had survived the palace revolutions of her brother's reign and the Roman Catholicism of her sister's; she was the product of a fine Renaissance education, and she had learned the need for strong secular leadership devoid of religious bigotry. Moreover, she possessed her father's magnetism without his egotism or ruthlessness. She was also her mother's daughter, and the offspring of Anne Boleyn had no choice but to reestablish the royal supremacy and once again sever the ties with Rome.

Elizabeth's religious settlement was constructed on the doctrine of adiaphorism, the belief that, except for a few fundamentals, there exists in religion a wide area of "things indifferent" that could be decided by the government on the basis of expediency. Conservative opposition was blunted by entitling the queen "supreme governor," not "head," of the church and by combining the words of the 1552 prayer book with the more conservative liturgical actions of the 1549 prayer book. At the same time, many of the old papal trappings of the church were retained. Protestant radicals went along with this compromise in the expectation that the principle of "things indifferent" meant that Elizabeth would, when the political dust had settled, rid her church of the "livery of Antichrist" and discard its "papal rags." In this they were badly mistaken, for the queen was determined to keep her religious settlement exactly as it had been negotiated in 1559. As it turned out, Roman Catholics proved to be better losers than Protestants: of the 900 parish clergy, only 189 refused to accept Elizabeth as supreme governor, but the Protestant radicals the future Puritans were soon at loggerheads with their new sovereign.

The Tudor ideal of government

The religious settlement was part of a larger social arrangement that was authoritarian to its core. Elizabeth was determined to be queen in fact as well as in name. She tamed the House of Commons with tact combined with firmness, and she carried on a love affair with her kingdom in which womanhood, instead of being a disadvantage, became her greatest asset. The men she appointed to help her run and stage-manage the government were politiques like herself: William Cecil, Baron Burghley, her principal secretary and in 1572 her lord treasurer; Matthew Parker, archbishop of Canterbury; and a small group of other moderate and secular men.

In setting her house in order, the queen followed the hierarchical assumptions of her day. All creation was presumed to be a great chain of being, running from the tiniest insect to the Godhead itself, and the universe was seen as an organic whole in which each part played a divinely prescribed role. In politics every element was expected to obey "one head, one governor, one law" in exactly the same way as all parts of the human body obeyed the brain. The crown was divine and gave leadership, but it did not exist alone, nor could it claim a monopoly of divinity, for all parts of the body politic had been created by God.

The organ that spoke for the entire kingdom was not the king alone but "king in Parliament," and, when Elizabeth sat in the midst of her Lords and Commons, it was said that "every Englishman is intended to be there present from the prince to the lowest person in England." The Tudors needed no standing army in "the French fashion" because God's will and the monarch's decrees were enshrined in acts of Parliament, and this was society's greatest defense against rebellion. The controlling mind within this mystical union of crown and Parliament belonged to the queen.

The Privy Council, acting as the spokesman of royalty, planned and initiated all legislation, and Parliament was expected to turn that legislation into law. Inside and outside Parliament the goal of Tudor government was benevolent paternalism in which the strong hand of authoritarianism was masked by the careful shaping of public opinion, the artistry of pomp and ceremony, and the deliberate effort to tie the ruling elite to the crown by catering to the financial and social aspirations of the landed country gentleman.

Every aspect of government was intimate because it was small and rested on the support of probably no more than 5,000 key persons. The bureaucracy consisted of a handful of privy councillors at the top and possibly 500 paid civil servants at the bottom the 15 members of the secretariat, the 265 clerks and custom officials of the treasury, a staff of 50 in the judiciary, and approximately 150 more scattered in other departments. Tudor government was not predominantly professional. Most of the work was done by unpaid amateurs: the sheriffs of the shires, the lord lieutenants of the counties, and, above all, the Tudor maids of all work, the 1,500 or so justices of the peace. Meanwhile, each of the 180 "corporate" towns and cities was governed by men chosen locally by a variety of means laid down in the particular royal charter each had been granted.

Smallness did not mean lack of government, for the 16th-century state was conceived of as an organic totality in which the possession of land carried with it duties of leadership and service to the throne, and the inferior part of society was obligated to accept the decisions of its elders and betters. The Tudors were essentially medieval in their economic and social philosophy. The aim of government was to curb competition and regulate life so as to attain an ordered and stable society in which all could share according to status. The Statute of Apprentices of 1563 embodied this concept, for it assumed the moral obligation of all men to work, the existence of divinely ordered social distinctions, and the need for the state to define and control all occupations in terms of their utility to society. The same assumption operated in the famous Elizabethan Poor Law of 1601 the need to ensure a minimum standard of living to all men and women within an organic and noncompetitive society (see Poor Law). By 1600 poverty, unemployment, and vagrancy had become too widespread for the church to handle, and the state had to take over, instructing each parish to levy taxes to pay for poor relief and to provide work for the able-bodied, punishment for the indolent, and charity for the sick, the aged, and the disabled. The Tudor social ideal was to achieve a static class structure by guaranteeing a fixed labour supply, restricting social mobility, curbing economic freedom, and creating a kingdom in which subjects could fulfill their ultimate purpose in life spiritual salvation, not material well-being.

Elizabethan society

Social reality, at least for the poor and powerless, was probably a far cry from the ideal, but for a few years Elizabethan England seemed to possess an extraordinary internal balance and external dynamism. In part the queen herself was responsible. She demanded no windows into men's souls, and she charmed both great and small with her artistry and tact. In part, however, the Elizabethan Age was a success because men had at their disposal new and exciting areas,

A revolution in reading (and to a lesser extent writing) was taking place. By 1640 a majority of men, and just possibly a majority of men and women, could read, and there were plenty of things for them to read. In the year that Henry VIII came to the throne (1509), the number of works licensed to be published was 38. In the year of Elizabeth's accession (1558), it was 77; in the year of her death (1603), it was 328. In the year of Charles I's execution (1649), the number had risen to 1,383. And by the time of the Glorious Revolution (1688–89), it had reached 1,570. These figures do not include the ever-rising tide of broadsheets and ballads that were intended to be posted on the walls of inns and alehouses as well as in other public places. Given that a large proportion of the illiterate population spent at least part of their lives in service in homes with literate members and given that reading in the early modern period was frequently an aural experience official documents being read aloud in market squares and parish churches and all manner of publications being read aloud to whole households a very high proportion of the population had direct or indirect access to the printed word.

There was very little church building in the century after the Reformation, but there was an unprecedented growth of school building, with grammar schools springing up in most boroughs and in many market towns. By 1600 schools were provided for more than 10 percent of the adolescent population, who were taught Latin and given an introduction to Classical civilization and the foundations of biblical faith. There was also a great expansion of university education; the number of colleges in Oxford and Cambridge doubled in the 16th century, and the number of students went up fourfold to 1,200 by 1640

The aim of Tudor education was less to teach the "three Rs" (reading, writing, and arithmetic) than to establish mind control: to drill children "in the knowledge of their duty toward God, their prince and all other[s] in their degree." A knowledge of Latin and a smattering of Greek became, even more than elegant clothing, the mark of the social elite. The educated Englishman was no longer a cleric but a justice of the peace or a member of Parliament, a merchant or a landed gentleman who for the first time was able to express his economic, political, and religious dreams and his grievances in terms of abstract principles that were capable of galvanizing people into religious and political parties. Without literacy, the spiritual impact of the Puritans or, later, the formation of parties based on ideologies that engulfed the kingdom in civil war would have been impossible. So too would have been the cultural explosion that produced William Shakespeare, Christopher Marlowe, Edmund Spenser, Francis Bacon, and John Donne.

Poets, scholars, and playwrights dreamed and put pen to paper. Adventurers responded differently; they went "a-voyaging." From a kingdom that had once been known for its "sluggish security," Englishmen suddenly turned to the sea and the world that was opening up around them. The first hesitant steps had been taken under Henry VII when John Cabot in 1497 sailed in search of a northwest route to China and as a consequence discovered Cape Breton Island. The search for Cathay became an economic necessity in 1550 when the wool trade collapsed and merchants had to find new markets for their cloth. In response, the Muscovy Company was established to trade with Russia; by 1588, 100 vessels a year were visiting the Baltic.

Martin Frobisher made a series of voyages to northern Canada during the 1570s in the hope of finding gold and a shortcut to the Orient; John Hawkins encroached upon Spanish and Portuguese preserves and in 1562 sailed for Africa in quest of slaves to sell to West Indian plantation owners; and Sir Francis Drake circumnavigated the globe (December 13, 1577–September 26, 1580) in search of the riches not only of the East Indies but also of Terra Australis, the great southern continent.

Suddenly, Englishmen were on the move: Sir Humphrey Gilbert and his band of settlers set forth for Newfoundland (1583); Sir Walter Raleigh organized what became the equally ill-fated "lost colony" at Roanoke (1587–91); John Davis in his two small ships, the Moonshine and the Sunshine, reached 72 north (1585–87), the farthest north any Englishman had ever been; and the honourable East India Company was founded to organize the silk and spice trade with the Orient on a permanent basis. The outpouring was inspired not only by the urge for riches but also by religion the desire to labour in the Lord's vineyard and to found in the wilderness a new and better nation. As it was said, Englishmen went forth "to seek new worlds for gold, for praise, for glory." Even the dangers of the reign the precariousness of Elizabeth's throne and the struggle with Roman Catholic Spain somehow contrived to generate a self-confidence that had been lacking under "the little Tudors."

The first decade of Elizabeth's reign was relatively quiet, but after 1568 three interrelated matters set the stage for the crisis of the century: the queen's refusal to marry, the various plots to replace her with Mary of Scotland, and the religious and economic clash with Spain. Elizabeth Tudor's virginity was the cause of great international discussion, for every bachelor prince of Europe hoped to win a throne through marriage with Gloriana (the queen of the fairies, as she was sometimes portrayed), and was the source of even greater domestic concern, for everyone except the queen herself was convinced that Elizabeth should marry and produce heirs. The issue was the cause of her first major confrontation with the House of Commons, which was informed that royal matrimony was not a subject for commoners to discuss. Elizabeth preferred maidenhood it was politically safer and her most useful diplomatic weapon but it gave poignancy to the intrigues of her cousin Mary, Queen of Scots.

Mary, Queen of Scots.

Mary had been an unwanted visitor-prisoner in England ever since 1568, after she had been forced to abdicate her Scottish throne in favour of her 13-month-old son, James VI (later James I). She was Henry VIII's grandniece and, in the eyes of many Roman Catholics and a number of political malcontents, the rightful ruler of England, for Mary of Scotland was a Roman Catholic. As the religious hysteria mounted, there was steady pressure put on Elizabeth to rid England of this dangerous threat, but the queen delayed a final decision for almost 19 years. In the end, however, she had little choice.

Mary played into the hands of her religious and political enemies by involving herself in a series of schemes to unseat her cousin. One plot helped to trigger the rebellion of the northern earls in 1569. Another, the Ridolfi plot of 1571 (see Ridolfi, Roberto), called for an invasion by Spanish troops stationed in the Netherlands and for the removal of Elizabeth from the throne and resulted in the execution in 1572 of Thomas Howard, duke of Norfolk, the ranking peer of the realm. Yet another, the Babington plot of 1586, led by Anthony Babington, allowed the queen's ministers to pressure her into agreeing to the trial and execution of Mary for high treason.

The clash with Spain

Mary was executed on February 8, 1587. By then England had moved from cold war to open war against Spain. Philip II was the colossus of Europe and leader of resurgent Roman Catholicism. His kingdom was strong: Spanish troops were the best in Europe, Spain itself had been carved out of territory held by the infidel and still retained its Crusading zeal, and the wealth of the New World poured into the treasury at Madrid. Spanish preeminence was directly related to the weakness of France, which, ever since the accidental death of Henry II in 1559, had been torn by factional strife and civil and religious war.

In response to this diplomatic and military imbalance, English foreign policy underwent a fundamental change. By the Treaty of Blois in 1572, England gave up its historic enmity with France, accepting by implication that Spain was the greater danger. It is difficult to say at what point a showdown between Elizabeth and her former brother-in-law became unavoidable there were so many areas of disagreement but the two chief points were the refusal of English merchants-cum-buccaneers to recognize Philip's claims to a monopoly of trade wherever the Spanish flag flew throughout the world and the military and financial support given by the English to Philip's rebellious and heretical subjects in the Netherlands.

The most blatant act of English poaching in Spanish imperial waters was Drake's circumnavigation of the Earth, during which Spanish shipping was looted, Spanish claims to California ignored, and Spanish world dominion proved to be a paper empire. But the encounter that really poisoned Anglo-Iberian relations was the Battle of San Juan de Ulúa in September 1568, where a small fleet captained by Hawkins and Drake was ambushed and almost annihilated through Spanish perfidy. Only Hawkins in the Minion and Drake in the Judith escaped. The English cried foul treachery, but the Spanish dismissed the action as sensible tactics when dealing with pirates. Drake and Hawkins never forgot or forgave, and it was Hawkins who, as treasurer of the navy, began to build the revolutionary ships that would later destroy the old-fashioned galleons of the Spanish Armada.

If the English never forgave Philip's treachery at San Juan de Ulúa, the Spanish never forgot Elizabeth's interference in the Netherlands, where Dutch Protestants were in full revolt. At first, aid had been limited to money and the harbouring of Dutch ships in English ports, but, after the assassination of the Protestant leader, William I, in 1584, the position of the rebels became so desperate that in August 1585 Elizabeth sent over an army of 6,000 under the command of Robert Dudley, earl of Leicester. Reluctantly, Philip decided on war against England as the only way of exterminating heresy and disciplining his subjects in the Netherlands. Methodically, he began to build a fleet of 130 vessels, 31,000 men, and 2,431 cannons to hold naval supremacy in the English Channel long enough for Alessandro Farnese, duke of Parma, and his army, stationed at Dunkirk, to cross over to England.

Nothing Elizabeth could do seemed to be able to stop the Armada Catholica. She sent Drake to Spain in April 1587 in a spectacular strike at that portion of the fleet forming at Cádiz, but it succeeded only in delaying the sailing date. That delay, however, was important, for Philip's admiral of the ocean seas, the veteran Álvaro de Bazán, marqués de Santa Cruz, died, and the job of sailing the Armada was given to Alonso Pérez de Guzmán, duque de Medina-Sidonia, who was invariably seasick and confessed that he knew more about gardening than war. What ensued was not the new commander's fault. He did the best he could in an impossible situation, for Philip's Armada was invincible in name only. It was technologically and numerically outclassed by an English fleet of close to 200.

Worse, its strategic purpose was grounded on a fallacy: that Parma's troops could be conveyed to England. The Spanish controlled no deepwater port in the Netherlands in which the Armada's great galleons and Parma's light troop-carrying barges could rendezvous. Even the Deity seemed to be more English than Spanish, and in the end the fleet, buffeted by gales, was dashed to pieces as it sought to escape home via the northern route around Scotland and Ireland. Of the 130 ships that had left Spain, perhaps 85 crept home; 10 were captured, sunk, or driven aground by English guns, 23 were sacrificed to wind and storm, and 12 others were "lost, fate unknown."

Internal discontent

When the Armada was defeated during the first weeks of August 1588, the crisis of Elizabeth's reign was reached and successfully passed. The last years of her reign were an anticlimax, for the moment the international danger was surmounted, domestic strife ensued. There were moments of great heroism and success as when Robert Devereux, earl of Essex, Raleigh, and Thomas Howard, earl of Suffolk, made a second descent on Cádiz in 1596, seized the city, and burned the entire West Indian treasure fleet but the war so gloriously begun deteriorated into a costly campaign in the Netherlands and France and an endless guerrilla action in Ireland, where Philip discovered he could do to Elizabeth what she had been doing to him in the Low Countries. Even on the high seas, the days of fabulous victories were over, for the king of Spain soon learned to defend his empire and his treasure fleets. Both Drake and Hawkins died in 1596 on the same ill-conceived expedition into Spanish Caribbean waters symbolic proof that the good old days of buccaneering were gone forever. At home the cost of almost two decades of war (£4 million) raised havoc with the queen's finances. It forced her to sell her capital (about £800,000, or roughly one-fourth of all crown lands) and increased her dependence upon parliamentary sources of income, which rose from an annual average of £35,000 to over £112,000 a year.

The expedition to the Netherlands was not, however, the most costly component of the protracted conflict; indeed, the privateering war against Spain more than paid for itself. The really costly war of the final years of Elizabeth's reign was in Ireland, where a major rebellion in response to the exclusion of native Catholics from government and to the exploitation of every opportunity to replace native Catholics with Protestant English planters tied down thousands of English soldiers. The rebellion was exacerbated by Spanish intervention and even by a Spanish invasion force (the element of the Armada that temporarily succeeded). This Nine Years War (1594–1603) was eventually won by the English but only with great brutality and at great expense of men and treasure.

Elizabeth's financial difficulties were a symptom of a mounting political crisis that under her successors would destroy the entire Tudor system of government. The 1590s were years of depression bad harvests, soaring prices, peasant unrest, high taxes, and increasing parliamentary criticism of the queen's economic policies and political leadership. Imperceptibly, the House of Commons was becoming the instrument through which the will of the landed classes could be heard and not an obliging organ of royal control. In Tudor political theory this was a distortion of the proper function of Parliament, which was meant to beseech and petition, never to command or initiate.

Three things, however, forced theory to make way for reality. First was the government's financial dependence on the Commons, for the organ that paid the royal piper eventually demanded that it also call the governmental tune. Second, under the Tudors, Parliament had been summoned so often and forced to legislate on such crucial matters of church and state legitimizing monarchs, breaking with Rome, proclaiming the supreme headship (governorship under Elizabeth), establishing the royal succession, and legislating in areas that no Parliament had ever dared enter before that the Commons got into the habit of being consulted. Inevitably, a different constitutional question emerged: If Parliament is asked to give authority to the crown, can it also take away that authority? Finally, there was the growth of a vocal, politically conscious, and economically dominant gentry; the increase in the size of the House of Commons reflected the activity and importance of that class.

In Henry VIII's first Parliament, there were 74 knights who sat for 37 shires and 224 burgesses who represented the chartered boroughs and towns of the kingdom. By the end of Elizabeth's reign, borough representation had been increased by 135 seats. The Commons was replacing the Lords in importance because the social element it represented had become economically and politically more important than the nobility. Should the crown's leadership falter, there existed by the end of the century an organization that was quite capable of seizing the political initiative, for as one disgruntled contemporary noted: "the foot taketh upon him the part of the head and commons is become a king." Elizabeth had sense enough to avoid a showdown with the Commons, and she retreated under parliamentary attack on the issue of her prerogative rights to grant monopolies regulating and licensing the economic life of the kingdom, but on the subject of her religious settlement she refused to budge.

By the last decade of her reign, Puritanism was on the increase. During the 1570s and '80s, "cells" had sprung up to spread God's word and rejuvenate the land, and Puritan strength was centred in exactly that segment of society that had the economic and social means to control the realm the gentry and merchant classes. What set a Puritan off from other Protestants was the literalness with which he held to his creed, the discipline with which he watched his soul's health, the militancy of his faith, and the sense that he was somehow apart from the rest of corrupt humanity. This disciplined spiritual elite clashed with the queen over the purification of the church and the stamping out of the last vestiges of Roman Catholicism.

The controversy went to the root of society: Was the purpose of life spiritual or political? Was the role of the church to serve God or the crown? In 1576 two brothers, Paul and Peter Wentworth, led the Puritan attack in the Commons, criticizing the queen for her refusal to allow Parliament to debate religious issues. The crisis came to a head in 1586, when Puritans called for legislation to abolish the episcopacy and the Anglican prayer book. Elizabeth ordered the bills to be withdrawn, and, when Peter Wentworth raised the issue of freedom of speech in the Commons, she answered by clapping him in the

Tower of London. There was emerging in England a group of religious idealists who derived their spiritual authority from a source that stood higher than the crown and who thereby violated the concept of the organic society and endangered the very existence of the Tudor paternalistic monarchy. As early as 1573 the threat had been recognized:

At the beginning it was but a cap, a surplice, and a tippet [over which Puritans complained]; now, it is grown to bishops, archbishops, and cathedral churches, to the overthrow of the established order, and to the Queen's authority in causes ecclesiastical.

James I later reduced the problem to one of his usual bons mots "no bishop, no king." Elizabeth's answer was less catchy but more effective; she appointed as archbishop John Whitgift, who was determined to destroy Puritanism as a politically organized sect. Whitgift was only partially successful, but the queen was correct: the moment the international crisis was over and a premium was no longer placed on loyalty, Puritans were potential security risks.

Puritans were a loyal opposition, a church within the church. Elizabethan governments never feared that there would or could be a Puritan insurrection in the way they constantly feared that there could and would be an insurrection by papists. Perhaps 1 in 5 of the peerage, 1 in 10 of the gentry, and 1 in 50 of the population were practicing Catholics, many of them also being occasional conformists in the Anglican church to avoid the severity of the law. Absence from church made householders liable to heavy fines; associating with priests made them liable to incarceration or death. To be a priest in England was itself treasonous; in the second half of the reign, more than 300 Catholics were tortured to death, even more than the number of Protestants burned at the stake by Mary. Some priests, especially Jesuits, did indeed preach political revolution, but many others preached a dual allegiance to the queen in all civil matters and to Rome in matters of the soul. Most laymen were willing to follow this more moderate advice, but it did not stem the persecution or alleviate the paranoia of the Elizabethan establishment.

Catholicism posed a political threat to Elizabethan England. Witches posed a cultural threat. From early in Elizabeth's reign, concern grew that men and (more particularly) women on the margins of society were casting spells on respectable folk with whom they were in conflict. Explanations abound. Accusations seem to have often arisen when someone with wealth denied a request for personal charity to someone in need, with the excuse that the state had now taken over responsibility for institutional relief through the Poor Laws; guilt about this refusal of charity would give way to blaming the poor person who had been turned away for any ensuing misfortunes.

Sometimes magisterial encouragement of witchcraft prosecutions was related to the intellectual search for the causes of natural disasters that fell short of an explanation more plausible than the casting of spells. Sometimes there was concern over the existence of "cunning men and women" with inherited knowledge based on a cosmology incompatible with the new Protestantism. This was especially the case when the cunning men and women were taking over the casting of spells and incantations that had been the province of the Catholic priest but were not the province of the Protestant minister. Certainly, the rise in incidence of witchcraft trials and executions can be taken as evidence of a society not at peace with itself. As the century ended, there was a crescendo of social unrest and controlled crowd violence.

There were riots about the enclosure of common land, about the enforced movement of grain from producing regions to areas of shortage, about high taxes and low wages, and about the volatility of trade. The decades on either side of the turn of the century saw roaring inflation and the first real evidence of the very young and the very old starving to death in remote areas and in London itself.

Elizabethan England ended in a rich cultural harvest and real physical misery for people at the two ends of the social scale, respectively.

The final years of Gloriana's life were difficult both for the theory of Tudor kingship and for Elizabeth herself. She began to lose hold over the imaginations of her subjects, and she faced the only palace revolution of her reign when her favourite, the earl of Essex, sought to take her crown. There was still fight in the old queen, and Essex ended on the scaffold in 1601, but his angry demand could not be ignored:

What! Cannot princes err? Cannot subjects receive wrong? Is an earthly power or authority infinite? Pardon me, pardon me, my good Lord, I can never subscribe to these principles.

When the queen died on March 24, 1603, it was as if the critics of her style of rule and her concept of government had been waiting patiently for her to step down. It was almost with relief that men looked forward to the problems of a new dynasty and a new century, as well as to a man, not a woman, upon the throne.

The early Stuarts and the Commonwealth

England in 1603
Economy and society

At the beginning of the 17th century, England and Wales contained more than four million people. The population had nearly doubled over the previous century, and it continued to grow for another 50 years. The heaviest concentrations of population were in the southeast and along the coasts. Population increase created severe social and economic problems, not the least of which was a long-term price inflation. English society was predominantly rural, with as much as 85 percent of its people living on the land. About 800 small market towns of several hundred inhabitants facilitated local exchange, and, in contrast to most of western Europe, there were few large urban areas. Norwich and Bristol were the biggest provincial cities, with populations of around 15,000. Exeter, York, and Newcastle were important regional centres, though they each had about 10,000 inhabitants.

Only London could be ranked with the great continental cities. Its growth had outstripped even the doubling of the general population. By the beginning of the 17th century, it contained more than a quarter of a million people and by the end nearly half a million, most of them poor migrants who flocked to the capital in search of work or charity. London was the centre of government, of overseas trade and finance, and of fashion, taste, and culture. It was ruled by a merchant oligarchy, whose wealth increased tremendously over the course of the century as international trade expanded.

London not only ruled the English mercantile world, but it also dominated the rural economy of the southeast by its insatiable demand for food and clothing. The rural economy was predominately agricultural, with mixed animal and grain husbandry practiced wherever the land allowed. The population increase, however, placed great pressure upon the resources of local communities, and efforts by landlords and tenants to raise productivity for either profit or survival were the key feature of agricultural development. Systematic efforts to grow luxury market crops like wheat, especially in the environs of London, drove many smaller tenants from the land. So too did the practice of enclosure, which allowed for more productive land use by large holders at the expense of their poorer neighbours.

There is evidence of a rural subsistence crisis lasting throughout the first two decades of the century. Marginally productive land came under the plow, rural revolts became more common, and harvest failures resulted in starvation rather than hunger, both in London and in the areas remote from the grain-growing lowlands such as north Wales and the Lake District. It was not until the middle of the century that the rural economy fully recovered and entered a period of sustained growth. A nation that could barely feed itself in 1600 was an exporter of grain by 1700.

In the northeast and southwest the harsher climate and poorer soils were more suited for sheep raising than for large-scale cereal production. The northeast and southwest were the location of the only significant manufacturing activity in England, the woolen cloth industry. Wool was spun into large cloths for export to Holland, where the highly technical finishing processes were performed before it was sold commercially. Because spinning and weaving provided employment for thousands of families, the downturn of the cloth trade at the beginning of the 17th century compounded the economic problems brought about by population increase. This situation worsened considerably after the opening of the Thirty Years' War (1618–48), as trade routes became disrupted and as new and cheaper sources of wool were developed. But the transformation of the English mercantile economy from its previous dependence upon a single commodity into a diversified entrepôt that transshipped dozens of domestic and colonial products was one of the most significant developments of the century.

The economic divide between rich and poor, between surplus and subsistence producers, was a principal determinant of rank and status. English society was organized hierarchically with a tightly defined ascending order of privileges and responsibilities. This hierarchy was as apparent in the family as it was in the state. In the family, as elsewhere, male domination was the rule; husbands ruled their wives, masters their servants, parents their children. But if hierarchy was stratified, it was not ossified; those who attained wealth could achieve status. The social hierarchy reflected gradations of wealth and responded to changes in the economic fortunes of individuals. In this sense it was more open than most European societies. Old wealth was not preferred to new, and an ancient title conferred no greater privileges than recent elevation; the humble could rise to become gentle, and the gentle could fall to become humble.

During the early 17th century a small titular peerage composed of between 75 and 100 peers formed the apex of the social structure. Their titles were hereditary, passed from father to eldest son, and they were among the wealthiest subjects of the state. Most were local magnates, inheriting vast county estates and occupying honorific positions in local government. The peerage was the military class of the nation, and in the counties peers held the office of lord lieutenant. Most were also called to serve at court, but at the beginning of the century their power was still local rather than central.

Below them were the gentry, who probably composed only about 5 percent of the rural population but who were rising in importance and prestige. The gentry were not distinguished by title, though many were knights and several hundred purchased the rank of baronet (hereditary knighthoods) after it was created in 1611. Sir Thomas Smith defined a member of the gentry as "he that can bear the port and charge of a gentleman." The gentry were expected to provide hospitality for their neighbours, treat their tenants paternally, and govern their counties. They served as deputy lieutenants, militia captains, and most important, as justices of the peace. To the justices fell the responsibility of enforcing the king's law and keeping the king's peace. They worked individually to mediate local disputes and collectively at quarter sessions to try petty crimes. As the magistracy the gentry were the backbone of county governance, and they maintained a fierce local independence even while enforcing the edicts of the crown.

Beneath the gentry were those who laboured for their survival. There were many prosperous tenants who were styled yeomen to denote their economic independence and the social gulf between them and those who eked out a bare existence. Some were the younger sons of gentlemen; others aspired to enter the ranks of the gentry, having amassed sufficient wealth to be secure against the fluctuations of the early modern economy. Like the gentry, the yeomanry were involved in local government, performing most of the day-to-day, face-to-face tasks. Yeomen were village elders, constables, and tax collectors, and they composed the juries that heard cases at quarter sessions. Most owned sufficient freehold land to be politically enfranchised and to participate in parliamentary selections. Filling out the ranks of rural society were husbandmen, cottagers, and labourers. Husbandmen were tenant farmers at or near self-sufficiency; cottagers were tenants with cottages and scraps of land, dependent on a range of by-employments to make ends meet ("an economy of makeshifts"); and labourers were those who were entirely dependent on waged employment on the land of others. They were the vast majority of local inhabitants, and their lives were bound up in the struggle for survival.

In towns, tradesmen and shopkeepers occupied the ranks below the ruling elites, but their occupational status clearly separated them from artisans, apprentices, and labourers. They were called the middling sort and were active in both civic and church affairs, holding the same minor offices as yeomen or husbandmen. Because of the greater concentrations of wealth and educational opportunities, the urban middling sort were active participants in urban politics.

Government and society

Seventeenth-century government was inextricably bound together with the social hierarchy that dominated local communities. Rank, status, and reputation were the criteria that enabled members of the local elite to serve the crown either in the counties or at court. Political theory stressed hierarchy, patriarchy, and deference in describing the natural order of English society. Most of the aristocracy and gentry were the king's own tenants, whose obligations to him included military service, taxes, and local office holding. The monarch's claim to be God's vice-regent on earth was relatively uncontroversial, especially since his obligations to God included good governance. Except in dire emergency, the monarch could not abridge the laws and customs of England nor seize the persons or property of his subjects.

The monarch ruled personally, and the permanent institutions of government were constantly being reshaped. Around the king was the court, a floating body of royal servants, officeholders, and place seekers. Personal service to the king was considered a social honour and thus fitting to those who already enjoyed rank and privilege. Most of the aristocracy and many gentlemen were in constant attendance at court, some with lucrative offices to defray their expenses, others extravagantly running through their fortunes. There was no essential preparation for royal service, no necessary skills or experiences. Commonly, members of the elite were educated at universities and the law courts, and most made a grand tour of Europe, where they studied languages and culture. But their entry into royal service was normally through the patronage of family members and connections rather than through ability.

From among his court the monarch chose the Privy Council. Its size and composition remained fluid, but it was largely composed of the chief officers of state: the lord treasurer, who oversaw revenue; the lord chancellor, who was the crown's chief legal officer; and the lord chamberlain, who was in charge of the king's household. The archbishop of Canterbury was the leading churchman of the realm, and he advised the king, who was the head of the established church. The Privy Council advised the king on foreign and domestic policy and was charged with the administration of government. It communicated with the host of unpaid local officials who governed in the communities, ordering the justices to enforce statutes or the deputy lieutenants to raise forces. In these tasks the privy councillors relied not only upon the king's warrant but upon their own local power and prestige as well. Thus, while the king was free to choose his own councillors, he was constrained to pick those who were capable of commanding respect. The advice that he received at the council table was from men who kept one eye on their localities and the other on the needs of central policy.

This interconnection between the centre and the localities was also seen in the composition of Parliament. Parliament was another of the king's councils, though its role in government was less well defined than the Privy Council's and its summoning was intermittent. In the early 17th century, Parliament was less an institution than an event; it was convened when the king sought the aid of his subjects in the process of creating new laws or to provide extraordinary revenue. Like everything else in English society, Parliament was constituted in a hierarchy, composed of the king, Lords, and Commons.

Every peer of the realm was personally summoned to sit in the House of Lords, which was dominated by the greatest of the king's officers. The lower house was composed of representatives selected from the counties and boroughs of the nation. The House of Commons was growing as local communities petitioned for the right to be represented in Parliament and local gentry scrambled for the prestige of being chosen. It had 464 members in 1604 and 507 forty years later. Selection to the House of Commons was a mark of distinction, and many communities rotated the honour among their most important citizens and neighbours. Although there were elaborate regulations governing who could choose and who could be chosen, in fact very few members of the House of Commons were selected competitively. Contests for places were uncommon, and elections in which individual votes were cast were extremely rare.

Members of Parliament served the dual function of representing the views of the localities to the king and of representing the views of the king to the localities. Most were members of royal government, either at court or in their local communities, and nearly all had responsibility for enforcing the laws that were created at Westminster. Most Parliaments were summoned to provide revenue in times of emergency, usually for defense, and most members were willing to provide it within appropriate limits. They came to Parliament to do the king's business, the business of their communities, and their own personal business in London. Such conflicting obligations were not always easily resolved, but Parliament was not perceived as an institution in opposition to the king any more than the stomach was seen as opposing the head of the body. There were upsets, however, and, increasingly during the 17th century, king and Parliament clashed over specific issues, but until the middle of the century they were part of one system of royal government.

James I (1603–25)

James VI, king of Scotland (1567–1625), was the most experienced monarch to accede to the English throne since William the Conqueror, as well as one of the greatest of all Scottish kings. A model of the philosopher prince, James wrote political treatises such as The Trew Law of a Free Monarchy (1598), debated theology with learned divines, and reflected continually on the art of statecraft. He governed his poor by balancing its factions of clans and by restraining the enthusiastic leaders of its Presbyterian church. In Scotland, James was described as pleasing to look at and pleasing to hear. He was sober in habit, enjoyed vigorous exercise, and doted on his Danish wife, Anne, who had borne him two male heirs.

But James I was viewed with suspicion by his new subjects. Centuries of hostility between the two nations had created deep enmities, and these could be seen in English descriptions of the king. In them he was characterized as hunchbacked and ugly, with a tongue too large for his mouth and a speech impediment that obscured his words. It was said that he drank to excess and spewed upon his filthy clothing. It was also rumoured that he was homosexual and that he took advantage of the young boys brought to service at court. This caricature, which has long dominated the popular view of James I, was largely the work of disappointed English office seekers whose pique clouded their observations and the judgments of generations of historians.

In fact, James showed his abilities from the first. In the counties through which he passed on his way to London, he lavished royal bounty upon the elites who had been starved for honours during Elizabeth's parsimonious reign. He knighted hundreds as he went, enjoying the bountiful entertainments that formed such a contrast with his indigent homeland. He would never forget these first encounters with his English subjects, "their eyes flaming nothing but sparkles of affection." On his progress James also received a petition, putatively signed by a thousand ministers, calling his attention to the unfinished business of church reform.

Triple monarchy

James had one overriding ambition: to create a single unified monarchy out of the congeries of territories he now found himself ruling. He wanted a union not only of the crown but of the kingdoms. He made it plain to his first Parliament that he wanted a single name for this new single kingdom: he wanted to be king not of England, Scotland, and Ireland but of Great Britain, and that is what he put on his seals and on his coins. He wanted common citizenship, the end of trade barriers, and gradual movement toward a union of laws, of institutions, and of churches, although he knew this could not be achieved overnight.

The chauvinism of too many English elite, however, meant he was not to achieve all of his goals. A common coinage, a common flag, the abolition of hostile laws, and a joint Anglo-Scottish plantation of Ulster were all he was able to manage. Even free trade between the kingdoms was prevented by the amateur lawyers in the English House of Commons. Having failed to promote union by legislation, he tried to promote it by stealth, creating a pan-British court and royal household, elevating Scots to the English peerage and Englishmen to the Scottish and Irish peerage, rewarding those who intermarried across borders, and seeking to remove from each of the churches those features objectionable to members of the other national churches. Progress was negligible and, under his son Charles I, went into reverse.

Religious policy

The Millenary Petition (1603) initiated a debate over the religious establishment that James intended to defend. The king called a number of his leading bishops to hold a formal disputation with the reformers. The Hampton Court Conference (1604) saw the king in his element. He took a personal role in the debate and made clear that he hoped to find a place in his church for moderates of all stripes. It was only extremists that he intended to "harry from the land," those who, unlike the supporters of the Millenary Petition, sought to tear down the established church. The king responded favourably to the call for creating a better-educated and better-paid clergy and referred several doctrinal matters to the consideration of convocation. But only a few of the points raised by the petitioners found their way into the revised canons of 1604. In fact, the most important result of the conference was the establishment of a commission to provide an authorized English translation of the Bible, the King James Version (1611).

Indeed, James's hope was that moderates of all persuasions, Roman Catholic and Protestant alike, might dwell together in his church. He offered to preside at a general council of all the Christian churches Catholic and Protestant to seek a general reconciliation. Liberals in all churches took his offer seriously. He sought to find a formula for suspending or ameliorating the laws against Catholics if they would take a binding oath of political obedience. Most Catholics were attracted by the offer, but James's plans took a tremendous knock when an unrepresentative group of Catholics, disappointed that this son of a Catholic queen had not immediately restored Catholic liberties, plotted to kill him, his family, and his leading supporters by blowing up the Houses of Parliament in the course of a state opening, using gunpowder secreted in a cellar immediately beneath the House of Lords. The failure of the Gunpowder Plot (1605) led to reprisals against Catholics and prevented James from going any further than exhibiting humane leniency toward them in the later years of his reign. Nevertheless, James's ecumenical outlook did much to defuse religious conflict and led to 20 years of relative peace within the English church.

Finance and politics

To a king whose annual budget in Scotland was barely £50,000, England looked like the land of milk and honey. But in fact James I inherited serious financial problems, which his own liberality quickly compounded. Elizabeth had left a debt of more than £400,000, and James, with a wife and two sons, had much larger household expenses than the unmarried queen. Land and duties from customs were the major sources of royal revenue, and it was James's good fortune that the latter increased dramatically after the judges ruled in Bate's case (1606) that the king could make impositions on imported commodities without the consent of Parliament. Two years later, under the direction of James's able minister Robert Cecil, earl of Salisbury, impositions were levied on an expanded list of goods, and a revised book of rates was issued in 1608 that increased the level of duties. By these measures customs revenues grew by £70,000 per year.

But even this windfall was not enough to stem the effects of inflation on the one hand and James's own free spending on the other. By 1606 royal debt was more than £600,000, and the crown's financial ministers had turned their attention to prerogative income from wardships, purveyance, and the discovery of concealed lands (i.e., crown lands on which rents and dues were not being paid). The revival and rationalization of these ancient rights created an outcry. As early as 1604 Salisbury was examining proposals to commute these fiscal rights into an annual sum to be raised by a land tax. By 1610 negotiations began for the Great Contract between the king and his taxpaying subjects that aimed to raise £200,000 a year. But at the last moment both royal officials and leaders of the House of Commons backed away from the deal, the government believing that the sum was too low and the leaders of the Commons that a land tax was too unpopular. The failure of the Great Contract drove Salisbury to squeeze even more revenue out of the king's feudal rights, including the sale of titles. This policy violated the spirit of principles about property and personal liberty held by the governing classes and, along with impositions, was identified as a grievance during James's first Parliaments.

There was much suspicion that the Scottish king would not understand the procedures and privileges of an English Parliament, and this suspicion was reinforced by James's speeches in the first session of the Parliament of 1604–10. The conventional ban upon the selection of outlaws to the Commons led to the Buckinghamshire Election Case (1604). The Commons reversed a decision by the lord chancellor and ordered Francis Goodwin, an outlaw, to be seated in the House of Commons. James clumsily intervened in the proceedings, stating that the privileges of the Commons had been granted by the grace of the monarch, a pronouncement that stirred the embers of Elizabethan disputes over parliamentary privilege. Although a compromise solution to the case was found, from this time forward the Commons took an active role in scrutinizing the returns of its members. A standing committee on elections was formed, and the freedom of members from arrest during sessions was reasserted. Some wanted to go even further and present the king with a defense of the ancient rights of their house. But this so-called apology was the work of a minority and was never accepted by the whole House of Commons or presented to the king.

Factions and favourites

As in the previous reign, court politics were factionalized around noble groups tied together by kinship and interest. James had promoted members of the Howard family to places of leadership in his government; Henry Howard, earl of Northampton, adeptly led a family group that included Thomas Howard, earl of Suffolk, and Thomas Howard, earl of Arundel. All managed to enrich themselves at the expense of the king, whose debts reached £900,000 by 1618. A stink of corruption pervaded the court during these years. The Howards formed the core of a pro-Spanish faction that desired better relations with Spain and better treatment of English Catholics. They also played upon the king's desire for peace in Europe.

The Howards were opposed by an anti-Spanish group that included the queen; George Abbot, archbishop of Canterbury; and William Herbert, earl of Pembroke. This group wished to pursue an aggressively Protestant foreign policy and, after the opening of the Thirty Years' War, to support James's son-in-law, Frederick V, the elector of the Palatinate. It was the anti-Spanish group that introduced the king to George Villiers, reputedly one of the handsomest men in Europe. Through Villiers they sought a conduit to power.

Even at the time it was thought unseemly that a lover should be provided for the king at the connivance of the queen and the archbishop. But Villiers was nobody's fool, and, while he succeeded spectacularly in gaining James's confidence, he refused to be a cipher for those who had advanced him. Soon he had risen to the pinnacle of the aristocracy. First knighted in 1615, he was created duke of Buckingham in 1623, the first nonroyal duke in half a century. Buckingham proved an able politician. He supported the movement for fiscal reform that led to the disgrace of Lord Treasurer Suffolk and the promotion of Lionel Cranfield, later earl of Middlesex. Cranfield, a skilled London merchant, took the royal accounts in hand and made the unpopular economies that kept government afloat.

Buckingham, whose power rested upon his relationship with the king, wholeheartedly supported James's desire to reestablish peace in Europe. For years James had angled to marry his son Charles to a Spanish princess. There were, however, many obstacles to this plan, not the least of which was the insistence of the pope that the marriage lead to the reconversion of England to Roman Catholicism. When negotiations remained inconclusive, James, in 1621, called his third Parliament with the intention of asking for money to support the Protestant cause. By this means he hoped to bully Philip IV of Spain into concluding the marriage negotiations and into using his influence to put an end to the German war.

Parliament, believing that James intended to initiate a trade war with Spain, readily granted the king's request for subsidies. But some members mistakenly also believed that the king wished their advice on military matters and on the prince's marriage. When James learned that foreign policy was being debated in the lower house, he rebuked the members for their temerity in breaching the royal prerogative. Stunned, both because they thought that they were following the king's wishes and because they believed in their freedom to discuss such matters, members of the Commons prepared the Protestation of 1621, exculpating their conduct and setting forth a statement of the liberties of the house. James sent for the Commons journal and personally ripped the protestation from it. He reiterated his claim that royal marriages and foreign policy were beyond the ken of Parliament and dryly noted that less than one-third of the elected members of the house had been present when the protestation was passed.

The Parliament of 1621 was a failure at all levels. No legislation other than the subsidy bill was passed; a simple misunderstanding among the members had led to a dramatic confrontation with the king; and judicial impeachments were revived, costing the king the services of Lord Chancellor Bacon. James, moreover, was unable to make any progress with the Spaniards, and supporting the European Protestants drained his revenue. By 1624 royal indebtedness had reached £1 million. The old king was clearly at the end of his power and influence. His health was visibly deteriorating, and his policies were openly derided in court and country. Prince Charles (later Charles I) and Buckingham decided to take matters into their own hands. In 1623 they traveled incognito to Madrid.

Their gambit created as much consternation in England as it did in Spain. James wept inconsolably, believing that his son would be killed or imprisoned. The Spaniards saw the end of their purposely drawn-out negotiations. Every effort was made to keep Charles away from the infanta, and he only managed to catch two fleeting glimpses of the heavily veiled princess. Nevertheless, he confided in Buckingham that he was hopelessly in love. Buckingham and John Digby, earl of Bristol, the ambassador to Spain, were almost powerless to prevent the most damaging concessions. Charles even confessed himself willing to be instructed in the Catholic faith. Yet the more the prince conceded, the more embarrassed the Spaniards became. Nothing short of an ultimate Catholic reestablishment in England would be satisfactory, and they began to raise obviously artificial barriers. Even the lovesick prince realized that he was being humiliated. Shame turned to rage as he and Buckingham journeyed home.

There they persuaded the bedridden king to call another Parliament for the purpose of declaring war on Spain. The Parliament of 1624 was given free rein. All manner of legislation was passed; subsidies for a trade war with Spain were voted; and issues of foreign policy were openly discussed. Firmly in control of political decision making, Charles and Buckingham worked to stave off attacks on James's fiscal policies, especially the granting of monopolies to royal favourites. The last Parliament of James's reign was his most successful. On March 27, 1625, the old king died.

Charles I (1625–49)

Father and son could hardly be more different than were James and Charles. Charles was shy and physically deformed. He had a speech defect that made his pronouncements painful for him and his audiences alike. Charles had not been raised to rule. His childhood had been spent in the shadow of his brother, Prince Henry, who had died in 1612, and Charles had little practical experience of government. He was introverted and clung tenaciously to a few intimates. His wife, Henrietta Maria French, Roman Catholic, and hugely unpopular received Charles's loyalty despite great political cost. So did Buckingham, who survived the change in monarchs and consolidated his grip on government.

The politics of war

Along with his kingdom, Charles I inherited a domestic economic crisis and the war with Spain. A series of bad grain harvests, continued dislocation of the cloth trade, and a virulent plague that killed tens of thousands all conspired against the new king. Under the pressure of economic crisis, members of the Parliament of 1625 were determined to reform the customs and to limit the crown's right to levy impositions. The traditional lifelong grant of tonnage and poundage was thus withheld from Charles so that reform could be considered. But reform was delayed, and, despite the appearance of illegality, the king collected these levies to prevent bankruptcy.

The Spanish war progressed no better than the domestic economy. Buckingham organized an expedition to Cádiz, but its failure forced Charles to summon another Parliament. From the start the Parliament of 1626 was badly managed, and members of both houses thirsted for Buckingham's blood. Where James had sacrificed his ministers to further policy, Charles would not. Parliament was dissolved without granting any subsidies.

Charles now fell back upon desperate remedies. All his predecessors had collected "forced loans" at times of imminent crisis when there was no time to await parliamentary elections, returns, and the vote of subsidies. It was widely accepted that the king must have discretion to require loans from his subjects in such circumstances loans that were routinely converted into grants when the next Parliament met. What was unprecedented was the collection of forced loans to replace lost parliamentary subsidies. The £260,000 Charles collected in 1627 was precisely the sum he had turned down when it was made conditional upon his surrender of Buckingham to the wrath of the Commons. But he collected it at a heavy price: Charles was compelled to lock up 180 refusers, including many prominent gentry. However, he refused to show cause for his imprisonment of five leading knights, controversially relying on a rarely used discretionary power to arrest "by special commandment" those suspected of crimes it was not in the general interest to make public a contingency normally used to nip conspiracies in the bud.

The inevitable result was furor in the next Parliament, to which he again had to go cap in hand because he was desperate for money to fund simultaneous naval wars against the two superpowers, France and Spain. Lawyers, such as Sir Edward Coke, and country gentlemen, such as Sir John Eliot, now feared that the common law insufficiently protected their lives and liberties. This sentiment was compounded by the fact that soldiers were being billeted in citizens' homes; local militias were forced to raise, equip, and transport men to fight abroad;

and provost marshals declared martial law in peaceful English communities.

Yet the extremity of these expedients was matched by the seriousness of the international situation. Incredibly, England was now at war with both France and Spain, and Buckingham was determined to restore his reputation. Instead, the campaign of 1627 was a disaster, and the duke's landing at the Île de Ré a debacle. It was hard to see how Charles could protect him from his critics once the Parliament of 1628–29 assembled.

The defeats of 1627 made emergency taxation more necessary than ever, and the new Parliament, 27 of whose members had been imprisoned for refusing to contribute to the loan, assembled with a sense of profound disquiet. It was proposed to grant the king five subsidies for defense but to delay their passage until the Petition of Right (1628) could be prepared. The petition asserted four liberties: freedom from arbitrary arrest, freedom from nonparliamentary taxation, freedom from the billeting of troops, and freedom from martial law. Couched in the language of tradition, it was presented to the king as a restatement of ancient liberties. In this spirit he accepted it, more in hope of receiving his subsidies than in fear that the petition would restrain his actions.

Between the two sessions of this Parliament, the duke of Buckingham was assassinated (Aug. 23, 1628). While the king wept in his palace, people drank to the health of the assassin in the streets; Buckingham had become a symbol of all that was wrong in the country. But with the king's favourite removed, there was a void in government. Buckingham had been in charge of military and domestic policy, and there was no one else who had the confidence of the king or the ability to direct the royal program. When Charles I, grief-stricken, attempted to manage the second session of Parliament by himself, all the tensions came to a head. In the Commons some members wanted to challenge violations of the Petition of Right, especially the continued collection of tonnage and poundage without parliamentary authority. Others were equally agitated about changes in religious policy caused by the emergence of Arminianism. When the level of bitterness reached new heights, the king decided to end the session. But before he could do so, two hotheaded members physically restrained the speaker while the Three Resolutions (1629), condemning the collection of tonnage and poundage as well as the doctrine and practice of Arminianism, were introduced. Parliament broke up in pandemonium, with both king and members shocked by the "carriage of diverse fiery spirits."

Peace and reform

The dissolution of the Parliament of 1628 in 1629 and the king's clear intention to govern for a period without this troublesome institution necessitated a reversal of policy. Over the next two years, peace treaties ended England's fruitless involvement in continental warfare in which more than £2 million had been wasted and royal government brought into disrepute. The king was also able to pacify his subjects by launching a campaign of administrative and fiscal reform that finally allowed the crown to live within its own revenues. Customs increased to £500,000 as both European and North American trade expanded. Under capable ministers such as Richard Weston, earl of Portland, prerogative income also increased. Ancient precedents were carefully searched to ensure that the crown received its full and lawful dues. Fines were imposed on those who had not come forward to be knighted at the king's accession. These distraints of knighthood yielded more than £170,000. The boundaries of royal forests were resurveyed and encroachers fined. Fees in the court of wards were raised and procedures streamlined. With effort and application annual royal revenue reached £1 million.

The most important of Charles's fiscal schemes was not technically a design to squeeze monies into the royal coffers. While the king's own rights might underwrite the needs of government, they could do nothing toward maintaining the navy, England's sole military establishment. Thus, Charles expanded the collection of ship money, an ancient levy by which revenue was raised for the outfitting of warships. Although ship money was normally only collected in the ports in times of emergency, Charles extended it to inland communities and declared pirates a national menace. At first there was little resistance to the collection of ship money, but, as it was levied year after year, questions about its legitimacy were raised. The case of John Hampden (1637) turned upon the king's emergency powers and divided the royal judges, who narrowly decided for the crown. But legal opinion varied so significantly that revenue dropped, and the stirring of a taxpayer revolt could be felt.

Religious reform

Fears about the state of the church, which erupted at the end of the Parliament of 1628, had been building for several years. Charles had become drawn to a movement of church reform that aroused deep hostility among his Calvinist subjects. The doctrines of predestination and justification by faith alone formed the core of beliefs in the traditional English church. Yet slowly competing doctrines of free will and the importance of works along with faith, advocated by the Dutch theologian Jacobus Arminius, spread to the English church. Arminians were viewed as radical reformers despite the fact that their leaders were elevated to the highest positions in church government. In 1633 William Laud, one of the ablest of the Arminians, became archbishop of Canterbury. Laud stressed ceremony over preaching. He believed in the "beauty of holiness" and introduced measures to decorate churches and to separate the communion table from the congregation. Both of these practices were reminiscent of Roman

Catholicism, and they came at a time when Protestants everywhere feared for the survival of their religion. Nor did it help that the queen openly attended mass along with some highly placed converted courtiers. Anti-popery was the single strain that had united the diverse elements of Protestant reform, and it was now a rallying cry against innovations at home rather than abominations abroad.

But perhaps Laud's greatest offense was to promote the authority of the clergy in general and of the bishops in particular, against the laity. He challenged head-on the central thrust of the English Reformation: the assault on the institutional wealth and power of the church as a clerical corporation. He wanted to restore the authority of the church courts and threatened to excommunicate the king's judges if they persisted in trying cases that belonged to ecclesiastical jurisdiction. He also tried to restore the value of tithes and prevent the misappropriation of churchyards for secular purposes.

Moreover, he sought to penalize those who did not pay the (much-enhanced) levies for the refurbishment of church buildings. Menacingly, in Scotland and Ireland (as a prelude, many assumed, to actions to come in England) he tried to renegotiate by a policy of surrender the terms on which all former monastic and cathedral lands were held. In all this he appeared to act more like an aggressive papal nuncio than a compliant appointee of the royal supreme governor of the church, and Charles I's purring complaisance in Laud's activities was unendurable to most of his subjects. The master of Westminster School was whipped in front of his pupils for saying of Laud that, like "a busie, angry wasp, his sting is in the tayl of everything." Others were flogged through the streets of London or had their ears cut off for "libeling" Laud and his work. He alienated not only everyone with a Puritan scruple but everyone with a strong sense of the supremacy of common law or with an inherited suspicion of clerical pride. No wonder the archbishop had so few friends by 1640.

His program extended to Ireland and especially disastrously to Scotland. Without consulting Parliament, the General Assembly, the Scottish bishops in conclave, or even the Scottish Privy Council, but rather by royal diktat, Laud ordered the introduction of new canons, a new ordinal, and a new prayer book based not on the English prayer book of 1559 but on the more ceremonialist and crypto-Catholic English prayer book of 1549. This was met by riot and, eventually, rebellion. Vast numbers of Scots bound themselves passively to disobey the "unlawful" religious innovations. Charles I decided to use force to compel them, and he twice sought to use troops raised by a loyal (largely Catholic) Scottish minority, troops from Ireland, and troops from England to achieve this end.

The Bishops' Wars (1639–40) brought an end to the tranquillity of the 1630s. Charles had to meet rebellion with force, and force required money from Parliament. He genuinely believed that he would be supported against the rebels, failing to comprehend the profound hostility that Laud's innovations had created in England. The Short Parliament (1640) lasted less than a month before the king dissolved it rather than permit an extended discussion of his inadequacies. He scraped some money together and placed his troops under the command of his able and ruthless deputy, Thomas Wentworth, earl of Strafford. But English troops fighting for pay proved no match for Scottish troops fighting for religion. In 1640 the Scots invaded England and captured Newcastle, the vital source of London's coal. Charles was forced to accept a humiliating treaty whereby he paid for the upkeep of the Scottish army and agreed to call another Parliament.

The Long Parliament

With his circumstances more desperate than ever, Charles I summoned Parliament to meet in November 1640. The king faced a body profoundly mistrustful of his intentions. The reform movement in the Commons was led by John Pym, a minor Somerset landowner, who was prominent by his oratorical skills in debate and his political skills in committee. Pym was a moderate, and for the next three years he ably steered compromises between those who wanted too much and those who would settle for too little. In the Lords, Viscount Saye and Sele and the earl of Warwick and the earl of Bedford worked in tandem with Pym and his allies, leading or following as occasion required.

The Long Parliament (1640–53) opened with the imprisonment of Strafford and Laud, the architects of the Scottish fiasco. Strafford was put on trial and ultimately attainted for treason. The dubious legality of the charges against him forced the Commons to proceed by bill rather than impeachment, and thus both the House of Lords and the monarch had to approve the charge. The Lords were cowed by crowds of angry London citizens and apprentices and Charles by the mistaken belief that Strafford's blood would placate his opponents. But Strafford's execution in May was just the beginning.

In fact, parliamentary reform took two different tacks. The first was to limit the king's constitutional authority in order to protect the existence of Parliament and the liberties of subjects. The second was to reconstitute the church. In February the Triennial Act (1641) was passed, mandating the summoning of Parliament every three years. In May the king's power to dissolve the Long Parliament was removed. Charles was forced to accept both bills. Meanwhile, the Commons relentlessly investigated the legal basis of the king's fiscal expedients, amending the laws that Charles had so scrupulously followed. Ship money and distraints of knighthood were declared illegal, royal forests were defined, and the prerogative courts of High Commission and Star Chamber were abolished. Again the king acceded.

Church reform proved more treacherous. Parliamentary leaders agreed that Charles and Laud had introduced intolerable innovations, but where some were satisfied by their removal, others wished that they be replaced by even greater novelties. In December 1640 an orchestrated petitioning campaign called upon Parliament to abolish episcopacy, root and branch. Pym and his supporters were as yet unwilling to propose such a sweeping change, fearing lest it divide the Commons and create a crisis with the Lords. Nevertheless, the equally radical proposal to remove the bishops from the upper house was passed in May, and, when the Lords rejected it, the Commons responded with the Root and Branch Bill.

Pym's fear that the religious issue might break apart the parliamentary consensus was compounded by his fear of provoking the king to counterattack. Throughout the first six months of the session, Charles had meekly followed Parliament's lead. But there were ominous signs that the worm would turn. His leading advisers, the queen among them, were searching for military options. The radical attack upon the church allowed the king to portray himself as the conservator of "the pure religion of Queen Elizabeth and King James" without "any connivance of popery or innovation" a coded repudiation of Laudianism and Arminianism. Week by week, sympathy for the king was growing, and in August Charles determined to conclude a peace treaty with the Scots. This successful negotiation removed the crisis that had brought the Long Parliament into being. When Charles returned to London at the end of November, he was met by cheering crowds and a large body of members of the two houses, who were unaware that he had been behind a failed attempt to arrest the leading conservator and overturn the Scottish settlement.

While the king resolved one crisis in Scotland, another emerged in Ireland. Catholics, stung by the harsh repression of Strafford's rule and by the threat of plantation and of the direct rule from England planned by the Long Parliament, rose against their Protestant overlords and slaughtered thousands in a bloody rebellion. Though the reality was grim enough, the exaggerated reports that reached London seemed to fulfill the worst fears of a popish plot. Urgently an army had to be raised, but only the king had military authority, and in the present circumstance he could not be trusted with a force that might be used in London rather than Londonderry. In despair over the situation in Ireland and deeply suspicious of the king's intentions, the leaders of the Long Parliament debated the Grand Remonstrance, a catalog of their grievances against the king.

The Grand Remonstrance (1641) divided the Commons as nothing else had. It passed by only 11 votes, and the move to have it printed failed. Many were appalled that the remonstrance was to be used as propaganda "to tell stories to the people." For the first time, members of Commons began to coalesce into opposing factions of royalists and parliamentarians.

The passage of the Grand Remonstrance was followed by Pym's attempt to transfer control of the militia (the appointment of lords, lieutenants, military officers, etc.) from the crown to Parliament. The political situation had reached a state of crisis. In Parliament, rumours spread of a royal attack upon the houses, and at court wild talk of an impeachment of the queen was reported. It was Charles who broke the deadlock. On Jan. 4, 1642, he rode to Westminster intending to impeach five members of the Commons and one of the Lords on charges of treason. It was the same device that had already failed in Scotland. But, because the king's plan was no secret, the members had already fled. Thus, Charles's dramatic breach of parliamentary privilege badly backfired. He not only failed to obtain his objective but also lost the confidence of many of the moderates left in Parliament. After ensuring the safe departure of his wife and children out of the country, Charles abandoned his capital and headed north.

The initiative had returned to Pym and his allies, who now proceeded to pass much of their stalled legislation, including the exclusion of the bishops from the Lords and the Impressment Bill (1642), which allowed Parliament to raise the army for Ireland. In June a series of proposals for a treaty, the Nineteen Propositions (1642), was presented to the king. The proposals called for parliamentary control over the militia, the choice of royal counselors, and religious reform. Charles rejected them outright, though in his answer he seemed to grant Parliament a coordinate power in government, making the king but one of the three estates. The king, however, had determined to settle the matter by main force. His principal advisers believed that the greatest lords and gentlemen would rally to their king and that Parliament would not have the stomach for rebellion. On Aug. 22, 1642, the king raised his standard bearing the device "Give Caesar His Due."

Civil war and revolution

The war that began in 1642 was a war within three kingdoms and between three kingdoms. There was a civil war in Ireland that pitted the Catholic majority against the Protestant minority, buttressed by English and Scottish armies. This war festered nastily throughout the 1640s and was settled only by a devastating use of force and terror by Oliver Cromwell in 1649–50 and his successors in 1651–54. Whenever they were in the ascendancy, the Catholic Irish were willing to send armies into England to assist Charles I, on condition that he give them religious freedom and effective control of the political institutions of the Irish kingdom. After the Cromwellian conquest, the English set out to destroy the power and wealth of the Catholic elite at one point even proposing to transport every native Catholic from 26 of the 32 counties of Ireland into the western region comprising the 5 counties of Connacht and County Clare; in the event, they settled for a confiscation of two-fifths of the land and its redistribution to Protestant Englishmen.

Scotland also was embroiled in civil war, but, at one time or another, all the groups involved demonstrated a willingness to send armies into England. The Anglo-Scottish wars were fought from 1643 to 1646, resumed from 1648 to 1651, and resulted in an English military occupation and complete political subjugation (the incorporation of Scotland into an enhanced English state) that lasted until the Restoration in 1660.

And then there was the English Civil War that began in 1642, a war that neither king, Parliament, nor the country wanted. It was a war that was as dangerous to win as to lose. The parliamentarians could only maintain the fiction that they were fighting to "preserve the safety of the king," as the commission of their commander, Robert Devereux, earl of Essex, stated. The king's fiction was that he was opposing a rebellion. Most of the country remained neutral, hoping that differences would be composed and fighting ended.

The first years of war were as halfhearted as these justifications. Parliament held the tactical advantages of controlling the navy and London. While the navy protected the coast from foreign invasion, London provided the funds and manpower for battle. The king held the strategic advantage of knowing that he had to recapture his capital. He relied upon the aristocracy for men and arms. In the first substantial engagement of the war, the Battle of Edgehill (1642), Charles's cavalry proved superior to Parliament's, and he followed this first encounter by marching on the capital. At Brentford (1642), on the outskirts of London, the City militia narrowly averted the king's triumph. For the next two years, however, the war was fought to a desultory standstill.

Almost from the beginning, the members of Parliament were divided over their goals. A war group argued that Charles could not be trusted until he learned the lesson of military defeat. A peace group countered that the longer the war ground on, the less likely Charles would be to compromise. Both of these groups were loose coalitions, and neither of them dominated parliamentary politics. Until his death in 1643, Pym steered a course between them, supporting the Oxford

Propositions (1643) for peace as well as creating the administrative machinery to raise and finance armies. The excise, modeled on impositions, and the monthly assessments, modeled on ship money, increased levels of taxation to new heights. The king burdened the communities his forces controlled just as heavily.

In 1643 the war widened. Charles negotiated a cease-fire with the Catholic rebels in Ireland that allowed him to bring Irish troops to England. Parliament negotiated the Solemn League and Covenant (1643) with the Scots, who brought an army to England in return for guarantees of a presbyterian church establishment. Initially Parliament benefited most. A combination of English and Scottish troops defeated royalist forces at the Battle of Marston Moor (1644) and took York. But ultimately religious differences between Scottish Presbyterians and English Independents vitiated the alliance. As the parliamentary commanders bickered, their forces were defeated at Lostwithiel (1644) and Newbury (1644). While another round of peace negotiations began, the unsuccessful Uxbridge Proposals (1645), Parliament recast its military establishment and formed the New Model Army.

There was little new about the New Model Army other than centralization. Remnants of three armies were combined to be directed by a parliamentary committee. This committee included the parliamentary generals who were displaced by the Self-Denying Ordinance (1645), an act that excluded members of Parliament from civil and military office. The New Model Army was commanded by Thomas Fairfax, Baron Fairfax, and eventually the cavalry was led by Lieut. Gen. Oliver Cromwell.

The new parliamentary army was thought so weak that the king hoped to crush it in a single blow and thus end the war. Instead, the Battle of Naseby on June 14, 1645, delivered the decisive blow to the royalists. Even though the parliamentary forces only just managed to carry the day despite their numerical superiority, their victory was decisive. It destroyed the king's main armies and left open a path to the west, where his other substantial forces were defeated at Langport (1645). The following year, the king surrendered to the Scots, erroneously believing that they would strike a better bargain.

For four years the political divisions at Westminster had been held in check by the military emergency. But the king's defeat released all restraints. In Parliament coherent parties began to form around the religious poles provided by Presbyterians and Independents and around the political poles of peace and war. Denzil Holles, one of the five members of Parliament Charles had tried to arrest in 1642, came to head the most powerful group. He pushed through a presbyterian church settlement, negotiated a large loan from the City of London, and used the money to ransom the king from the Scots. Holles's peace plan was to remove the main points of difference between king and Parliament by disbanding the army and settling the disputes about the church, the militia, and the rebellion in Ireland. His party was opposed by a group led by Sir Henry Vane the Younger and Oliver Cromwell, who desired toleration for Independents and were fearful of disbanding the army before an agreement was reached with Charles I.

But war weariness in both Parliament and the country swept all before it. In January 1647 Charles was returned to English custody, and Holles moved forward with his plan to send a portion of the army to Ireland, assign a small force to English garrisons, and disband the rest. But in this he reckoned without the army. In the rank and file, concern about arrears of pay, indemnity, and liability for impressment stirred the soldiers to resist Irish service. A movement that began over material grievances soon turned political as representatives were chosen from the rank and file to present demands through their officers to Parliament. Holles attempted to brush this movement aside and push through his disbandment scheme. At this the army rose up, driving out those of its officers who supported the disbandment, seizing Charles at Holmby House on June 3 and demanding the impeachment of Holles and his main supporters. At the beginning of August 1647, the army marched into London, and Holles, with 10 of his allies, fled the capital.

The army's intervention transformed civil war into revolution. Parliament, which in 1646 had argued that it was the fundamental authority in the country, by 1647 was but a pawn in a new game of power politics. The perceived corruption of Parliament made it, like the king, a target of reform. Initiative was now in the hands of the king and the army, and Charles I tried to entice Cromwell and Henry Ireton, the army's leading strategist, to bargain his restoration for a tolerant church settlement. But the officers were only one part of a politicized army that was bombarded with plans for reorganizing the state. Among the most potent plans were those of the Levelers, led by John Lilburne, who desired that a new compact between ruler and ruled, the Agreement of the People (1647), be made. This was debated by the council of the army at Putney in October. The Levelers' proposals, which had much in common with the army's, called for the reform of Parliament through elections based upon a broad franchise and for a generally tolerant church settlement. Turmoil in the army led Fairfax and Cromwell to reassert military discipline, while the machinations of Charles led to the second Civil War (1648).

Charles had now managed to join his English supporters with discontented Scots who opposed the army's intervention in politics. Though the fighting was brief, it was bloody. Fairfax stormed Colchester (1648) and executed the ringleaders of the English rebellion, and Cromwell and several New Model regiments defeated the invading Scots at the Battle of Preston (1648).

The second Civil War hardened attitudes in the army. The king was directly blamed for the unnecessary loss of life, and for the first time alternatives to Charles Stuart, "that man of blood," were openly contemplated. Parliament too was appalled by the renewal of fighting. Moderate members believed that there was still a chance to bring the king to terms, despite the fact that he had rejected treaty after treaty. While the army made plans to put the king on trial, Parliament summoned its strength for one last negotiation, the abortive Treaty of Newport. Even now the king remained intransigent, especially over the issue of episcopacy. New negotiations infuriated the army, because it believed that Parliament would sell out its sacrifices and compromise its ideals. On Dec. 6, 1648, army troops, under the direction of Col. Thomas Pride, purged the House of Commons. Forty-five members were arrested, and 186 were kept away. A rump of about 75 active members were left to do the army's bidding. They were to establish a High Court of Justice, prepare a charge of treason against the king, and place him on trial in the name of the people of England. Pride's Purge was a last-minute compromise made to prevent absolute military rule. With Cromwell deliberately absent in the north, Ireton was left to stave off the argument, made by the Levelers, that Parliament was hopelessly corrupt and should be dissolved. The decision to proceed by trial in the High Court of Parliament was a decision in favour of constitutional forms, however much a shadow they had become.

The king's trial took place at the end of January. The Court of Justice was composed of members of Parliament, civilians, and army officers. There was little enthusiasm for the work that had to be done. No more senior judge than John Bradshaw could be found to preside, and he wore a hat ringed with iron in fear of assassination. The charges against the king, however politically correct, had little legal basis, and Charles deftly exposed their weakness. But like Strafford before him, Charles was to be sacrificed to the law of necessity if not the law of England. On Jan. 30, 1649, at the wall of his own palace, Charles I was beheaded. A witness recorded in his diary, "Such a groan went up as I had never before heard."

Commonwealth and Protectorate

The execution of the king aroused hostility not only in England but also throughout Europe. Regicide was considered the worst of all crimes, and not even the brilliance of John Milton in The Tenure of Kings and Magistrates (1649) could persuade either Catholic or Protestant powers that the execution of Charles I was just. Open season was declared against English shipping, and Charles II was encouraged to reclaim his father's three kingdoms.

Despite opposition and continued external threats, the government of the Commonwealth was declared in May 1649 after acts had been passed to abolish the monarchy and the House of Lords. Political power resided in a Council of State, the Rump Parliament (which swelled from 75 to 213 members in the year following the king's execution), and the army. The military was now a permanent part of English government. Though the soldiers had assigned the complex tasks of reform to Parliament, they made sure of their ability to intervene in political affairs.

At first, however, the soldiers had other things to occupy them. For reasons of security and revenge, Ireland had to be pacified. In the autumn of 1649, Cromwell crossed to Ireland to deal once and for all with the Irish Confederate rebels. He came first to Drogheda. When the town refused to surrender, he stormed it and put the garrison of 3,000 to the sword, acting both as the avenger of the massacres of 1641 ("I am persuaded that this is a righteous judgement of God upon those barbarous wretches who have imbrued their hands in so much innocent blood") and as a deliberate instrument of terror to induce others to surrender. He repeated his policy of massacre at Wexford, this time choosing not to spare the civilian population. These actions had the desired effect, and most other towns surrendered at Cromwell's approach. He departed Ireland after nine months, leaving his successors with only a mopping-up operation. His reputation at a new high, Cromwell was next put in charge of dealing with those Scots who had welcomed Charles I's son, Charles II, to Scotland and who were soon to crown him at Scone as king of all of Great Britain and Ireland. Although outnumbered and in a weak defensive position, Cromwell won a stunning victory in the Battle of Dunbar on Sept. 3, 1650. A year later to the day, having chased Charles II and a second Scottish army into England, he gained an overwhelming victory at Worcester. Charles II barely escaped with his life.

Victorious wars against the Irish, Scots, and Dutch (1652) made the Commonwealth a feared military power. But the struggle for survival defined the Rump's conservative policies. Little was done to reform the law. An attempt to abolish the court of chancery created chaos in the central courts. Little agreement could be reached on religious matters, especially on the vexing question of the compulsory payment of tithes. The Rump failed both to make long-term provision for a new "national church" and to define the state's right to confer and place limits on the freedom of those who wished to worship and gather outside the church. Most ominously, nothing at all had been done to set a limit for the sitting of the Rump and to provide for franchise reform and the election of a new Parliament.

This had been the principal demand of the army, and the more the Rump protested the difficulty of the problem, the less patient the soldiers became. In April, when it was clear that the Rump would set a limit to its sitting but would nominate its own members to judge new elections, Cromwell marched to Westminster and dissolved Parliament. The Rump was replaced by an assembly nominated mostly by the army high command. The Nominated Parliament (1653) was no better able to overcome its internal divisions or untangle the threads of reform than the Rump. After five months it dissolved itself and returned power to Cromwell and the army.

The problems that beset both the Rump and the Nominated Parliament resulted from the diversity of groups that supported the revolution, ranging from pragmatic men of affairs, lawyers, officeholders, and local magistrates whose principal desire was to restore and maintain order to zealous visionaries who wished to establish heaven on earth. The republicans, like Sir Henry Vane the Younger, hoped to create a government based upon the model of ancient Rome and modern Venice. They were proud of the achievements of the Commonwealth and reviled Cromwell for dissolving the Rump. But most political reformers based their programs on dreams of the future rather than the past. They were millenarians, expecting the imminent Second Coming of Christ.

Some were social reformers, such as Gerrard Winstanley, whose followers, agrarian communists known as Diggers, believed that the common lands should be returned to the common people. Others were mystics, such as the Ranters, led by Laurence Claxton, who believed that they were infused with a holy spirit that removed sin from even their most reprehensible acts. The most enduring of these groups were the Quakers (Society of Friends), whose social radicalism was seen in their refusal to take oaths or doff their hats and whose religious radicalism was contained in their emphasis upon inner light. Ultimately, all these groups were persecuted by successive revolutionary governments, which were continually being forced to establish conservative limits to individual and collective behaviour.

The failure of the Nominated Parliament led to the creation of the first British constitution, the Instrument of Government (1653). Drafted by Maj. Gen. John Lambert, the Instrument created a lord protector, a Council of State, and a reformed Parliament that was to be elected at least once every three years. Cromwell was named protector, and he chose a civilian-dominated Council to help him govern. The Protectorate tackled many of the central issues of reform head-on. Commissions were appointed to study law reform and the question of tithes. Social legislation against swearing, drunkenness, and stage plays was introduced. Steps were taken to provide for the training of a godly ministry, and even a new university at Durham was begun.

But the protector was no better able to manage his Parliaments than had been the king. The Parliament of 1654 immediately questioned the entire basis of the newly established government, with the republicans vigorously disputing the office of lord protector. The Parliament of 1656, despite the exclusion of many known opponents, was no more pliable. Both were a focus for the manifold discontents of supporters and opponents of the regime.

Nothing was more central to the Cromwellian experiment than the cause of religious liberty. Cromwell believed that no one church had a monopoly on truth and that no one form of government or worship was necessary or desirable. Moreover, he believed in a loosely federated national church, with each parish free to worship as it wished within very broad limits and staffed by a clergy licensed by the state on the basis of their knowledge of the Bible and the uprightness of their lives, without reference to their religious beliefs. On the other hand, Cromwell felt that there should be freedom for "all species of protestant" to gather if they wished into religious assemblies outside the national church. He did not believe, however, that religious liberty was a natural right, but one conferred by the Christian magistrate, who could place prudential limits on the exercise of that liberty.

Thus, those who claimed that their religion permitted or even promoted licentiousness and sexual freedom, who denied the Trinity, or who claimed the right to disrupt the worship of others were subject to proscription or penalty. Furthermore, for the only time between the Reformation and the mid-19th century, there was no religious test for the holding of public office. Although Cromwell made his detestation of Catholicism very plain, Catholics benefited from the repeal of the laws requiring attendance at parish churches, and they were less persecuted for the private exercise of their own faith than at any other time in the century. Cromwell's policy of religious tolerance was far from total, but it was exceptional in the early modern world.

Among opponents, royalists were again active, though by now they were reduced to secret associations and conspiracies. In the west, Penruddock's rising, the most successful of a series of otherwise feeble royalist actions in March 1655, was effectively suppressed, but Cromwell reacted by reducing both the standing army and the level of taxation on all. He also appointed senior army officers "major generals," raising ultra-loyal militias from among the demobbed veterans paid for by penal taxation on all those convicted of active royalism in the previous decade. The major generals were also charged with superintending "a reformation of manners" the imposition of strict Puritan codes of social and sexual conduct. They were extremely unpopular, and, despite their effectiveness, the offices were abolished within a year.

By now it was apparent that the regime was held together by Cromwell alone. Within his personality resided the contradictions of the revolution. Like the gentry, he desired a fixed and stable constitution, but, like the zealous, he was infused with a millenarian vision of a more glorious world to come (see millennialism). As a member of Parliament from 1640, he respected the fundamental authority that Parliament represented, but, as a member of the army, he understood power and the decisive demands of necessity. In the 1650s many wished him to become king, but he refused the crown, preferring the authority of the people to the authority of the sword. When he died in 1658, all hope of continued reform died with him.

For a time, Richard Cromwell was elevated to his father's titles and dignity, but he was no match in power or skill. The republicans and the army officers who had fought Oliver tooth and nail now hoped to use his son to dismantle the civil government that under the Humble

Petition and Advice (1657) had come to resemble nothing so much as the old monarchy. An upper House of Lords had been created, and the court at Whitehall was every bit as ceremonious as that of the Stuarts. While some demanded that the Rump be restored to power, others clamoured for the selection of a new Parliament on the basis of the old franchise, and this took place in 1659. By then there was a vacuum of power at the centre; Richard Cromwell, incapable of governing, simply left office. A rebellion of junior officers led to the reestablishment of the Rump.

But all was confusion. The Rump was incapable of governing without financial support from the City and military support from the army. Just as in 1647, the City demanded military disbandment and the army demanded satisfaction of its material grievances. But the army was no longer a unified force. Contentions among the senior officers led to an attempt to arrest Lambert, and the widely scattered regiments had their own grievances to propound. The most powerful force was in Scotland, commanded by George Monck, once a royalist and now one of the ablest of the army's senior officers. When one group of officers determined to dissolve the Rump, Monck marched his forces south, determined to restore it. Arriving in London, Monck quickly realized that the Rump could never govern effectively and that only the restoration of Charles II could put an end to the political chaos that now gripped the state. In February 1660 Monck reversed Pride's Purge, inviting all of the secluded members of the Long Parliament to return to their seats under army protection. A month later the Long Parliament dissolved itself, paving the way for the return of the king.

The later Stuarts

Charles II (1660–85)
The Restoration

Charles II arrived in London on the 30th birthday of what had already been a remarkably eventful life. He came of age in Europe, a child of diplomatic intrigues, broken promises, and unfulfilled hopes. By necessity he had developed a thick skin and a shrewd political realism. This was displayed in the Declaration of Breda (1660), in which Charles offered something to everyone in his terms for resuming government. A general pardon would be issued, a tolerant religious settlement would be sought, and security for private property would be assured. Never a man for details, Charles left the specifics to the Convention Parliament (1660), which was composed of members of the competing religious and political parties that contended for power amid the rubble of the Commonwealth.

The Convention declared the restoration of the king and the lords, disbanded the army, established a fixed income for the king by maintaining the parliamentary innovation of the excise tax, and returned to the crown and the bishops their confiscated estates. But it made no headway on a religious settlement. Despite Charles's promise of a limited toleration and his desire to accept Presbyterians into the Anglican fold as detailed in the Worcester House Declaration (1660), enthusiasts from both left and right wrecked every compromise.

It was left to the Cavalier Parliament (1661–79) to make the hard choices and to demonstrate that one of the changes that had survived the revolution was the independence of Parliament. Despite Charles's desire to treat his father's adversaries leniently and to find a broad church settlement, the Cavalier Parliament sought to establish a rigid Anglican orthodoxy. It began the alliance between squire and parson that was to dominate English local society for centuries. The bishops were returned to Parliament, a new prayer book was authorized, and repressive acts were passed to compel conformity.

The imposition of oaths of allegiance and nonresistance to the crown and an oath recognizing the king's supremacy in the church upon all members of local government in the Corporation Act (1661) and then upon the clergy in the Act of Uniformity (1662) led to a massive purge of officeholders. Town governors were put out of their places, and nearly one-fifth of all clergymen were deprived of their livings. Authority in the localities was now firmly in the hands of the gentry. The Conventicle Act (1664) barred Nonconformists (Dissenters) from holding separate church services, and the Five Mile Act (1665) prohibited dispossessed ministers from even visiting their former congregations.

This program of repressive religious legislation was the first of many missed opportunities to remove the underlying causes of political discontent. Though religious dissenters were not a large percentage of the population, their treatment raised the spectre of permanently divided local communities and of potentially arbitrary government. This legislation (the Clarendon Code) is inappropriately associated with the name of Lord Chancellor Clarendon, for he, as well as the king, realized the dangers of religious repression and attempted to soften its effects. Indeed, in central government the king relied upon men of diverse political backgrounds and religious beliefs. Clarendon, who had lived with the king in exile, was his chief political adviser, and Charles's brother James, duke of York (later James II), was his closest confidant and was entrusted with the vital post of lord admiral. Monck, who had made the restoration possible, was raised to duke of Albemarle and continued to hold military authority over the small standing army that, for the first time in English history, the king maintained.

War and government

Charles II could not undo the effects of the revolution, but they were not all negative. The Commonwealth had had to fight for its survival, and in the process England had become a potent military power. Wars against France and Spain had expanded English colonial dominions. Dunkirk and Jamaica were seized, Barbados was colonized, and the

North American colonies flourished. Colonial trade was an important source of royal revenue, and Charles II continued Cromwell's policy of restricting trade to English ships and imposing duties on imports and exports. The Navigation Acts (1660 and 1663) were directed against the Dutch, still the most powerful commercial force in Europe. The Cromwellian Navigation Act (1651) had resulted in the first Anglo-Dutch War (1652–54), and Charles's policy had the same effect. In military terms the Dutch Wars (1665–67; 1672–74) were a standoff, but in economic terms they were an English triumph (see Anglo-Dutch Wars). The American colonies were consolidated by the capture of New York, and the policy of the Navigation Acts was effectively established. Colonial trade and English shipping mushroomed.

In the long run Charles's spasmodically aggressive foreign policy solved the crown's perpetual fiscal crises. But in the short run it made matters worse. The Great Plague of London (1664–66) and the Great Fire of London (1666) were interpreted as divine judgments against a sinful nation. These catastrophes were compounded when the Dutch burned a large portion of the English fleet in 1667, which led to the dismissal and exile of Clarendon. The crown's debts led to the Stop of the Exchequer (1672), by which Charles suspended payment of his bills. The king now ruled through a group of ministers known as the Cabal, an anagram of the first letters of their names. None of the five was Anglican, and two were Roman Catholic.

Charles had wearied of repressive Anglicanism, underestimating its strength among rural gentry and clergy, and desired comprehension and toleration in his church. This fit with his foreign-policy objectives, for in the Treaty of Dover (1670) he allied himself with Catholic France against Protestant Holland. In exchange he received a large subsidy from Louis XIV and, in the treaty's secret clauses, known only to the king's Catholic ministers, the promise of an even larger one if Charles undertook, at some unspecified moment, to declare himself a Catholic. That moment came for the king on his deathbed, by which time his brother and heir, the duke of York, had already openly professed his conversion. In 1672 Charles promulgated the Declaration of Indulgence, which suspended the penal code against all religious Nonconformists, Catholic and Dissenter alike. But a declaration of toleration could not bring together these mortal enemies, and the king found himself faced by a unified Protestant front. Parliamentary Anglicans would not vote money for war until the declaration was abrogated. The passage of the Test Act (1673), which the king reluctantly signed, effectively barred all but Anglicans from holding national office and forced the duke of York to resign the admiralty.

The Popish Plot

Anti-Catholicism united the disparate elements of English Protestantism as did nothing else. Anglicans vigorously persecuted the Protestant sects, especially Quakers and Baptists, who were imprisoned by the thousands whenever the government claimed to have discovered a radical plot. John Bunyan's Pilgrim's Progress (1678), which became one of the most popular works in the English language, was composed in jail. Yet dissenters held out against persecution and continued to make their converts in towns and cities. They railed against the debauchery of court life, naming the duke of York, whose shotgun wedding had scandalized even his own family, and the king himself, who acknowledged 17 bastard children but did not produce one legitimate heir. Most of all they feared a Catholic revival, which by the late 1670s was no paranoid delusion. The alliance with Catholic France and rumours of the secret treaty, the open conversion of the duke of York, heir to the throne, and the king's efforts to suspend the laws against Catholic officeholders were potent signs.

Not even the policy of Charles's new chief minister, Thomas Osborne, earl of Danby, could stem the tide of suspicion. An Anglican, Danby tried to move the crown back into alliance with the majority of country gentry, who wanted the enforcement of the penal code and the end of the pro-French foreign policy. He arranged the marriage of Mary (later Mary II), the eldest daughter of the duke of York, to William of Orange (later William III), the Dutch stadtholder. Yet, like the king, Danby admired Louis XIV and the French style of monarchy. He attempted to manage Parliament, centralize crown patronage, shore up royal finance, and maintain a standing army in short, to build a base for royal absolutism. Catholicism and absolutism were so firmly linked in the popular mind that Danby was soon tarred by this broad brush. In 1678 a London Dissenter named Titus Oates revealed evidence of a plot by the Jesuits to murder the king and establish Roman Catholicism in England.

Although both the evidence and the plot were a total fabrication, England was quickly swept up in anti-Catholic hysteria. The murder of the Protestant magistrate who had first heard Oates's revelations lent credence to a tissue of lies. Thirty-five alleged conspirators in the Popish Plot were tried and executed, harsh laws against Catholics were revived and extended, and Danby's political position was undermined when it was revealed that he had been in secret negotiation with the French. Parliament voted his impeachment and began to investigate the clauses of the Anglo-French treaties. A second Test Act (1678) was passed, barring all but Anglicans from Parliament, and an exception for the duke of York to sit in the Lords was carried by only two votes. After 18 years Charles II dissolved the Cavalier Parliament.

The exclusion crisis and the Tory reaction

The mass hysteria that resulted from the Popish Plot also had its effects on the country's governors. When Parliament assembled in 1679, a bill was introduced to exclude the duke of York from the throne. This plunged the state into its most serious political crisis since the revolution. But, unlike his father, Charles II reacted calmly and decisively. First he co-opted the leading exclusionists, including the earl of Shaftesbury, the earl of Halifax, and the earl of Essex, into his government, and then he offered a plan for safeguarding the church during his brother's reign. But when the Commons passed the Exclusion Bill, Charles dissolved Parliament and called new elections. These did not change the mood of the country, for in the second Exclusion Parliament (1679) the Commons also voted to bypass the duke of York in favour of his daughter Mary and William of Orange, though this was rejected by the Lords. Again Parliament was dissolved, again the king appealed to the country, and again an unyielding Parliament met at Oxford (1681). By now the king had shown his determination and had frightened the local elites into believing that there was danger of another civil war. The Oxford Parliament was dissolved in a week, the "Whig" (Scottish Gaelic: "Horse Thief") councillors, as they were now called, were dismissed from their places, and the king appealed directly to the country for support.

The king also appealed to his cousin Louis XIV, who feared exclusion as much as Charles did, if for different reasons. Louis provided a large annual subsidy to increase Charles's already plentiful revenues, which had grown with English commerce. Louis also encouraged him to strike out against the Whigs. An attempt to impeach the earl of Shaftesbury was foiled only because a Whig grand jury refused to return an indictment. But the earl was forced into exile in Holland, where he died in 1683. The king next attacked the government of London, calling in its charter and reorganizing its institutions so that "Tories" (Irish: "Thieving Outlaws"), as his supporters were now called, held power. Quo warranto proceedings against the charters of many urban corporations followed, forcing surrenders and reincorporations that gave the crown the ability to replace disloyal local governors. (See Whig and Tory.)

In 1683 government informants named the earl of Essex, Lord William Russell, and Algernon Sidney as conspirators in the Rye House Plot, a plan to assassinate the king. Though the evidence was flimsy, Russell and Sidney were executed and Essex took his own life. There was hardly a murmur of protest when Charles II failed to summon a Parliament in 1684, as he was bound to do by the Triennial Act. He was now fully master of his state financially independent of Parliament and politically secure, with loyal Tory servants predominating in local and national government. He died in 1685 at the height of his power.

James II (1685-88)

Church and king

Unlike his brother, James II did not dissimulate for the sake of policy. He dealt plainly with friend and foe alike. James did not desire to establish Catholicism or absolutism and offered ironclad guarantees for the preservation of the Anglican church. He did desire better treatment for his coreligionists and the repeal of the Test Acts. James came to the throne amid declarations of loyalty from the ruling elite. The Parliament of 1685 was decidedly royalist, granting the king customs revenues for life as well as emergency military aid to suppress Monmouth's Rebellion (1685). James Scott, duke of Monmouth, an illegitimate son of Charles II, was Shaftesbury's personal choice for the throne had Exclusion succeeded. Monmouth recruited tradesmen and farmers as he marched through the west country on the way to defeat at the Battle of Sedgemoor. The rebellion was a fiasco, as the local gentry refused to sanction civil war. Monmouth was executed, and more than 600 of his supporters were either hanged or deported in the brutal aftermath of the rebellion, the Bloody Assizes (1685).

The king misinterpreted Monmouth's failure to mean that the country would place the legitimate succession above all else. During the rebellion, James had dispensed with the Test Act and appointed Catholics to military command. This led to a confrontation with Parliament, but the king's dispensing power was upheld in Godden v.

Hales (1686). James made it clear that he intended to maintain his large military establishment, to promote Catholics to positions of leadership, and to dispense with the penal code.

These decisions could hardly have come at a worse moment. In France Louis XIV revoked the Edict of Nantes, the legislation that had protected the rights of French Protestants for nearly a century. The repression of Huguenot congregations inflamed English public opinion. Thus, the king's effort on behalf of Catholics was doomed from the start. He had vainly hoped the Parliament of 1685 would repeal the Test Acts. When his attempt to open the universities to Catholics was met by rigid opposition, he forced a Catholic head upon Magdelan College, Oxford, but only after an open break with the fellows and unpleasant publicity. Moreover, his effort to forge an alliance with Dissenters proved unsuccessful. When James showed favour to William Penn and the Quakers, his leading Anglican ministers, Henry Hyde, earl of Clarendon, and Lawrence Hyde, earl of Rochester, resigned.

By now the king was set upon a collision course with his natural supporters. The Tory interest was made up of solid support for church and king; it was James's mistake to believe that they would support one without the other. In 1687 he reissued the Declaration of Indulgence, which suspended the penal laws against Catholics and Dissenters. This was a temporary measure, for James hoped that his next Parliament would repeal the penal code in its entirety. To that end he began a systematic investigation of the parliamentary boroughs. Agents were sent to question mayors, lieutenants, and justices of the peace about their loyalty to the regime and their willingness to vote for members of Parliament (MPs) who would repeal the Test Acts. Most gave temporizing answers, but those who stood out were purged from their places. For the first time in English history, the crown was undertaking to pack Parliament.

The Revolution of 1688

The final crisis of James's reign resulted from two related events. The first was the refusal of seven bishops to instruct the clergy of their dioceses to read the Declaration of Indulgence in their churches. The king was so infuriated by this unexpected check to his plans that he had the bishops imprisoned, charged with seditious libel, and tried. Meanwhile, in June 1688 Queen Mary (Mary of Modena) gave birth to a male heir, raising the prospect that there would be a Catholic successor to James. When the bishops were triumphantly acquitted by a London jury, leaders of all political groups within the state were persuaded that the time had come to take action. Seven leading Protestants drafted a carefully worded invitation for William of Orange to come to England to investigate the circumstances of the birth of the king's heir. In effect, the leaders of the political nation had invited a foreign prince to invade their land.

This came as no surprise to William, who had been contemplating an invasion since the spring of 1688. William, who was organizing the Grand Alliance against Louis XIV, needed England as an ally rather than a rival. All Europe was readying for war in the summer of 1688, and James had powerful land and sea forces at his disposal to repel William's invasion. The crossing, begun on October 19, was a feat of military genius, however propitious the strong eastern "Protestant wind" that kept the English fleet at anchor while Dutch ships landed at Torbay (November 5). William took Exeter and issued a declaration calling for the election of a free Parliament. From the beginning, the Anglican interest flocked to him. James could only watch as parts of his army melted away.

Yet there was no plan to depose the king. Many Tories hoped that William's presence would force James to change his policies; many Whigs believed that a free Parliament could fetter his excesses. When James marched out of London, there was even the prospect of battle.

But the result was completely unforeseen. James lost his nerve, sent his family to France, and followed after them, tossing the Great Seal into the Thames. James's flight was a godsend, and, when he was captured en route, William allowed him to escape again. At the end of December, William arrived in London, summoned the leading peers and bishops to help him keep order, and called Parliament into being.

The Convention Parliament (1689) met amid the confusion created by James's flight. For some Tories, James II was still the king. Some were willing to contemplate a regency and others to allow Mary to rule with William as consort. But neither William nor the Whigs would accept such a solution. William was to be king in his own right, and in February the Convention agreed that James had "abdicated the government and that the throne has thereby become vacant." At the same time, the leaders of the Convention prepared the Declaration of Rights to be presented to William and Mary. The declaration was a restatement of traditional rights, but the conflicts between Whigs and Tories caused it to be watered down considerably. Nevertheless, the Whigs did manage to declare the suspending power and the maintenance of a standing army in peacetime illegal. But many of the other clauses protecting free speech, free elections, and frequent Parliaments were cast in anodyne formulas, and the offer of the throne was not conditional upon the acceptance of the Declaration of Rights.

William III (1689–1702) and Mary II (1689–94)

The revolution settlement
The Glorious Revolution (the Revolution of 1688) was a constitutional crisis, which was resolved in England, if not in Scotland and Ireland, through legislation. The Bill of Rights (1689), a more conservative document than even the declaration, was passed into law, and it established the principle that only a Protestant could wear the crown of England. A new coronation oath required the monarch to uphold

Protestantism and the statutes, laws, and customs of the realm as well. A Triennial Act (1694) reestablished the principle of regular parliamentary sessions.

Two other pieces of legislation tackled problems that had vexed the country since 1640. The Mutiny Act (1689) restrained the monarch's control over military forces in England by restricting the use of martial law. It was passed for one year only; however, when it lapsed between 1698 and 1701, the crown's military power was not appreciably affected. The Toleration Act (1689) was the most disappointing part of the whole settlement. It was originally intended to be part of a new comprehensive religious settlement in which most mainline Dissenters would be admitted into the church. This failed for the same reasons that comprehension had been failing for 30 years; the Anglican clergy would not give up its monopoly, and Dissenters would not compromise their principles. The Toleration Act permitted most forms of Protestant worship; Unitarians were explicitly excluded, as were Catholics and Jews. But the Test Acts that prevented Dissenters from holding government office or sitting in Parliament were continued in force.

A new society

In the decades before, and especially following, the Glorious Revolution, profound realignments can be seen in English society. Hitherto, the great divide was between landed wealth and urban wealth derived from trade and the law. A new fault line became ever clearer within landed society, and new ties emerged between the super-rich of the city and countryside. The old social values that had tied the peerage, or nobilitas maior (greater nobility), and gentry, or nobilitas minor (lesser nobility), withered. A new social term emerged, the aristocracy. Previously it had been used to describe not a social group but a system of government; now it referred to an elite whose wealth was vicarious, encompassing not only vast estates but also great profits from urban redevelopment such as the Russells' redevelopment of Covent Garden and later of Bloomsbury (from the time of Francis Russell, 4th earl of Bedford) and the Grosvenors' development of Mayfair, Belgravia, and Pimlico (from the time of Sir Thomas Grosvenor in the early 18th century).

Profits also came to them from investment in overseas trading companies and from government stock. They built elegant town houses to go with their huge country houses, often pulling down or shifting whole villages (as Sir Robert Walpole did at Houghton Hall and Philip Yorke, earl of Hardwicke, did at Wimpole) so as to produce spacious parks and noble vistas for themselves. They patronized the secular arts in one sense and the "squires" (another new term for the "mere" gentry) in another sense. The squires faced financial decline as their rent rolls sagged and new, expensive forms of capital-intensive rather than labour-intensive agriculture passed them by. Two new political epithets were introduced: Whig aristocrat and Tory squire. They represented two social realities and two political visions: the Whig vision of a cosmopolitan, religiously and culturally liberal society and the Tory vision of a world gone bad that had abandoned the paternalism of manor house and parish church and of the confessional state and the organic society (the body politic) in favour of a materialistic possessive individualism.

Post-revolution society was based much less on the rule of social leaders voluntarily leading in public service and on private philanthropy than on a rule of law made by the elite for the elite and upon the professionalism of government. These changes to the social order made many Tories temperamentally Jacobite, not in the sense that they believed in the cause of James Edward, the Old Pretender, or Charles Edward, the Young Pretender, but in the sense that they were in perpetual mourning for the world they had lost.

The sinews of war

William III had come to England to further his continental designs, but English politics conspired against him. The first years of his reign were dominated by the constitutional issues of the revolution settlement, and he became increasingly frustrated with the political squabbling of Whigs and Tories. Moreover, holding the English throne was proving more difficult than taking it. In 1690, with French backing, James II invaded Ireland. William personally led an army to the Battle of the Boyne (1690), where James's forces were crushed. But the compromise settlement that his plenipotentiaries reached with the Catholic leaders as the price of their abandonment of resistance (the Treaty of Limerick) was rejected by the Irish Parliament, which executed the full rigours of the penal code upon Irish Catholics.

The Irish wars impressed upon William's English subjects that, as long as the French backed James, they were now part of the great European struggle. Parliament granted William vast subsidies for the War of the Grand Alliance (1688–97), more than £4.5 million in a two-year period alone, but also established a right to oversee the expenditure of public monies. This led to both economies and accountability, and it forged a new political alliance among "country" (that is, anti-court) forces that were uneasy about foreign entanglements and suspicious of corruption at court. William's war was going badly on land and sea. The French fleet inflicted heavy losses on a combined Anglo-Dutch force and heavier losses on English merchant shipping. The land war was a desultory series of sieges and reliefs, which again tipped in favour of France.

For some time it looked as if Scotland might go its own way. Whereas in England the centre held and compromises were reached, in Scotland James's supporters first held their ground and then crumbled, and a vindictive Parliament not only decreed a proscription of his supporters but set out to place much greater limits on the crown. James was formally deposed. Moreover, measures were taken to ensure that Westminster could not dictate what was done in

Edinburgh. And there was to be religious toleration in Scotland. Episcopacy was abolished, and all those who had taken part in the persecution of covenanting conventicles in previous years were expelled from a vengeful kirk (church). There was spasmodic resistance from Jacobites, and it took several years and some atrocities most notoriously, the slaughter of the MacDonalds, instigated by their ancient enemies the Campbells, in the Massacre of Glencoe in 1692 for William to secure complete control.

Year by year the financial costs mounted. Between 1688 and 1702 England accumulated more than £14 million of debt, which was financed through the creation of the Bank of England (1694). The bank was a joint-stock company empowered to discount bills and issue notes. It lent to the government at a fixed rate of interest initially 8 percent and this interest was secured by a specific customs grant. Investors scrambled for the bank's notes, which were considered gilt-edged securities, and more than £1.2 million was raised on the initial offering. Not surprisingly, a growing funded debt created inflation and led to a financial crisis in 1696. But the underlying English economy was sound, and military expenditures fueled production.

The establishment of a funded national debt and the Bank of England was the work of the Whigs in alliance with the London mercantile establishment. The Tories and the country party were alternately suspicious and jealous of Whig success. In order to secure funds for his campaigns, William had been forced to allow the Whigs to dominate government, much against his inclination. An attempted assassination of the king in 1696 gave the Whigs an opportunity to impose an oath on the political nation that William was the "rightful and lawful king." This directly challenged Tory consciences, which had been tender since the death of Queen Mary in 1694. Many resigned office rather than affirm what they did not believe. The ascendancy of the so-called Junto Whigs might have been secured had not European events once again intruded into English affairs. In 1697 the War of the Grand

Alliance ended with the Treaty of Rijswijk, in which Louis XIV formally recognized William III as king of England.

A great revulsion and war weariness now took hold of the country. Parliament voted to disband most of the military establishment, including William's own Dutch guards, and a vigorous public debate against the existence of a standing army ensued. Taxes were slashed, accounts were audited, and irregularities were exposed. The Junto Whigs, who were associated with war and war profiteers, fell. A new coalition of country and Tory MPs, led by Robert Harley, earl of Oxford, launched a vigorous campaign of retrenchment. It had not progressed very far by 1700, when the deaths of the duke of Gloucester and Charles II of Spain redefined English and European priorities.

The duke of Gloucester was the only surviving child of Queen Mary's sister, Princess Anne, despite her 18 pregnancies. Because William and Mary were childless, the duke was the long-term Protestant heir to the throne. His death created a complicated problem that was resolved in the Act of Settlement (1701), which bypassed 48 legitimate but Catholic heirs and devolved the throne upon a granddaughter of James I, that is, on Sophia of Hanover and her son George (later George I). In clauses that read like a criticism of the policies of William III, the act stipulated that the sovereign must be and could only be married to a member of the Anglican church and that his foreign policy was to be directed by Parliament and his domestic policy by the Privy Council. It also limited the right of the king to dismiss judges at pleasure. Although many of the more restrictive clauses of the act were repealed in 1706, the Act of Settlement asserted a greater degree of parliamentary control over the monarchy than had been obtained since 1649.

The consequences of the death of Charles II of Spain were no less momentous. Years of futile negotiations to divide the vast Spanish empire among several claimants came to an end when Louis XIV placed his grandson on the Spanish throne and began making preparations to unite the kingdoms into a grand Bourbon alliance. Louis's aggressive stance overcame even the torpor of British public opinion, especially when he renounced William's legitimacy and welcomed James Edward, the Old Pretender, to his court as rightful king of England. William constructed another anti-French coalition and bequeathed to Queen Anne the War of the Spanish Succession (1701–14).

Anne (1702–14)

Queen Anne, daughter of James II and the last of the Stuarts, inherited a country that was bitterly divided politically. Her weak eyesight and indifferent health forced her to rely more upon her ministers than had any of her Stuart predecessors, but she was no less effective for that. Anne had decided views about people and policies, and these did much to shape her reign. She detested the party divisions that now dominated central politics and did all she could to avoid being controlled by either Whigs or Tories. While she only briefly achieved her ideal of a nonpartisan ministry, Anne did much to disappoint the ambitions of nearly all party leaders.

Whigs and Tories

The most significant development in political life over the previous quarter century had been the growth of clearly defined and opposing parties, which had taken the opprobrious titles Whigs and Tories. Parties had first formed during the exclusion crisis of 1679–81, but it was the Triennial Act (1694) that unintentionally gave life to party conflict. Nine general elections were held between 1695 and 1713, and these provided the structure whereby party issues and party leaders were pushed to the fore. Though party discipline was still in its infancy and ideology was a novel aspect of politics, clearly recognizable political parties had emerged by the end of the reign of William III. In general, the Tories stood for the Anglican church, the land, and the principle of passive obedience. They remained divided over the impending Hanoverian succession (see house of Hanover), wistfully dreaming that James Edward might convert to Protestantism so that the sanctity of the legitimate succession could be reaffirmed. From their country houses, the Tories opposed an expensive land war and favoured the "blue sea" strategy of dominating the Atlantic and Mediterranean shipping lanes. Their leaders had a self-destructive streak. Only Robert Harley, earl of Oxford, was a politician of the first rank, and he always shrank from being labeled a Tory. The Tories generally had a majority in the Commons and a friend on the throne, but they rarely attained power.

The Whigs stood for Parliament's right to determine the succession to the throne, for all necessary measures to blunt the international pretensions of Catholic-absolutist France, and for a latitudinarian approach to religion and a broad, generous interpretation of the Toleration Act. They were blessed with brilliant leadership and an inexhaustible supply of good luck. John Churchill, duke of Marlborough, was the outstanding military figure of his day. His victories at the Battle of Blenheim (1704) and the Battle of Ramillies (1706) rank among the greatest in British history. During the first part of the reign, his wife, Sarah, duchess of Marlborough, was the queen's confidante, and together the Marlboroughs were able to push Anne to support an aggressive and expensive foreign policy.

Continental warfare was costing £4 million a year, paid for by a tax on land, and, after the early years, successes were few and far between. Sidney Godolphin kept the duke supplied and financed and ably managed the Whig interest by disciplining government officeholders to vote for Whig policies in Parliament. Among these policies was support for Dissenters who, to avoid the rigours of the Test Acts, would take Anglican communion. Both the queen and the Tories were opposed to these occasional conformists, and three bills to outlaw the practice were passed through the Commons but defeated in the Lords. When the Tories attempted to attach one of these to the military appropriations bill, even the queen condemned the maneuver.

For the first half of Anne's reign, Whig policies were dominant. The duke of Marlborough's victories set off a wave of nationalistic pride and forced even Tories to concede the wisdom of a land war. Unfortunately, military success built overconfidence, prompting the Whigs to adopt the fruitless policy of "no peace without Spain," which committed them to an increasingly unattainable conquest of Iberia. Yet the capture of both Gibraltar (1704) and Minorca (1708) made England the dominant sea power in the western Mediterranean and paid handsome commercial dividends. So too did the unexpected union with Scotland in 1707 (see Act of Union). Here again, Godolphin was the dominant figure, calling the Scottish Parliament's bluff when it announced it would not accept the Hanoverian succession. Godolphin passed the Aliens Act (1705), which would have prohibited all trade between England and Scotland no mere scare tactic in light of the commercial policy that was crippling the Irish economy. Rather than risk economic strangulation, Scottish leaders negotiated for a permanent union, a compact the English monarchy had sought for more than a century. The union was a well-balanced bargain: free trade was established; Scottish Presbyterianism and the Scottish legal system were protected; and provisions were made to include 45 Scottish members in the English House of Commons and 18 members in the House of Lords. England gained security on its northern border, and the Whigs gained the promise of a peaceful Hanoverian succession.

Tories and Jacobites

Whig successes were not welcomed by the queen, who had a personal aversion to most of their leaders, especially after her estrangement from Sarah Churchill. As in the reign of William, war weariness and tax resistance combined to bring down the Whigs. The earl of Oxford and Henry St. John, Viscount Bolingbroke, vied for leadership of a reinvigorated Tory party that rallied support with the cry "church in danger." In 1710 a Whig prosecution of a bigoted Anglican minister, Henry Sacheverell, badly backfired. Orchestrated mob violence was directed against dissenting churches, and Sacheverell was impeached by only a narrow margin and given a light punishment. When the Tories gained power, they were able to pass legislation directed against Dissenters, including the Occasional Conformity Act (1711), which forbade Dissenters to circumvent the test acts by occasionally taking Anglican communion, and the Schism Act, which prevented them from opening schools (they were barred from Anglican schools and colleges). The Tories also concluded the War of the Spanish Succession. By the Treaty of Utrecht (1713), England expanded its colonial empire in Canada and the Caribbean and maintained possession of Gibraltar and Minorca in the Mediterranean.

But the Tories had their own Achilles' heel. They were deeply divided over who should succeed Anne, which became public during the queen's serious illness in 1713. Though there were far more Hanoverian Tories than Jacobite Tories (supporters of James II and his son, James Edward, the Old Pretender), the prospect of the succession of a German Lutheran prince with continental possessions to defend did not warm the hearts of isolationist Anglican country gentlemen. Both Oxford and Bolingbroke were in correspondence with James Edward, but Oxford made it plain that he would only support a Protestant succession.

Bolingbroke's position was more complicated. A brilliant politician, he realized that the Tories would have little to hope for from the Hanoverians and that they could only survive by creating huge majorities in Parliament and an unshakable alliance with the church. Conflict between Tory leaders and divisions within the rank and file combined to defeat Bolingbroke's plans. After Anne died in August 1714, George I acceded to the British throne, and Bolingbroke, having tainted the Tory party with Jacobitism for the next half century, fled to France.

18th-century Britain, 1714–1815

The state of Britain in 1714

When Georg Ludwig, elector of Hanover, became king of Great Britain on August 1, 1714, the country was in some respects bitterly divided. Fundamentally, however, it was prosperous, cohesive, and already a leading European and imperial power. Abroad, Britain's involvement in the War of the Spanish Succession had been brought to a satisfactory conclusion by the Treaty of Utrecht (1713). It had acquired new colonies in Gibraltar, Minorca, Nova Scotia, Newfoundland, and Hudson's Bay, as well as trading concessions in the Spanish New World. By contrast, Britain's rivals, France, Spain, and the Dutch Republic, were left weakened or war-weary by the conflict. It took France a decade to recover, and Spain and Holland were unable to reverse their military and economic decline. As a result Britain was able to remain aloof from war on the Continent for a quarter of a century after the Hanoverian succession, and this protracted peace was to be crucial to the new dynasty's survival and success.

War had also strengthened the British state at home. The need to raise men and money had increased the size and scope of the executive as well as the power and prestige of the House of Commons. Taxation had accounted for 70 percent of Britain's wartime expenditure (£93,644,560 between 1702 and 1713), so the Commons' control over taxation became a powerful guarantee of its continuing importance.

Britain's ability to pay for war on this scale demonstrated the extent of its wealth. Agriculture was still the bedrock of the economy, but trade was increasing, and more men and women were employed in industry in Britain than in any other European nation. Wealth, however, was unequally distributed, with almost a third of the national income belonging to only 5 percent of the population. But British society was not polarized simply between the rich and the poor; according to writer Daniel Defoe there were seven different and more subtle categories:

1. The great, who live profusely.

2. The rich, who live plentifully.

3. The middle sort, who live well.

4. The working trades, who labour hard, but feel no want.

5. The country people, farmers etc., who fare indifferently.

6. The poor, who fare hard.

7. The miserable, that really pinch and suffer want.

From 1700 to the 1740s Britain's population remained stable at about seven million, and agricultural production increased. So, although men and women from Defoe's 6th and 7th categories could still die of hunger and hunger-related diseases, in most regions of Britain there was usually enough basic food to go around. This was crucial to social stability and to popular acquiescence in the new Hanoverian regime.

But early 18th-century Britain also had its weaknesses. Its Celtic fringe Wales, Ireland, and Scotland had been barely assimilated. The vast majority of Welsh men and women could neither speak nor understand the English language. Most Irish men and women spoke Gaelic and belonged to the Roman Catholic church, in contrast with the population of the British mainland, which was staunchly Protestant. Scotland, which had only been united to England and Wales in 1707, still retained its traditional educational, religious, legal, and cultural practices. These internal divisions were made more dangerous by the existence of rival claimants to the British throne. James II, who had been expelled in the Glorious Revolution of 1688, died 13 years later, but his son, James Francis Edward Stuart, the Old Pretender, pressed his family's claims from his exile in France. His Catholicism and Scottish ancestry ensured him wide support in Ireland and the Scottish Highlands; his cause also commanded sympathy among sections of the Welsh and English gentry and, arguably, among the masses.

Controversy over the succession sharpened partisan infighting between the Whig and Tory parties. About 50 Tory MPs (less than a seventh of the total number) may have been covert Jacobites in 1714. More generally, Tories differed from Whigs over religious issues and foreign policy. They were more anxious to preserve the privileges of the Anglican church and more hostile to military involvement in continental Europe than Whig politicians were inclined to be. These attitudes made the Tories vulnerable in 1714. The new king was a Lutheran by upbringing and wanted to establish wider religious toleration in his new kingdom. As a German he was deeply interested in European affairs. Consequently he regarded the Tory party as insular in its outlook as well as suspect in its allegiance.

Britain from 1715 to 1742

The supremacy of the Whigs

Even before he arrived in Britain, George I had decided to exclude the two leading Tory ministers, Robert Harley, earl of Oxford, and Henry St. John, Viscount Bolingbroke. In their place he appointed two Whig politicians, Charles, Viscount Townshend, and James, Viscount Stanhope, as secretaries of state. Townshend's brother-in-law, Robert Walpole, became paymaster general. Walpole, who came from a minor Norfolk gentry family, was an extremely able politician, shrewd, greedy, and undeviatingly Whig. He encouraged the new king's partisan bias, turning it unremittingly to his advantage. A general election was held in February 1715, and, due in part to royal influence, the Whigs won 341 seats to the Tories' 217. In December the Old Pretender landed in Scotland, provoking an armed rebellion that was quickly suppressed.

The proved involvement of a small number of Tory landowners led to Tories being purged not only from state office but also from the higher ranks of the army and navy, the diplomatic service, and the judicial system. To make their capture of the state even more secure, the Whigs passed the Septennial Act in 1716. It allowed general elections to occur at seven-year intervals instead of every three years, as mandated by the Triennial Act of 1694. The intention was to tame the electorate, which during Anne's reign had shown itself to be volatile and far more inclined to vote Tory than Whig.

Having defeated their Tory opponents, the Whig leaders began to quarrel among themselves. In 1717 Walpole and Townshend left office and went into open opposition. Stanhope stayed on, with Charles Spencer, earl of Sunderland, now serving as secretary of state. At the same time the heir apparent to the throne, George, prince of Wales, quarreled with his father and began to flirt with Opposition groups in Parliament. These events set the pattern for future political conflicts. From then on until the 1750s the Opposition in Parliament would be a hybrid group of Whig and Tory sympathizers. And from then on until the early 19th century Oppositions in Parliament would enjoy sporadic support from successive princes of Wales. In 1717 the rebel Whigs were a serious threat in large part because Walpole was such a skillful House-of-Commons politician. As peers, Sunderland and Stanhope were confined to the House of Lords and lacked spokesmen in the Commons who could match Walpole's ruthlessness and talent. He showed his power by mobilizing a majority of MPs against the Peerage Bill in 1719. Had this legislation passed, it would have limited the king's prerogative to create new peers, thereby cementing the Whig administration's majority in the House of Lords. To prevent further blows of this kind, the Whig elite ended its schism in April 1720. The royal family temporarily buried its differences at the same time.

The restoration of unity was just as well, as 1720 saw the bursting of what became known as the South Sea Bubble. The South Sea Company had been founded in 1711 as a trading and finance company. In 1719 its directors offered to take over a large portion of the national debt previously managed by the Bank of England. The Whig administration supported this takeover, and in return the company made gifts (in effect, bribes) of its new stock to influential Whig politicians, including Stanhope and Sunderland, and to the king's mistress, the Duchess of Kendal. In 1720 investing in the South Sea Company became a mania among those who could afford it and some who could not; South Sea stock was at 120 in January and rose to 1,000 by August. But in September the inevitable crash came.

Many landed and mercantile families were ruined, and there was a nationwide shortage of specie. Parliament demanded an inquiry, thus raising the possibility that members of the government and the royal family would be openly implicated in financial scandal. This disaster proved to be Walpole's opportunity, and he did not waste it. He used his influence in the Commons to blunt the parliamentary inquiry and managed gradually to restore financial confidence. The strain of the investigation killed Stanhope, and Sunderland too died in 1722. Walpole duly became first lord of the treasury and chancellor of exchequer, while Townshend returned to his post as secretary of state.

Walpole's position as the king's favourite minister was finally assured when he exposed the Atterbury plot. Francis Atterbury was bishop of Rochester. Always a Tory and High Churchman, he drifted after the Hanoverian succession into Jacobite intrigue. In 1721–22 he and a small group of conspirators plotted an armed invasion of Britain on behalf of the Old Pretender. The plot was uncovered by the secret service, which was more efficient in this period than it was until World War II. Atterbury was tried for treason by Parliament and sent into exile. This coup, one politician aptly wrote at the time, was the "most fortunate and greatest circumstance of Mr Walpole's life. It fixed him with the King, and united for a time the whole body of Whigs to him, and gave him the universal credit of an able and vigilant Minister."

Robert Walpole

Walpole has often been referred to as Britain's first prime minister, but historically this is incorrect. The title had in fact been applied to certain ministers in Anne's reign and was commonly used as a slur or simply as a synonym for first minister. During Walpole's period of dominance it was certainly used more frequently, but it did not become an official title until the early 20th century. Some historians have also claimed that Walpole was the architect of political stability in Britain, but this interpretation needs to be qualified. There is no doubt that from 1722 to his resignation in 1742 Walpole stabilized political power in himself and a section of the Whig party. Nor can there be any doubt that his foreign and economic policies helped the Hanoverian dynasty to become securely entrenched in Britain. But it should not be forgotten that Walpole inherited a nation that was already wealthy and at peace. He built on foundations that were already very strong. And, although he was to dominate political life for 20 years, he never succeeded in stamping out political, religious, and cultural opposition entirely, nor did he expect to do so.

Opposition to Walpole in Parliament began to develop as early as 1725. When William Pulteney, an ambitious and talented politician, was dismissed from state office, he and 17 other Whig MPs aligned themselves with the 150 Tory MPs remaining in the House of Commons. These dissidents (who called themselves Patriot Whigs) grew in number until, by the mid-1730s, more than 100 Whig MPs were collaborating with the Tories against Walpole's nominally Whig administration. Some were motivated primarily by disappointed ambition. But many Whigs and Tories genuinely believed that Walpole had arrogated too much power to himself and that he was corrupt and an enemy to liberty.

These accusations were expressed not just among politicians in London but also in the growing number of newspapers and periodicals in Britain at large. In 1726 Pulteney and the one-time Tory minister Lord Bolingbroke founded their own journal, The Craftsman (the implication of the title being that Walpole governed by craft alone). It was widely read among the political classes, not least because many of the most gifted writers working in London had been drawn into the Opposition camp. Jonathan Swift, Alexander Pope, and, for a time, Henry Fielding all wrote against Walpole. So did John Gay, whose triumphantly successful The Beggar's Opera (1728) was a satire on ministerial corruption.

But, despite its flamboyance and innovative tactics, the Opposition for a long time lacked high-level support. Frequent disagreements occurred between its Patriot Whig and Tory sectors. These weaknesses helped Walpole to keep the Opposition at bay until 1742. But there were other reasons for his prolonged stay in power: he retained the support of the crown, resisted military involvement in Europe, pursued a moderate religious policy, and adopted a skillful economic policy. Moreover, in the general elections of 1727 and 1734 he was able to manipulate the electoral system to maintain himself in power.

George II and Walpole

George I died in June 1727 and was buried in Hanover. He was succeeded by his eldest son, who became George II. Initially the new king planned to dismiss Walpole and appoint his personal favourite,

Spencer Compton, in his place. Closer familiarity with Walpole's gifts, however, dissuaded him from taking this step, as did his formidable wife, Queen Caroline, who remained an important ally of the minister until her death in 1737. Walpole cemented his advantage by securing the king a Civil List (money allowance) from Parliament of £800,000, a considerably larger sum than previous monarchs had been able to enjoy. Royal favour, in turn, shored up Walpole's parliamentary majority. Because the monarch appointed and promoted peers, he had massive influence in the House of Lords. In addition, he appointed the 26 bishops of the Church of England, who also possessed seats in the House of Lords. He alone could promote men to high office in the army, navy, diplomatic service, and bureaucracy. Consequently, MPs who held such offices (the so-called placemen), and those who wanted to hold them in the future, were likely to support Walpole as the king's minister out of self-interest, if for no other reason. Walpole, however, could never take royal support for granted. George II was an irritable but by no means an insignificant figure who retained great influence in terms of patronage, military affairs, and foreign policy. He demanded respect from his minister and had to be carefully managed.

Foreign policy

Once the Hanoverian succession had taken place, Whig ministers became as eager to remain at peace with France as the Tories had been. Walpole certainly adhered to this view, and for good reasons. Although Britain now possessed the world's most powerful navy, it could not match France in land forces. War with France, moreover, was likely to lead to an invasion of Hanover, which was naturally unwelcome to George I and his successor. It would also give the Old Pretender the prospect of French military aid to launch an invasion against Britain itself. In 1717 Stanhope negotiated a Triple Alliance with the French and the Dutch. This treaty was maintained by Walpole and Townshend throughout the 1720s. By 1730, however, it was attracting considerable criticism from the Opposition, and in the Second Treaty of Vienna, signed in March 1731, Walpole jettisoned the Anglo-French alliance in favour of an alliance with Austria. But whether forming an alliance with the French or the Austrians, Walpole always considered it his primary aim to keep Britain out of war in continental Europe.

In 1733 Austria, Saxony, and Russia went to war against France, Spain, and Sardinia in the War of the Polish Succession (1733–38). The Austrians asked for British aid under the terms of the Treaty of Vienna, but Walpole refused to give it. By keeping out of European entanglements for so long, Walpole appeased some of the traditionally insular Tory MPs. He also kept direct taxation low, which pleased many landed families. The land tax was cut to two shillings in the pound (10 percent) in 1730 and to one shilling in the pound two years later.

Religious policy

Walpole's religious policy was also designed to foster social and political quiescence. Traditionally the Whig party had supported wider concessions to the Protestant dissenters (Protestants who believed in the doctrine of the Trinity but who refused to join in the worship of the state church, the Church of England). They had been given freedom of worship under the Toleration Act of 1689 but were barred from full civil rights and access to university education in England. In 1719 the Whigs had repealed two pieces of Tory legislation aimed against dissent, the Schism and the Occasional Conformity acts. These concessions ensured that Protestant dissenters would be able to establish their own educational academies and hold public office in the localities, if not in the state.

There was always a danger, however, that too many concessions to Protestant dissent would alienate the Church of England, which enjoyed wide support in England and Wales. There were 5,000 parishes in these two countries, each containing at least one church served by a vicar (minister) or a curate (his deputy). For much of the 18th century these Anglican churches provided the only large, covered meeting places available outside of towns. They served as sources of spiritual comfort and also as centres for village social life. At religious services vicars would not only preach the word of God but also explain to congregations important national developments: wars, victories, and royal deaths and births.

Thus churches often supplied the poor, the illiterate, and particularly women with the only political information available to them. Weakening the Church of England therefore struck Walpole as unwise, for at least two reasons. Its ministers provided a vital service to the state by communicating political instruction to the people. The church, moreover, commanded massive popular loyalty, and assaults on its position would arouse nationwide discontent. Walpole therefore determined to reach an accommodation with the church, and in 1723 he came to an agreement with Edmund Gibson, Bishop of London. Gibson was to ensure that only clergymen sympathetic to the Whig administration were appointed to influential positions in the Church of England. In return, Walpole undertook that no further extensive concessions would be made to Protestant dissenters. This arrangement continued until 1736.

Economic policies

Finally, Walpole's long tenure of power was assisted by national prosperity. The gross national product rose from £57.5 million in 1720 to £64.1 million in 1740, an increase of 11.5 percent. Walpole encouraged trade by abolishing some customs duties, but his main economic concerns were to reduce interest payments on the national debt and to foster agriculture by switching taxation from land to consumption. He succeeded in reducing interest payments on the debt by 26 percent during his time in office, but his efforts to reduce the land tax in favour of more excises almost led to political disaster. In 1732 he revived a duty on salt, which enabled him to cut the land tax to one shilling in the pound.

In 1733 he proposed to levy excise taxes on the sale of wine and tobacco, but the Opposition in Parliament launched a ferocious and successful campaign against these proposals. It claimed that excises weighed unfairly on the poor, whereas the land tax was mainly paid by the prosperous. It claimed, too, that excise collectors, and there were more than 6,000 of them employed by the state by this time, intruded into citizens' private affairs and were a danger to British liberties. This crisis led to nationwide riots and demonstrations, and Walpole's House-of-Commons majority seemed in jeopardy. In April 1733 he decided to retreat. He continued, however, until 1740 to keep the land tax at a low rate, thereby winning important support from the nation's dominant landed class.

The electoral system

The fiasco over the excise might have toppled Walpole, since a general election was scheduled for 1734. In fact, however, his administration retained a comfortable majority in the House of Commons. One reason for this was that Britain's electoral system at this time did not adequately reflect the state of public opinion. Until the Reform Act of 1832 England returned 489 MPs. Eighty of these were elected by the 40 county constituencies; 196 smaller constituencies called boroughs returned two MPs each, and two other boroughs, including London, the capital city, returned four MPs each. Oxford and Cambridge universities were also allowed four representatives in Parliament. Wales returned only 24 members of Parliament and Scotland 45. Their limited representation indicated the extent to which these countries were subordinated to England in the British political system at this time.

The system was not even remotely democratic. Power in this society was intimately and inextricably connected with the possession of property, particularly landed property. To be eligible for election as an MP, a man had to possess land worth £600 per annum if he was representing a county constituency and worth £300 per annum in the case of a borough constituency. To vote, adult males had to possess some kind of residential property or, in certain borough constituencies, be registered as freemen. Women were not given the vote until 1918.

In all, some 350,000 Britons may have been able to vote in the 1720s, which was roughly one in four of the adult male population. There was no secret ballot, and voting took place in public. Consequently, many voters were liable to be influenced or coerced by their landlords or employers or bribed by the candidates themselves. Bribery was particularly widespread and effective in the smaller boroughs where there were often fewer than 100 voters and sometimes fewer than 50. These constituencies were called rotten or pocket boroughs. In the borough of Malmesbury, for example, in the English county of Wiltshire, there were only 13 voters, few of whom voted strictly in accordance with their own conscience or opinions: "It was no odds to them who they voted for," one inhabitant declared, "it was as master pleased."

Large electorates could be found, however, in some areas. The northern English county constituency of Yorkshire had 15,000 voters in 1741. In Bristol, a major port on the western coast of England, 5,000 men had the vote approximately one-third of the city's adult male population. In these larger constituencies public opinion could make itself felt at election time. The problem for the Opposition in 1734 was that there were few such populous, open constituencies but very many rotten borough seats such as Malmesbury. Since government candidates usually had more to bribe voters with in the way of money and favours, Walpole was able to win the majority of these boroughs and therefore retain his majority in the House of Commons despite his unpopularity after the excise crisis.

Walpole's loss of power

Walpole's luck and political grasp only began to fail in 1737. In that year Queen Caroline, one of his most important allies, died. At this time, too, Frederick Louis, prince of Wales, George II's eldest son and heir apparent, followed Hanoverian family tradition; he quarrelled with his father and aligned himself with the Opposition. This damaged Walpole's position in two ways. The king, born in 1683, was now in his 50s, which was elderly by the standards of the time. Many young ambitious MPs, such as William Pitt, were inclined to join Prince Frederick, because they saw in him the political future. Moreover, as Prince of Wales, Frederick owned a large part of the county of Cornwall and consequently controlled numerous rotten boroughs. In the 1734 election the Cornish constituencies had returned 32 pro-government MPs to Parliament; but at the next general election in 1741, when Prince Frederick used his electoral influence against Walpole, only 17 pro-government candidates were returned by this county. Walpole lost another important ally to the opposition, John, duke of Argyll. Argyll was a member of the Cabinet, the most important Whig landowner in Scotland, and head of Clan Campbell. In the 1734 election his influence in Scotland helped to ensure that 34 of the country's 45 elected MPs were pro-government. But by the 1741 election he had defected to the Opposition, and the electoral repercussions were serious. On this occasion Scottish constituency only elected 17 pro-government MPs.

But Walpole's main enemies were time and war. By 1737 he was in his 60s and had dominated politics for 15 years. Some ambitious Whigs resented his prolonged monopoly on power; others anticipated his retirement or death and judged it prudent to distance themselves from his administration. And some of Walpole's policies were now widely viewed as dubious, even anachronistic. Whereas he wanted to keep Britain out of war, many government and Opposition MPs, and even some members of Walpole's own Cabinet, favoured going to war with Spain to gain colonial and commercial objectives. Such a war policy was strongly backed by commercial opinion in London and in the nation's main trading cities.

It was a sign of Walpole's declining powers that he was unable to prevent the drift into war in 1739. The War of Jenkins' Ear (so called after an alleged Spanish atrocity against a British merchant navy officer, Captain Robert Jenkins) was initially successful. Admiral Edward Vernon became a popular and Opposition hero when he captured the Spanish settlement of Portobelo (in what is now Panama) in November 1739. But his victory was followed by several defeats, and Britain soon became embroiled in a wider European conflict, the War of the Austrian Succession. Walpole survived the general election of 1741, but with a greatly reduced majority. His political doom was sealed in the fall of that year when the Tory and Whig sectors of the Opposition managed finally to agree on a strategy to defeat him.

Walpole eventually resigned from his offices in early 1742. He still retained the king's favour, and, although sections of the Opposition wanted to impeach him for corruption, he was given a peerage, entered the House of Lords as earl of Orford, and died in his bed in 1745. Nonetheless, the fact that he had to resign despite George II's continuing support indicated an important development in the British political system. Although monarchs retained the rights to choose their own ministers, they could no longer retain a chief minister who was unable to command a majority of votes in the House of Commons. If they wanted to remain in office, chief ministers now needed to possess parliamentary as well as royal support.

Britain from 1742 to 1754

Political events after Walpole's resignation demonstrated once again the artificiality and inner tensions of the Opposition. Its Tory sector (some 140 MPs strong) had expected that a new administration would be formed in which some of their leaders would be given state office. They hoped that the proscription of their party, implemented after 1714, would be reversed and that various changes in domestic and foreign policy would be made. But now that Walpole was out of the picture many of their Patriot Whig allies wanted nothing more to do with Tories or Tory measures. The leading Patriot Whig, William Pulteney, accepted a peerage and became earl of Bath. Six other Patriot Whigs accepted government office, including John, Baron Carteret (later earl of Granville), who became the new secretary of state.

Spencer Compton, now earl of Wilmington, became the new first lord of the treasury and nominal head of the government. Fourteen former members of Walpole's administration retained their posts, including Henry Pelham and his older brother, Thomas Pelham-Holles, duke of Newcastle. The Tories, as well as many people outside Parliament, had expected the fall of Walpole to result in a revolution in government and society, but this did not occur. Instead, all that had happened was a reshuffling of state employment among patrician Whigs, which caused widespread disillusionment and anger. It was with the Patriot Whigs in mind that Samuel Johnson, a staunch Tory, was later to describe patriotism in his Dictionary as the last resort of the scoundrel.

When Wilmington died in 1743, Carteret took over as head of the administration. He was a clever and subtle man, able to speak many European languages, and fascinated by foreign affairs. These qualities naturally endeared him to the king. His status as a royal favourite was confirmed when he accompanied George on a military expedition to Germany in defense of the electorate of Hanover. In June George commanded his British and Hanoverian troops at the Battle of Dettingen (the last battle in which a British monarch commanded), defeating the opposing French forces. But the victory was not followed up and aroused little patriotic enthusiasm in Britain. Instead, accusations that the king and Carteret were sacrificing British interests to Hanoverian priorities were openly expressed in Parliament and in the press. The Pelham brothers took advantage of this discontent (and Carteret's absence) to undermine his political position. In November 1744 he was forced to resign, though during the next 18 months George II continued to consult with him privately on political business. These intrigues infuriated Henry Pelham, who was now first lord of the treasury and chancellor of the exchequer, and his brother Newcastle, who was secretary of state.

The Jacobite rebellion

Britain's involvement in the War of the Austrian Succession, Tory and popular anger at the political deals that followed Walpole's resignation, and the infighting among the Whig elite were the background to the Jacobite rebellion of 1745–46 (the Forty-five). Since Britain was now at odds with France, the latter power was willing to sponsor an invasion on behalf of the Stuart dynasty. It hoped that such an invasion would win support from the masses and from the Tory sector of the landed class. Although a handful of Tory conspirators encouraged these hopes, the degree of their commitment is open to question. A large-scale French naval invasion of Britain in early 1744 failed in part because these men would not commit themselves to action. In July 1745 the Old Pretender's eldest son, Charles Edward Stuart (the Young Pretender), landed in Scotland without substantial French aid. In September he and some 2,500 Scottish supporters defeated a British force of the same size at the Battle of Prestonpans. In December, with an army of 5,000 men, he marched into England and got as far south as the town of Derby, some 150 miles from London.

Charles's initial success owed much to the ineptitude, the unconcern even, of Britain's rulers. One problem was that the standing army was too small, consisting of some 62,000 men. Because of Britain's involvement in the War of the Austrian Succession, the bulk of this force was in Flanders and Germany. Only 4,000 men had been left to defend Scotland, and most of them were raw recruits. Moreover, hampered by internal divisions, the administration was slow to respond. When the Young Pretender landed, the Pelhams were anxious but Carteret, now earl of Granville, was not. Nor, at the beginning, was George II, who was actually in Hanover when his rival for the throne landed. As a result of these squabbles and misunderstandings, Parliament did not assemble until October 17, 1745. Because by law only Parliament could authorize money to pay the militia (Britain's civil defense force), this delay seriously impeded early resistance to the Jacobite force. The city of Carlisle in the north of England surrendered to the rebels in November largely because its militia had received no pay from the government or from anyone else for two months.

Some historians have argued that the mass of Britain's population cared little which dynasty ruled them at this time and that the Young Pretender would have regained the kingdom for the Stuarts if only he had pressed on to London. Clearly, this thesis can never be proved one way or the other. The Jacobites, however, did not try to march on to London but retreated to Scotland. Nonetheless, it is probably significant that the Young Pretender attracted scarcely any English supporters on his march to Derby. Only in Manchester, which had a large Catholic population, did he gain recruits some 200 men, mostly unemployed weavers. No Tory landowner or politician joined him, nor did any men of influence or wealth come out in his favour. By contrast, once the seriousness of the invasion was recognized, many individuals joined home-defense units or subscribed money against it. Between September and December 57 civilian loyal associations are known to have been founded in 38 different counties. Merchants and traders in the prosperous towns Liverpool, Norwich, Exeter, Bristol, and most of all London were particularly prominent in loyalist activity.

Although many Britons had become disillusioned by events after Walpole's fall, probably few were seriously tempted by the prospect of a Jacobite restoration. The Young Pretender, a Roman Catholic, was viewed as the pawn of France, Britain's enemy and prime commercial and imperial competitor. Traditionally the Catholic religion and French politics were associated with absolutist government, religious persecution, and assaults on liberty. These prejudices worked against the Young Pretender's appeal, as did prejudices against the Scottish Highlanders, the bulk of his armed supporters, who were regarded as terrifying barbarians by many of the English. The lack of mass English support for the Stuarts in 1745 dissuaded the French government from sending substantial military aid to the rebels. On April 16, 1746, the duke of Cumberland (George II's second son) defeated the Jacobite army at Culloden in northern Scotland. This was the last major land battle to occur in Great Britain. The Young Pretender escaped to France and finally died in 1788, sodden with drink and disillusionment.

The main result of the Forty-five was the British government's decision to integrate Scotland, and particularly the Scottish Highlands, more fully into the rest of the kingdom. Despite the Act of Union of 1707, clan chieftains had retained considerable judicial and military powers over their followers. But these powers were destroyed by the Abolition of Heritable Jurisdictions (Scotland) Act of 1747. Other statutes required oaths of allegiance to the Hanoverian dynasty from the Episcopalian clergy, banned the wearing of kilts and tartans in an attempt to erode distinctive Highlands practices, and confiscated arms.

The administration also confiscated the estates of Highlands chieftains who had rebelled and used the proceeds to encourage trade and agriculture in Scotland. Indeed, the gradual pacification of Scotland and its partial integration into a united Britain probably owed more to growing prosperity than to legal changes. By the mid-1750s Scotland's population was estimated at 1,265,380, and it continued to grow at a rapid rate until the 1830s. Linen production doubled between 1750 and 1775, and coal mining, iron smelting, and agricultural productivity also began to expand. Economic and demographic growth was particularly dramatic in towns such as Glasgow, Edinburgh, Aberdeen, and Dundee. The Act of Union had made Britain the largest free-trade area in Europe, and, as more Scots came to profit from trading and manufacturing links with England, more had a vested interest in maintaining the status quo.

The rule of the Pelhams

Defeating the rebellion also strengthened the position of the Pelhams. In February 1746, George II attempted to replace them with Granville but failed. Thereafter Henry Pelham and Newcastle insisted upon and received the king's full confidence. The attempted invasion widened once again the gulf between the Whig and Tory parties. The Whigs became for a time more united, and the Tories did badly in the general election of 1747, winning only 110 seats. The only serious opposition Pelham faced after that date came from the heir to the throne, Frederick, prince of Wales. Although Frederick had abandoned the Opposition in 1742, his impatience to succeed to the throne soon prompted him to drift back into political intrigue against his father and his father's ministers.

He claimed to be motivated by some of Lord Bolingbroke's political ideas. In 1738, during Frederick's earlier phase of opposition, Bolingbroke had written The Idea of a Patriot King, arguing that a future ideal monarch could unify and purify the nation by seizing the initiative to abolish faction and ruling over an administration based on virtue rather than on party. Frederick's avowed commitment to a nonparty government attracted Tory as well as a few Whig MPs to his support in the late 1740s. But their schemes and hopes were dashed when Frederick died in 1751. His eldest son, George (the future George III), became heir to the throne, and serious opposition to Pelham effectively ceased. Debate in Parliament became so muted, one politician wrote, that a bird might have built its nest in the Speaker's wig and never be disturbed.

Both Pelham and Newcastle were overshadowed by their more famous predecessor Robert Walpole and by their charismatic successor, William Pitt the Elder. Like Walpole, both brothers regarded themselves as staunchly Whig though their ideology was by no means clear-cut. Like Walpole, they had little enthusiasm for British involvement in European wars. They helped to negotiate the Treaty of Aix-la-Chapelle (1748), which ended the War of the Austrian Succession. Like Walpole, too, the Pelhams sought to reduce the national debt and to keep taxation on land low. But unlike Walpole, they avoided corruption; both lost rather than made money during their political careers. And Henry Pelham was more interested in domestic reform than Walpole had been.

Domestic reforms

The Gin Act of 1751 was designed to reduce consumption of raw spirits, regarded by contemporaries as one of the main causes of crime in London. In 1752 Britain's calendar was brought into conformity with that used in continental Europe. Throughout the continent, the calendar reformed in the 16th century by Pope Gregory XIII had gained widespread use by the mid-18th century and was 11 days ahead of the Julian calendar, which had been used in Britain. It was once believed that protests against this change "give us back our 11 days," crowds are supposed to have chanted represented nothing more than parochial ignorance. In fact the adoption of the new calendar, though it ultimately benefited commerce and international relations, initially played havoc with monthly rental payments and wages in the short term. In 1753 the Marriage Act was passed to prevent secret marriages by unqualified clergymen. From then on, every bride and groom had to sign a marriage register or, if they were illiterate, make their mark upon it. This innovation has been of enormous value to historians, enabling them to establish how many Britons were able to write at this time and, by inference, how many could read.

British society by the mid-18th century

Joseph Massie's categories

From the Hanoverian succession to the mid-18th century the texture and quality of life in Britain changed considerably but by no means evenly. Change was far more pronounced in the towns than in the countryside and among the prosperous than among the poor. The latter category was still very large; in the late 1750s an economist named Joseph Massie estimated that the bottom 40 percent of the population had to survive on less than 14 percent of the nation's income. The rest of his calculations can be summarized as follows:

Massie's calculations were not exact since no official census was implemented in Britain until 1800. But his figures were probably broadly correct and are the best available for this period. It is noticeable that his top three categories had close connections with the land, still the bedrock of wealth, status, and power. The greatest landowners (Massie's 310 families) owned estates ranging from 10,000 to 20,000 acres. Many of them belonged to the peerage, that is, they were dukes, marquesses, earls, viscounts, or barons. Such hereditary titles, which could only be granted by the crown, carried with them the right to sit in the House of Lords. In the reigns of George I and George II there were some 170 of these peers. Almost all of them possessed fine houses in London as well as one or more mansions in the counties where their land lay. The dukes of Marlborough (Winston Churchill's ancestors), for example, dominated large parts of Oxfordshire from their stately home of Blenheim (built 1705–30). The earls of Carlisle in Cumberland built Castle Howard in the same period, spending £35,000 on the house and a further £24,000 on the gardens. Together with the greater gentry and the squires, listed in Massie's second and third categories, great landowners such as these owned considerably more than half of the cultivatable land in Britain.

Not all wealthy men were landowners. The foundation of the Bank of England in 1694 and other finance companies made it possible to make fortunes on the stock market, and the expansion of trade and industry forged powerful mercantile dynasties such as the Whitbreads (brewing), Smiths (banking), and Strutts (textiles). Some of these self-made families purchased landed estates to advertise their new wealth; others made do with smart town houses or country villas. But, although it was possible to be rich and influential in this society without owning broad acres, it was the landed elite that set the cultural tone and dominated positions of power in both central and local government. Every peer in the House of Lords and a majority of MPs in the House of Commons owned land.

Landowners also monopolized the office of lord lieutenant. Lords lieutenant were the crown's leading representatives in each of the English and Welsh counties. (Only in the 1790s was this office extended to Scotland.) Appointed by the king, they were responsible for maintaining law and order in their counties and for organizing civil defense measures during time of war. To assist them in these tasks, they appointed deputy lieutenants and justices of the peace offices usually held by the squires and lesser gentry in the countryside and by merchants and landed gentlemen in the towns. None of these offices carried salaries a clear indication that they were confined to the prosperous. But they brought with them considerable local influence and status and were often much sought after.

Less is known about Massie's 4th, 5th, and 6th social categories than about the landowning classes. And much less is known about small merchants, tradesmen, professionals, artisans, and labourers in Wales and Scotland than about their English equivalents. Most historians believe that the middle-income groups were increasing in number in the mid-18th century. Professional opportunities in law, medicine, schoolteaching, banking, and government service certainly expanded at this time. In the town of Preston in Lancashire, for example, there was only one attorney in 1702; by 1728 there were 17. Growing prosperity also increased job opportunities in the leisure and luxury industries. Urban directories show that there were more musicians and music teachers and more dancing masters, booksellers, caterers, and landscape gardeners than in the 17th century. And there were more shops. Shops had expanded even into rural areas by the 1680s, but in the 18th century they proliferated at a much faster rate. By 1770 the new town of Birmingham in Warwickshire had 129 shops dealing in buttons and 56 selling toys, as well as 35 jewelers. Not for nothing would Napoleon Bonaparte later describe Britain as a nation of shopkeepers.

Urban development

The centre of this commercial culture was the city of London. As the only real national metropolis, London was unique in its size and multiplicity of functions. By 1750 it contained more than 650,000 citizens just under one in 10 of Britain's population. By contrast, only one in 40 Frenchmen lived in Paris in this period. The Hague held only one in 50 of the inhabitants of the Netherlands, and Madrid was the home of just one in 80 Spaniards. Some of these great European capitals had no resident sovereign. Many others, such as Vienna and St. Petersburg, were grand ceremonial and cultural centres but effectively isolated from the economic life of their national hinterland. London was different.

It was not only the location of the Court and of Parliament but also the nation's chief port, its financial centre, the home of its printing industry, and the hub of its communications network. Britain's rulers were brought into constant proximity with powerful economic lobbies from all parts of the nation and with a large and constantly fluctuating portion of their subjects. Britons seem to have been more mobile than their fellow Europeans in this period, and then as now many traveled to the capital to find work and excitement. Perhaps as many as one in six Britons spent a portion of their working life in London in the 18th century.

London easily dwarfed the other British towns. In 1750 its nearest rival, Norwich, had fewer than 50,000 people. Nonetheless, the provincial towns, although functioning on quite a different scale from that of the metropolis, were also growing in size and importance at this time. In 1700 only 10 of them contained more than 10,000 people. By 1750 there were 17 towns with populations of that size, and by 1800 there were more than 50. As towns grew, they became better organized and safer, more pleasant places to live in. Because more stone was used in buildings, the risk of destruction by fire began to lessen. Towns acquired insurance companies and fire engines to protect their citizens.

Supplies of clean water improved. Urban planning and architecture became more sophisticated and splendid, and the results can still be seen today in towns like Stamford in Lincolnshire or Bath in Somerset. These provincial centres developed cultural lives of their own, with new theatres, assembly rooms, libraries, Freemason lodges, and coffeehouses. By mid-century there were at least nine coffeehouses in Bristol, six in both Liverpool and Chester, two in Northampton, and at least one in most substantial market towns. Such establishments supplied their customers with newspapers and a place to gossip as well as with liquid refreshments. They also often served as a base for clubs, debating societies, and spontaneous political activity. Schools grew in number, in both the towns and the surrounding countryside. In just one English county, Northamptonshire, the local newspaper press advertised the establishment of more than 100 new schools between 1720 and 1760.

Change and continuity

Historians have differed sharply over the impact these commercial and cultural innovations had on British society as a whole. Some have argued that only a minority of men and women were touched by them and that the countryside, which contained the majority of the population, continued on in its traditional ways and values. This is certainly true of parts of Britain. The Scottish Highlands, the mountainous central regions of Wales, and some English regions such as East Anglia remained predominately rural and agricultural. Old beliefs and superstitions lingered on there and elsewhere, often into the late 19th century. Although Parliament repealed the laws against witchcraft in the 1730s, for example, many men and women, and not just the illiterate, continued to believe in its power. (John Wesley, the founder of Methodism, was convinced that witches and the Devil had a real corporeal existence on earth.) It is true, too, that many of the new consumer goods that improved the quality of life for the prosperous porcelain china, armchairs, fine mirrors, newspapers, and manufactured toys were beyond the economic reach of the poor.

And, although new styles of interior decoration transformed the dwellings of the landed and mercantile classes the sale of wallpaper, for example, had risen from 197,000 yards in 1713 to more than two million yards in 1785, a 10-fold increase they rarely reached the impoverished. Some agricultural labourers and miners had only one set of clothes and lived in mud-lined cottages, caves, or cellars.

Beggars, vagrants, and the unemployed might not possess even these basic commodities.

Yet it would be wrong to postulate too stark a contrast in life-styles between the town and countryside, between the wealthy and the lower orders. Points of contact between the various layers of British society were in fact increasing at this time. More and more country landowners, their womenfolk, and their servants succumbed (without, one suspects, too much trouble) to the temptation of spending some months every year sampling the pleasures of their neighbourhood provincial town, consulting its lawyers and financial agents, and patronizing its shops. Many urban merchants, taking advantage of better roads and coach services, went to live in the countryside while maintaining their businesses in town.

Lower down the social scale, hawkers and peddlers (itinerant traders) carried town-produced goods into the country areas and sold them there. Conversely, the growing demand for food in urban areas sucked in men and goods from the countryside. English drovers braved the old Roman roads and faltering bridle paths, the only routes available in Welsh counties such as Caernarvon and Anglesey, in order to purchase meat cattle for London and other towns. Every year tens of thousands of black cattle from the Scottish Highlands were driven southward until they reached the Smithfield meat market in London. Demand for manufactured goods fostered the spread of inland trade, as did increasing industrial specialization in the different British regions. Daniel Defoe illustrated this point by describing the multiple provenance of an affluent man's suit of clothes:

A coat of woollen cloth from Yorkshire, a waistcoat of cullamancoe from Norwich, breeches of strong drugget from Devizes and Wiltshire, stockings of yarn from Westmoreland, a hat of felt from Leicestershire, gloves of leather from Somerset, shoes from Northampton, buttons from Macclesfield, or, if metal, from Birmingham, garters from

Manchester, and a shirt of handmade linen from Lancashire or Scotland.

In short, Britain was not a static society, and the towns and the countryside were not entirely separate spheres. Men and women moved about to seek pleasure, to do business, to sell goods, to marry, or to find work; and their ideas and impressions shifted over time.

The revolution in communications

Increased mobility was made possible by a revolution in communications. In the earlier 18th century long-distance travel was rare and the idea of long-distance travel for pleasure was a contradiction in terms. The speediest coach journey between London and Cambridge (just 60 miles) took at least a day. Traveling from the capital to the town of Shrewsbury by coach took more than three days, and the journey to Edinburgh could last as long as 10 days. Some travelers made their wills before starting, as coaches easily overturned on bad roads or in swollen rivers. By 1750, however, privately financed turnpike roads had spread from London and its environs to major English provincial centres like Bristol, Manchester, Newcastle, Leeds, and Birmingham. In the 1760s and '70s they spread further into Wales and Scotland. The postal service also improved in this period, though again much more slowly in the Celtic fringe than in England. In 1765 only 30 Scottish towns enjoyed a daily postal service.

But the most dramatic advance in inland communication came in the form of the printed word. London's first daily newspaper appeared in 1702. By 1760 it had four dailies and six tri-weekly evening papers that circulated in the country at large as well as in the capital. But the provinces also generated their own newspapers, their own books, dictionaries, magazines, printed advertisements, and primers. In 1695 Parliament passed legislation allowing printing presses to be established freely outside London. Between 1700 and 1750 presses were founded in 57 English provincial towns, and they proliferated at an even faster rate in the last third of the 18th century:

By 1725 no fewer than 22 provincial newspapers had emerged. By 1760 there were 37 such papers and by 1780, 50. In Scotland seven newspapers and periodicals were in existence by 1750, including the monthly Scots Magazine, which was printed in Edinburgh but could also be purchased from booksellers at Aberdeen, Glasgow, Dundee, Perth, and Stirling. Wales had no English-language newspaper until 1804, but many English papers found their way there.

By 1760 more than nine million newspapers were sold in Britain every year. Because they were expensive by the standards of the time (three or four pennies), one copy of a paper may have been shared and read by as many as 20 different people. There is little doubt that this explosion of newsprint helped to integrate the nation. All provincial newspapers and periodicals were parasitic on the London press. They borrowed large extracts from the more popular and controversial London papers and pamphlets. Increasingly, too, they broke the law and reprinted London journalists' accounts of debates in the House of Commons and House of Lords (printing parliamentary debates was illegal until 1770). Consequently, by the time of the Seven Years' War (1756–63), larger numbers of Britons than ever before had some access to political information. They were more aware of their country's military victories and defeats and more conscious of political scandals and protest. Politics was no longer just the preserve of the politicians at court, in Parliament, and in the country houses.

Britain from 1754 to 1783

Henry Pelham died in 1754 and was replaced as head of the administration by his brother, the duke of Newcastle. Newcastle was shrewd, intelligent, and hard-working and possessed massive political experience. But he lacked self-confidence and a certain breadth of vision, and he was hampered by being in the House of Lords. In 1755 Henry Fox was appointed secretary of state and acted as the administration's spokesman in the Commons. Fox's promotion alienated a man who was far more interesting and remarkable than either of these ministers, William Pitt the Elder. Pitt had entered Parliament as an Opposition MP in the 1730s. In 1746 he had been appointed paymaster general, a highly lucrative state office. But Pitt, whose ambition was for fame and recognition rather than money, remained unsatisfied. The king, however, disliked him and successfully obstructed his career. In 1755 he dismissed Pitt, who began to attack Newcastle on imperial and foreign policy issues.

Conflict abroad

Although Britain and France had technically been at peace since 1748, both powers continued to harass each other in their colonial settlements in North America, the West Indies, and India. When the French attacked the British colony of Minorca in May 1756, war broke out; Britain allied itself with Prussia and France with Austria. Like every 18th-century war, this one began badly for Britain; it lost Oswego in North America as well as Minorca. There was an outcry in the press, and Newcastle and Fox resigned. In November Pitt was appointed secretary of state with William Cavendish, duke of Devonshire, serving as nominal head of the new administration. But Pitt, still lacking royal approval or an adequate majority in the Commons, was dismissed by the king in April 1757. He returned to power in June, forming what was to be a highly effective wartime coalition with Newcastle.

Pitt captured the attention and imagination of Parliament and of the people by his rhetoric and charisma; Newcastle employed his experience and industry to raise more than £160 million during the course of the war. But what cemented the coalition was Britain's naval and military successes. In India, where Britain and France were keen competitors, General Robert Clive captured the French settlement of

Chandernagore and then, with the forces of the East India Company, defeated the army of Siraj-ud-Dawlah, the nawab (ruler) of Bengal, at the Battle of Plassey on June 23, 1757. The battle lasted only a few hours but decided the fate of India by establishing British dominance in Bengal and the Carnatic, the two most profitable regions of India for European traders.

The year 1757, as a consequence, is often cited as the beginning of Britain's supremacy over India, the start of Calcutta's significance as the headquarters of the East India Company, and the beginning of the end of French influence on the subcontinent. Two years later large sections of the French fleet were destroyed at the naval battle of Quiberon Bay. When Quebec fell to General James Wolfe in 1759, British control of Canada was effectively secured. The island of Guadeloupe was captured in the same dramatic year, as were French trading bases on the west coast of Africa.

Most of these gains were confirmed by the Treaty of Paris (1763), though Britain restored Guadeloupe to the French in return for control of Canada. In the short term these victories resulted in a mood of patriotic exultation, especially among merchants. They looked to the new colonies to provide both fresh stocks of raw materials and eager markets for British manufactured goods: "Trade," Edmund Burke gloated, "had been made to flourish by war." This global victory, however, had been purchased at a high price. The conquest of Canada freed the American colonists from the fear of a French invasion from the north.

Anxiety on this score had helped to foster American attachment to Britain. Now these fears had been relieved, and as early as 1760 some Britons and Americans anticipated that this would lead to difficulties. Furthermore, the enormous cost of the conflict led to drastic and sometimes damaging postwar economies, not least the deterioration of the Royal Navy, which would be an important factor in Britain's defeat in the American Revolution (1775–83). Postwar economies also forced British governments to explore new fiscal expedients, which aroused discontent at home and in the American colonies. Finally, the apparent unity and strength of Britain's elite during the Seven Years' War was deceptive: Newcastle and many of his allies were elderly men, Pitt was difficult and unstable, and old Whig and Tory alignments had ceased to have much meaning. All these factors helped to make the early reign of George III a period of conflict and instability.

Political instability in Britain

George II died in October 1760 and was succeeded by his grandson, who became George III. The new king became one of the most controversial British monarchs. In the first 10 years of his reign administrations changed no fewer than seven times. In October 1761 Pitt resigned and Newcastle was made to share power with the royal favourite, John Stuart, earl of Bute. In May 1762 Newcastle too resigned, and Bute alone led the government until his resignation in April 1763. Bute was replaced by George Grenville, who was in turn dismissed in July 1765. For the next year Charles Watson-Wentworth, marquess of Rockingham, served as first lord of the treasury. But in July 1766 Rockingham was sacked and replaced by Pitt, now elevated to the House of Lords as earl of Chatham. Chatham soon lapsed into manic depression, and from 1768 to 1770 Augustus Henry Fitzroy, duke of Grafton, led the government. Only in 1770 did the king find a minister whom he felt he could trust and deal with: Frederick, Lord North. Such high political instability undoubtedly hampered British efforts to resolve the problem of its American colonies.

But division and instability were not just confined to the court and parliament. The 1760s were a period of bad harvests, rising food prices, and sporadic unemployment. These economic and social problems helped to fuel the public agitation over John Wilkes, a Protestant dissenter and the son of a London malt distiller. In 1757 he bribed a rotten borough to elect him as its member of Parliament. An interesting, irresponsible, and cheerfully immoral man, Wilkes became well known in London society but failed to obtain a government post. His disappointment, as well as a bent toward iconoclasm, pushed him into opposition journalism. In April 1763 issue number 45 of his paper, the North Briton (a reference to the then chief minister Lord Bute, who was Scottish), was judged seditious. The government reacted by issuing a general warrant under which Wilkes and 48 additional persons were arrested. But Sir Charles Pratt, chief justice of the court of commons pleas, determined that this was a breach of Wilkes's parliamentary privilege, and he acquitted him. Soon after Wilkes fled to France to avoid another trial, this time for obscenity. In 1764 he was expelled from the Commons and tried in absentia for sedition, libel, and obscenity. But, as he did not return, he was declared an outlaw for impeding royal justice. In 1768, deeply in debt, he returned and was elected MP for the county of Middlesex, the most populous county constituency in England.

Since Wilkes was still an outlaw, Parliament declared him ineligible for election, and for a time he was imprisoned in the Tower of London. Due in large part to Wilkes's organizational and propaganda skills, this precipitated a nationwide agitation; Wilkes was seen not only in England but also in the American colonies as a martyr for liberty. His plight raised the question of whether the will of the people or the decision of a Parliament elected by only a fraction of the people was supreme. In 1769 the Society for the Supporters of the Bill of Rights was founded to aid Wilkes and to press for parliamentary reform. Its members demanded parliamentary representation for important new towns such as Birmingham, Leeds, and Manchester, the abolition of rotten boroughs, and general admission to the franchise for men of movable property (i.e., traders, merchants, and professionals). The English, as well as the American colonists, were becoming more interested in the connection between parliamentary representation (or the lack of it) and the obligation to pay taxes.

The American Revolution

The American issue was the final and most volatile element in the instability of the 1760s. Tension mounted, as far as British governments were concerned, primarily for two reasons. First, from this decade onward imperial organization received increased attention, and attempts were made to tighten British rule in Ireland and India as well as in the American colonies, a development that caused friction. Fiscal need was the second and more pressing problem. In 1763 the national debt stood at £114 million, and it continued to grow. Since the burden of taxation was already heavy for Britons, the government naturally looked to other sources of revenue.

This was the background to George Grenville's decision, in 1765, to pass the Stamp Act, a measure designed to raise revenue in the American colonies by putting a tax on all legal and commercial papers. But it stirred up intense resentment in the colonies and, indirectly, in Britain, when the Americans boycotted British goods. In 1766 Rockingham repealed the Stamp Act while maintaining Parliament's right to legislate for the colonies. In 1767 Charles Townshend, then chancellor of exchequer, levied duties on certain imports into the colonies, including a duty on tea, and linked this proposal with plans to remodel colonial government. These measures exacerbated American discontent, though Parliament was not made to realize how much until 1774.

Historians have long disagreed over the question of how far George III himself was responsible for these tumultuous events. The Declaration of Independence (1776) unambiguously condemned the king as a tyrant. The so-called 19th-century British Whig historians also criticized the king in very harsh terms, maintaining, at their most extreme, that as a young prince he was indoctrinated with archaic and inflated ideas of royal power. When he came to the throne, he supposedly ousted his Whig ministers, replacing them with Tories, who were more sympathetic to royal ambitions. His arbitrary aims and policies, it was claimed, provoked the Wilkite agitation in Britain and drove the American colonists to rebel. George was consequently held directly responsible for the break-up of the British Empire. Finally, he was charged with employing bribery and corruption to persuade Parliament to do his bidding.

Twentieth-century historians, in particular the Polish-born scholar Lewis Namier, have revised many of these extreme judgments. It has now been established that the king was neither educated in arbitrary ideas, nor did he preside over a Tory revival. Ministers such as Bute, Grenville, Townshend, and North regarded themselves as Whigs. But by the 1760s and '70s "Whig" and "Tory" were terms that had lost precise ideological significance, and the breakdown of these old partisan divisions undoubtedly contributed to ministerial instability at this time. There is little evidence that the king used corrupt influence to make Parliament accept his American policy. Indeed, it is unlikely that he initially even possessed an American policy; royal correspondence shows that he was rarely closely interested in American affairs before 1774. The colonists' drift toward opposition and independence was probably caused as much by their distance from London and their increasing prosperity as it was by British fiscal measures.

But George III cannot be entirely exonerated. When he succeeded, he was only 22, immature, idealistic, and not well-educated. His appointment of his decorative favourite, Lord Bute, was a breach of the convention that monarchs should choose chief ministers possessed of political experience and proven abilities. In his dealings with other politicians George showed himself throughout his reign to be intransigent and obstinate, and he often confused his own personal feelings with the public welfare. He can scarcely be blamed for wanting to retain such an important part of his empire as the American colonies, but he can legitimately be criticized for insisting that the American war be continued after 1780, by which time it had become clear to his chief minister, Lord North, that Britain had lost.

Domestic responses to the American Revolution

Even at its outbreak in 1775 British attitudes to the American war were mixed. Many Protestant dissenters regarded the Americans as their brethren, for political and religious reasons. The City of London, and other commercial centres such as Glasgow, Norwich, and Newcastle, objected to the war because it disrupted highly profitable Anglo-American trade. Many British newspapers and cartoons adopted a pacifist and sometimes even a pro-American line. Other Britons believed, with George III, that rebellion against a monarch was sinful and that Parliament's authority must be preserved. Conventional patriotism became stronger after 1778, when France, Spain, and belatedly the Dutch, allied themselves with the Americans against Britain.

The next two years proved profoundly difficult. Fears that the French would invade Ireland as a prelude to invading the British mainland led ministers to encourage the creation of an Irish volunteer force some 40,000 strong. The Irish Protestant elite, led by Henry Grattan, used this force and the French threat to extract concessions from London. In 1783 Ireland was granted legislative independence, though it remained subject to George III. Declining British fortunes abroad also revived the issue of parliamentary reform. By 1779 three different reform groups had emerged, all of whom favoured peace with America. The marquess of Rockingham and his parliamentary supporters (including his secretary, Edmund Burke) wanted to reduce official corruption and George III's influence in government. Another group, led by Christopher Wyvill, a one-time Anglican clergyman, wanted a moderate reform of the representative system.

Wyvill and some of his supporters played with the idea of a national association, an assembly of reformers from each county in Britain, that would exist parallel to Parliament and be superior to it in constitutional zeal. A third small group, led by Charles James Fox, a Whig MP, and by former Wilkite activists, wanted more extensive political reform, including the secret ballot and annual general elections. In 1780 they founded the Society for Constitutional Information, which was designed to build public support for political change through the systematic production and distribution of libertarian propaganda.

It was unlikely that any of these reforms would be implemented. But the Gordon Riots of June 1780 made it certain that they would not be. In 1778 Parliament had made minor concessions to British Roman Catholics, who were excluded from civil rights. Anti-Catholic prejudice, however, had been a powerful emotion in Britain since the Reformation in the 16th century, and Roman Catholicism tended to be associated by many with political absolutism and persecution. A movement to repeal the Catholic Relief Act of 1778, the Protestant Association, started in Scotland under the leadership of an unstable individual called Lord George Gordon. The movement reached London and exploded there in riots that lasted for eight days. More than 300 people were killed, and more damage was done to property than would be done in Paris during the French Revolution. For a time these riots gave reform and popular agitation a bad name. To many, the very name of Wyvill's National Association was dangerously suggestive of the Protestant Association, and the parliamentary reform movement lapsed until the 1790s.

Disasters at home were followed by further disasters abroad. Late in 1781 Britain learned of General Charles Cornwallis's surrender in

America at the Battle of Yorktown. Parliamentary pressure to end the war now became irresistible. When in March 1782 Lord North's majority in the Commons fell to nine votes, he resigned, against the wishes of George III. A new administration, formed under Lord Rockingham, was committed to peace with America and moderate constitutional reform at home. When Rockingham died in July 1782, William Petty, earl of Shelburne, became first lord of the treasury. In November of that year it was he who had the thankless task of concluding peace with the Americans and formally acknowledging their independence and British defeat in the Treaty of Paris.

Britain from 1783 to 1815

Defeat abroad and division at home led many Britons to believe that their country was in irreversible decline. The war had cost more than £236.4 million and had apparently brought only humiliation and the loss of one of the most profitable regions of the British Empire. Yet recovery was rapid, and by the time Britain again went to war in 1793, against revolutionary France it was wealthier and more powerful than it had been at the beginning of George III's reign.

In February 1783 Britain made a far from disadvantageous peace with its European enemies. Minorca and Florida were ceded to the Spanish, but Gibraltar was retained. France was given settlements in Senegal and Tobago, but Britain recovered other West Indian islands lost during the war. Holland gave Britain freedom of navigation in its spice islands and an important trading base in India. Nonetheless, this peace damaged Shelburne's reputation, and he resigned. A coalition administration was formed, led by Lord North and Charles James Fox. The king disliked it and ruthlessly sabotaged it.

The Fox–North coalition planned to cement its authority by passing a bill to reform the government of British settlements in India, previously administered by the East India Company alone. The India

Bill passed the Commons but, like every other piece of legislation not directly concerned with taxation, it had to be approved by a majority in the House of Lords. In advance of the vote the king let it be known that he would regard any peer who supported the bill with disfavour. The Lords duly threw the bill out in December 1783, providing the king with an excuse to dismiss Fox and North and replace them with William Pitt the Younger, the second son of the late earl of Chatham. The general election of 1784 supplied Pitt with a parliamentary majority.

William Pitt the Younger

Pitt lived and died a bachelor, totally obsessed with political office. He was clever, single-minded, confident of his own abilities, and a natural politician. But perhaps his greatest asset in the early 1780s was his youth. He had entered Parliament in 1780 and was just 24 when he became first minister in 1783. Consequently, he was not associated in the public mind with the American debacle but seemed instead to promise a new era. Moreover, although he and George III never developed a close relationship, he did enjoy the king's support. Knowing that the alternative to Pitt was Fox (whom he hated), the king dealt with Pitt in a responsible manner. In 1788–89 the king suffered a major bout of insanity (or, according to some scholars, porphyria, a hereditary blood disease). Although he recovered, he thereafter interfered in politics far less than in his early reign. Pitt in turn treated the king tactfully. He dropped his early enthusiasm for parliamentary reform, and in 1801 he resigned over the issue of Roman Catholic emancipation (the extension of civil rights to Catholics) rather than force the king to accept it.

Royal support aided Pitt's control of his cabinet and political patronage. But what sustained him most in the 1780s and early 1790s was the quality and success of his measures. He reduced the national debt by £10 million between 1784 and 1793, in part by increasing tax revenue. He fostered legitimate trade and reduced smuggling by cutting import duties on certain commodities such as tea. In 1786 he signed an important commercial agreement, the Eden Treaty, with France. It was in keeping with the argument made by the economist Adam Smith in his The Wealth of Nations (1776) that Britain should be less economically dependent on trade with America and become more adventurous in exploring trading opportunities in continental Europe. At home, Pitt strove for cheaper and more efficient administration; for example, he set up a stationery department to supply government offices with the necessary paper at a more economical rate. Abroad, he restored Britain's links with continental Europe and implemented imperial reorganization. In 1788 he signed the Triple Alliance between Britain, Prussia, and Holland, thereby ensuring that in a future war his country would not be bereft of allies as it had been during the American Revolution. In 1790 he demonstrated Britain's renewed power and prestige by negotiating a peace between Austria and Turkey. In 1784 he passed his own India Act, creating a board of control regulating Indian affairs and the East India Company. The board's members were nominated by the king from among the privy councillors. Finally, in 1791 the Canada Constitutional Act was passed. London became responsible for the government of both Lower and Upper Canada, but both provinces were given representative assemblies.

Economic growth and prosperity

Many of Pitt's reforms and policies, such as his India Act, had been devised by previous ministers. But even though he did not originate all of his schemes, Pitt nonetheless deserves credit for actually implementing them. For all his priggish ruthlessness and occasional dishonesties (perhaps because of them), Pitt undoubtedly contributed to the restoration of national confidence; indeed, for many people, he became its very personification. But British recovery had wider and more complex causes than just one man's measures. At bottom, it was rooted in accelerating economic growth and unprecedented national prosperity:

These figures illustrate two striking points. First, in the 1770s British export performance and industrial productivity were perceptibly damaged by the American war. But, second, Britain's economic recovery after the war was rapid and dramatic. Particularly noticeable is the fact that the wars with revolutionary and Napoleonic France (1793–1802 and 1803–15) did not slow Britain's buoyant prosperity. Although Napoleon tried to blockade Britain in 1808 and again in 1811–12, he never succeeded in cutting the lifeline of its trade. In the period 1794–96 British exports averaged £21.7 million per annum. In the period 1804–06 the equivalent figure was £37.5 million, and during 1814–16, £44.4 million. These figures demonstrate how quickly Britain regained its American markets after 1783 and how extensive its other colonial markets were. But they are also one of many signs that the nation was experiencing the first Industrial Revolution.

The Industrial Revolution

Some historians have questioned whether the term Industrial Revolution can really be applied to the economic transformation of late 18th- and early 19th-century Britain. They point out that in terms of employment the industrial sector may not have overtaken the agricultural sector until the 1850s and that even then the average unit of production employed only 10 people. Large, anonymous factories did not become common until the late 19th century. Other scholars have argued, rightly, that industry did not suddenly take off in the 1780s and that even in 1700 Britain was a more industrialized state than its European competitors. But, despite all these qualifications, the available evidence suggests that by 1800 Britain was by far the most industrialized state in the world and that, because of this, its rate of economic growth must have accelerated in the last third of the 18th century.

Perhaps the most powerful evidence one can cite for these statements (which are inevitably controversial, given the ferocity and rapid fluctuations of the debate on the Industrial Revolution) is Britain's ability to sustain an unprecedented growth in its population from 1780 onward without suffering from major famines or acute unemployment. In 1770 the population was about 8.3 million. By 1790 it had reached 9.7 million; by 1811, 12.1 million; and by 1821, 14.2 million. By the latter date, it is estimated that 60 percent of Britain's population was 25 years of age or below. By comparison, while a similar rate of demographic growth occurred in Ireland, there was no Irish Industrial Revolution. Partly as a result of this, Ireland suffered the great famine in the 1840s, whereas there was no similar famine in Britain.

To say this is not to deny the dark side of early industrialization. The conditions of work were often brutal, particularly for the young. Industrial safety was minimal, and environmental pollution and unguarded machines led to horrific injuries. Mechanization ruined the livelihoods of some skilled craftsmen, most notably the handloom weavers. Nonetheless, it is probable that without industrialization the social costs of rapid population growth in Britain would have been far greater.

Although it is not easy to account for Britain's early industrialization, some facts stand out. Britain, unlike its prime European rival, France, was a small, compact island. Except in northern Scotland, it had no major forests or mountains to disrupt or impede its internal communications. The country possessed a range of natural ports facing the Atlantic, plenty of coastal shipping, and a good system of internal waterways. By the 1760s there were already 1,000 miles of inland canals in Britain; over the next 70 years 3,000 more miles of canals were constructed. Britain was also richly endowed with coal and iron ore, and these minerals were often located close together in counties such as Staffordshire, Northumberland, Lancashire, and Yorkshire.

Most importantly perhaps, Britain could draw on an ample supply of customers for its goods, both at home and overseas. Its colonies fed it with raw materials while also serving as captive customers. And its expanding population meant buoyant demand at home even in wartime when foreign trade was disrupted. The best illustration of these advantages is the cotton industry. Its Indian settlements supplied Britain with ever-increasing amounts of raw cotton, and annual cloth production soared from 50,000 pieces of cloth in 1770 to 400,000 pieces in 1800. Much of this output in textiles was consumed by the home market. Some scholars have argued that the increased wearing of cotton (which could be easily washed) as distinct from woolen clothes (which could not) improved health conditions, thus contributing to Britain's population expansion.

Britain during the French Revolution

The outbreak of the French Revolution in July 1789 initially heightened British national confidence. Some Britons welcomed it in the belief that civil commotion would weaken their prime European competitor. Many others, William Wordsworth, Samuel Taylor Coleridge, William Godwin, and Mary Wollstonecraft among them, felt confident that revolutionary France would become a new and enlightened state and that this process would in turn accelerate political, religious, and social change in Britain. By contrast, Edmund Burke's fierce denunciation in Reflections on the Revolution in France (1790) met with little immediate support, even among the political elite. Only when the new French regime guillotined Louis XVI and threatened to invade Holland did mainstream opinion in Britain begin to change and harden. In February 1793 Britain and France went to war.

There has been much debate over the degree to which British opinion on the war was united. Some historians have argued that Thomas Paine's best-seller, The Rights of Man (1791–92), fostered mass enthusiasm for democratic reform and mass alienation from Britain's ruling class. Paine attacked the monarchy, aristocracy, and all forms of privilege, and he demanded not only manhood suffrage and peace but also public education, old-age pensions, maternity benefits, and full employment. While he did not directly advocate a redistribution of property to fund these reforms, some contemporary radicals certainly did. A Newcastle schoolmaster, Thomas Spence, for example, issued a penny periodical, Pig's Meat (a reference to Burke's savage description of the British masses as "the swinish multitude"), calling for the forcible nationalization of land.

These developments in radical ideology were made more significant by simultaneous developments in radical organization. In January 1792 a small coterie of London artisans led by a shoemaker, Thomas Hardy, formed a society to press for manhood suffrage. It cost only a shilling to join, and the weekly subscription was set at a penny so as to attract as many members as possible. These plebeian reformers, making use of Britain's growing communications network, corresponded with similar societies that had sprung up in response to the Revolution in the English provinces and in Scotland. In October 1793 Scottish radicals held what they styled a British Convention in Edinburgh, and a few of the English corresponding societies managed to send delegates there. They issued a manifesto demanding universal manhood suffrage and annual elections and affirming their faith in the principles of the French Revolution.

In terms of the number of men involved, these initiatives were always limited. Corresponding societies were far more widespread in London and the industrial north than in predominantly rural areas such as central Wales. Only a small proportion of rural and industrial labourers, as distinct from artisans, seems to have joined them. Even in the radical bastion of Sheffield (population 31,000) the local corresponding society attracted only 2,000 members, and most of these did not attend its meetings regularly. A minority of these activists were overtly Francophile and some may have wanted a French invasion of Britain and the establishment of a republican regime. Most corresponding-society members, however, seem to have been deeply attached to the British constitution and to have wanted only to reform it. But if these societies were not extensive or proto-revolutionary, they were still important and recognized as such. Contemporaries realized that for the first time in the 18th century working men throughout the nation were beginning to organize to achieve political change.

Pitt's ministry acted ruthlessly to suppress them. Leading Scottish radicals were arrested and given harsh sentences. In England habeas corpus was temporarily suspended, laws were passed prohibiting public meetings and demonstrations, and Thomas Hardy was tried for treason but acquitted. By 1795 the corresponding societies had formally ceased to meet. A minority of radicals, however, continued to agitate for reform in secret, some of them engaging in sedition. Particularly prominent in this respect were Irish dissidents. By now large numbers of Irish immigrants lived and worked in British towns.

Some of them sympathized with the Irish Rising of 1798 and formed secret societies to overturn the government. Several Irish agitators were involved in the Spithead and Nore naval mutinies of 1797 that for a time immobilized the Royal Navy. In 1803 an Irishman and former shipmate of Horatio Nelson, Edward Despard, was executed in London for plotting a coup d'état. Just how dangerous and well-supported these various incidents were is uncertain. But there can be no doubt that successive British wartime administrations felt obliged to devote extensive resources to maintaining order at home. even though they were also fighting an unprecedentedly massive war abroad.

The Napoleonic Wars

The Napoleonic Wars were massive in their geographic scope, ranging, as far as Britain was concerned, over all of the five continents. They were massive, too, in terms of expense. From 1793 to the Battle of Waterloo in June 1815 the wars cost Britain more than £1,650,000,000. Only 25 percent of this sum was raised by government loans, the rest coming largely from taxation, not least from the income tax that was introduced in 1798. But the wars were massive most of all in terms of manpower. Between 1789 and 1815 the British army had to expand more than sixfold, to about a quarter of a million men. The Royal Navy, bedrock of British defense, aggression, trade, and empire, grew further and faster still. Before the wars it had employed 16,000 men; by the end of them, it employed more than 140,000. Because there was an acute danger between 1797 and 1805 that France would invade Britain, the civil defense force also had to be expanded. The militia was increased, and by 1803 more than 380,000 men were acting as volunteers in home-based cavalry and infantry regiments. In all, one in four adult males in Britain may have been in uniform by the early 19th century.

Despite these financial and military exertions, British governments found it extremely difficult to defeat France. In part this was because Pitt the Younger's abilities were more suited to peace than to war. But the main reason the conflict was so protracted was France's overwhelming military superiority on land. The historian Paul Kennedy has written of British and French power in this period:

Like the whale and the elephant, each was by far the largest creature in its own domain. But British control of the sea routes could not by itself destroy the French hegemony in Europe, nor could Napoleon's military mastery reduce the islanders to surrender.

The first coalition of anti-French states, consisting of Britain, Russia, Prussia, Spain, Holland, and Austria, disintegrated by 1796. A British expeditionary force to aid Flanders and Holland was defeated, and Holland was occupied by the French. By 1797 the cost of maintaining its own forces and subsidizing those of its European allies had brought Britain to the verge of bankruptcy. For a time the Bank of England suspended payments in cash.

The British response to these developments was to concentrate on home defense and to consolidate its imperial and naval assets. Britain won a string of important naval victories in 1797, and in 1798 at the Battle of the Nile, Nelson defeated the French fleet anchored off Egypt, thereby safeguarding British possessions in India. Pitt also tried to solve the problem of Ireland. In 1801 the Act of Union took effect amalgamating Ireland with Great Britain and creating the United Kingdom. The Dublin Parliament ceased to exist, and Ireland's Protestant voters were allowed to return 100 MPs to Westminster. Pitt had hoped to sweeten the union by accompanying it with Roman Catholic emancipation, that is, by allowing Irish Catholics to vote and hold state office if they possessed the necessary property qualifications. George III opposed this concession, however, and Catholics were not admitted to full British citizenship until 1829. Pitt resigned and was succeeded as first minister by Henry Addington, the deeply conservative son of a successful doctor. It was his administration that signed the short-lived Treaty of Amiens with France in 1802.

War broke out again in May 1803. Once again, Britain demonstrated its power at sea but, until 1809, was unable to win substantial victories on land. Its fleet captured St. Lucia, Tobago, Dutch Guiana, the Cape of Good Hope, French Guiana, Java, Martinique, and other West Indian and African territories. Most importantly, in October 1805 Nelson defeated the French and Spanish fleets at Trafalgar, thereby preventing an invasion of Britain. Napoleon, however, inflicted serious military defeats on the Austrians, Prussians, and Russians and invaded Spain. At one stage Britain's only remaining European allies were

Sweden, Portugal, Sicily, and Sardinia; in short, the country was without any significant allies at all. Political leadership was uneven and sometimes weak, and the long duration of the war and its damaging effects on trade aroused increasing criticism at home. Pitt had resumed his post as chancellor of the Exchequer and first lord of the Treasury in May 1804, but he died worn out by work and drink in January 1806. None of the three men who succeeded him as premier, William Wyndham Grenville, Baron Grenville (1806–07), William Henry Cavendish Bentinck, duke of Portland (1807–09), and Spencer Perceval (1809–12), was able to establish himself in power for very long or to capture the public imagination.

Yet the war began to turn in Britain's favour in 1809, in large part because of Napoleon's strategic mistakes. When the Spanish rebelled against French rule, substantial British armed forces were dispatched to assist them under the command of Arthur Wellesley, later duke of Wellington. Spain's new anti-French posture meant that Spain was once again open to British manufactured goods, as were its colonies in Latin America. For a time this helped to reduce the commercial community's criticism of the conduct of the war. But demands for peace revived during the slump of 1811–12 and intensified when British relations with the United States, a vitally important market, began to deteriorate. One of the main irritants was the so-called Orders in Council, prohibiting neutral powers (like the United States) from trading with France. In 1812 commercial lobbies in Liverpool, Sheffield, Leeds, and Birmingham succeeded in getting the orders repealed, an indication of the growing political weight exercised by the manufacturing interest in Britain. Although this failed to prevent the Anglo-American War of 1812, neither Britain's trade nor its war efforts in Europe was seriously damaged by that conflict. Russia's break with Napoleon in 1812 opened up large markets for British goods in the Baltic and in northern Europe.

From 1812 onward Napoleon's defeat was merely a matter of time. In June 1813 Wellington defeated the French army in Spain at Victoria. The forces of Austria, Sweden, Prussia, and Russia expelled the French from Germany in the Battle of Leipzig (October 1813). This victory allowed Wellington, who had already crossed the Pyrenees, to advance upon Bayonne and Toulouse. Robert Stewart, Viscount Castlereagh, the secretary of state for foreign affairs, played the leading part in negotiating the Treaty of Chaumont in March 1814, which clarified allied war aims (including the expulsion of Napoleon), tightened allied unity, and made provision for a durable European settlement. The subsequent squabbles over the spoils of war were interrupted for a time when Napoleon escaped from his genteel exile on Elba and fought his last campaign from March to June 1815. Although his final defeat at Waterloo was accomplished by the allied armies, Britain secured prime credit. This textbook victory was to help Britain dominate Europe and much of the world for the next 100 years.

Imperial expansion

Britain's ultimate success against Napoleon, like its importance in this period as a whole, owed much to its wealth its capacity to raise loans through its financial machinery and revenue through the prosperity of its inhabitants and the extent of its trade. But British success also owed much to the power of its navy and to the energy and aggressiveness of its ruling class, which was particularly apparent in the imperial expansion of this period. Britain sought to extend its control by legislation, by war, and by individual enterprise.

The Acts of Union with Scotland in 1707 and with Ireland in 1801 tightened London's rule over its Celtic periphery, as did the laws passed to erode the autonomy of the Scottish Highlands after the rebellion of 1745. In the 1760s Britain sought not only to increase the revenue it gained from its North American colonies but also to shore up its military and administrative influence there. These measures failed, but Britain had more success with its Indian possessions. Between 1768 and 1774, in fact, the House of Commons devoted far more time to Indian affairs than to those of North America. Its discussions culminated in the passing of the India Act in 1784, which indicatively increased the government's authority over the East India Company and therefore over Britain's possessions in India.

Every major war Britain engaged in during this period increased its colonial power. The Seven Years' War was particularly successful in this respect, and so were the Napoleonic Wars. Between 1793 and 1815 Britain gained 20 colonies, including Tobago, Mauritius, Malta, St. Lucia, the Cape, and the United Provinces of Āgra and Oudh in India. By 1820 the total population of the territories it governed was 200 million, 26 percent of the world's total population. Not all of these acquisitions were formally directed by London. Captain James Cook's explorations of Australia and New Zealand after 1770 were in part an exercise in private enterprise and scientific inquiry. Nonetheless, British settlement of Australia at New South Wales began in 1787, in part because the mother country needed another repository for transported convicts previously sent to the North American colonies. The East India Company also retained considerable initiative in its military strategies. In 1819 Sir Thomas Stamford Raffles seized Singapore for the company and not on London's instructions. But, however acquired, all these acquisitions added to Britain's power and reputation. It was no accident, perhaps, that its two national anthems, "God Save the King" and "Rule Britannia," were composed in this period. For the privileged and the rich, this was preeminently an era of confidence and arrogance.

Great Britain, 1815–1914

Britain after the Napoleonic Wars
State and society

The relationship between state and society in Britain after the Napoleonic Wars assumed the shape that was to remain apparent into the 20th and 21st centuries. In contrast to most other European societies, many of the functions performed by central government elsewhere were performed in Britain by groups of self-governing citizens, either on an elective, but unpaid, official basis, as in the institutions of local government, or through voluntary organizations. Britain in the 19th century did not develop a strong bureaucratic element with interests of its own, a strong sense of popular expectations concerning the role of the state, nor a strong popular sense of identification with it.

This understanding of the limited role of government (contemporaries would have used this term rather than the "state") reflected and served to further entrench what in the 18th century had become a relatively homogeneous and stable society relative to the great majority of European states, that is. This was particularly so after the integration of Scotland into what was increasingly, with the clear exception of Ireland, a United Kingdom. Internal differences of course remained strong, but, nonetheless, linguistic and geographical unity was paralleled by the increasing integration of communications, seen in the improved road system of the first three decades of the new century, a precursor of the integration later evident in the railway system.

However, this decentralized state combined considerable strength with considerable flexibility; indeed, these two characteristics were mutually reinforcing. Even in the 18th century, central government showed sensitivity to the dangers of trespassing upon the limits of consent. Although in no sense a democratic state, this combination of strength and liberality was made possible by the close link between central government and the decentralized channels through which it ruled. If ruling at a distance often, this rule was all the stronger for being experienced as a kind of freedom. This experience in turn strengthened central government, enabling it all the more firmly to coordinate decentralized rule.

Nonetheless, if liberal, the late 18th- and early 19th-century state was marked by a strong sense of rights, enforceable by law and enjoyed by all members of the community, however unequally, including rights of subsistence by means of the poor-relief system. However limited, the propertied and the powerful felt it their responsibility to uphold these rights, rights that they and the poor and unpropertied regarded as the birthright of the "Free-Born Englishman." Those with governmental responsibility did not generally try to exclude the mass of the population from at least some participation in the regulation of their own lives. In the courts, by the means of petition, and through attendance at parish meetings, for example, the less powerful could exert some influence. This influence, among both the high and the low in society, was felt to operate at the level of the representation of communities, rather than the individual, and was reflected in the system of parliamentary representation itself. This sense of rights also took the form of strong attachments to customary observances and regulations for instance, those associated with particular trades and localities, such as the parish. The country was governed through a process of negotiation and reciprocity, albeit between unequal sides, in which what has been called a "rebellious but traditional popular culture" set limits on the power of the governors, while at the same time respecting this power when justly implemented.

This was to change in the aftermath of the Napoleonic Wars. The moves of William Pitt, the Younger, toward more professional, economically liberal, politically authoritarian government were carried forward by the "liberal Tory" governments of the years after 1815. This new understanding of government built upon the old liberality of the 18th-century state but divested it of many of the rights intrinsic to it. This involved a reconstruction of the roles of Parliament, the executive, and the party, with the purpose of reducing these to the provision of a framework within which individuals and institutions could operate with maximum safety and freedom. While retaining and modernizing its basic public order and foreign policy functions thereby retaining at the centre a strong directive power this new notion of government involved stripping away what were perceived to be the great premodern accretions of intrusive legislation, regulation, and custom, particularly in relation to economic activity and the "Old Corruption" of the ancien régime.

Instead, what would be constructed were mechanisms that would facilitate the automatic operations of the "natural order" believed to lie beneath and to be prevented from its beneficial operation by the unnecessary weight of custom and regulation created over the centuries. Liberated in this way, it was thought, individuals and the economy would be set free to achieve their full potential. This understanding of government was supported by particular appropriations of political economy, utilitarian thought, and evangelical religion, whereby the workings of the political system could be equated with the workings of Providence. This understanding of government conflicted with older notions of rights and responsibilities, so that arguments about the role of a strong central state and institutional and personal freedom, as well as the question of what was public and what was private, were at the heart of political discussion throughout the century and, indeed, through the course of the 20th century too. These arguments were reflected in the uneven movement toward the liberalization of society and the economy in the first two decades of the century, though of the direction of this movement there could be no doubt.

The political situation

The end of the long wars against Napoleon did not usher in a period of peace and contentment in Britain. Instead, the postwar period was marked by open social conflicts, most of them exacerbated by an economic slump. As the long-run process of industrialization continued, with a rising population and a cyclic pattern of relative prosperity and depression, many social conflicts centred on questions of what contemporaries called "corn and currency" that is, agriculture and credit. Others were directly related to the growth of factories and towns and to the parallel development of middle-class and working-class consciousness.

The agriculturalists, who were predominant in Parliament, attempted to safeguard their wartime economic position by securing, in 1815, a new Corn Law designed to keep up grain prices and rents by taxing imported grain. Their political power enabled them to maintain economic protection. Many of the industrialists, an increasingly vociferous group outside Parliament, resented the passing of the Corn Law because it favoured the landed interests. Others objected to the return in 1819 of the gold standard, which was put into effect in 1821. Whatever their outlook, industrialists were beginning to demand a voice in Parliament.

The term middle classes began to be used more frequently in social and political debate. So too were working class and classes. Recent historical research indicates that the awareness of class identity was not simply the direct outcome of economic and social experience but was articulated in terms of public discourse, particularly in the political sphere. For example, claims to be middle-class were actively contested in the political life of the time, and different groups, for different purposes, sought to appropriate or stigmatize the term. In the same manner, working-class identity was formed differently by different political and social movements, and the poorer sections of society were politically mobilized around collective identities that were not only about class but also about the poor (versus the propertied) and especially "the people" (versus the privileged and the powerful). This understanding of how collective identity was politically shaped according to the cultural contexts of the time has marked the formation of collective identities more broadly in British history down to the present.

Town and village labourers were also unrepresented in Parliament, and they bore the main brunt of the postwar difficulties. Bad harvests and high food prices left them hungry and discontented, but it was as much their political as their economic situation that served as the basis of their mobilization. However, new forms of industrial production, as well as the growth of towns with structures of communication that were quite different from those of villages or preindustrial urban communities, enabled new kinds of political appeal and of collective identity to take root. There were radical riots in 1816, in 1817, and particularly in 1819, the year of the Peterloo Massacre, when there was a clash in Manchester between workers and troops of the yeomanry, or local citizenry.

The Six Acts of 1819, associated with Henry Addington, Viscount Sidmouth, the home secretary, were designed to reduce disturbances and to check the extension of radical propaganda and organization. They provoked sharp criticism even from the more moderate Whigs as well as from the radicals, and they did not dispel the fear and suspicion that seemed to be threatening the stability of the whole social order. There was a revival of confidence after 1821, as economic conditions improved and the government itself embarked on a program of economic reform. Even after the collapse of the economic boom of 1824–25, no attempt was made to return to policies of repression.

There was a change of tone, if not of principle, in foreign policy, as in home affairs, after the suicide of the foreign secretary, Robert Stewart, Viscount Castlereagh. Castlereagh, who had represented

Britain at the Congress of Vienna in 1815, pursued a policy of nonintervention, refusing to follow up the peace settlement he had signed, which entailed provisions for converting the Quadruple Alliance of the victorious wartime allies into an instrument of police action to suppress liberalism and nationalism anywhere in Europe. His successor at the Foreign Office, George Canning, propounded British objectives with a strong appeal to British public opinion and emphasized differences between British viewpoints and interests and those of the European great powers more than their common interests. In 1824 he recognized the independence of Spain's American colonies, declaring in a famous phrase that he was calling "the New World into existence to redress the balance of the Old." In 1826 he used British force to defend constitutional government in Portugal, whereas in the tension-ridden area of the eastern Mediterranean, he supported the cause of Greek independence. His policies and styles were reasserted by Henry John Temple, Viscount Palmerston, who became foreign minister in 1830.

The situation in Ireland heralded the end of one pillar of the old order namely, legal restrictions on the civil liberties of Roman Catholics. Irish disorders centred, as they had since the Act of Union in 1801, on the issue of Catholic emancipation, a favourite cause of the Whigs, who had been out of power since 1807. During the 18th century, Catholics in England had achieved a measure of unofficial toleration, but in Ireland restrictions against Catholics holding office were still rigorously enforced. In 1823 Daniel O'Connell, a Dublin Roman Catholic lawyer, founded the Catholic Association, the object of which was to give Roman Catholics in Ireland the same political and civil freedoms as Protestants. Employing pioneering techniques of organization, involving the mobilization of the large numbers of the poor and the excluded in great open-air demonstrations, O'Connell introduced a new form of mass politics that galvanized opinion in Ireland while at the same time mobilized radical allies in England. The result was the passing of the Catholic Emancipation Act in 1829.

The death in June 1830 of George IV (whose reign had begun in 1820) heralded the end of another pillar of the old order, the unreformed system of parliamentary representation. In a year of renewed economic distress and of revolution in France, when the political reform issue was being raised again at public meetings in different parts of Britain, Wellington, the military hero of the Napoleonic Wars who had assumed the premiership in 1828, had not made matters easier for himself by expressing complete confidence in the constitution as it stood. In consequence he resigned, and the new king, William IV (1830–37), invited Charles Grey, 2nd Earl Grey, to form a government. Grey's cabinet was predominantly aristocratic including Canningites as well as Whigs but the new prime minister, like most of his colleagues, was committed to introducing a measure of parliamentary reform. For this reason, 1830 marked a real parting of the ways. At last there was a break in the continuity of regime that dated from the victory of William Pitt, the Younger, over Charles James Fox in the 1780s and that had only temporarily been interrupted in 1806–07. Moreover, the new government, aristocratic or not, was the parent of most of the Whig-Liberal administrations of the next 35 years.

The year 1830 was also one of economic and social grievances, with religious issues still being thrown into the melee. In the Midlands and in northern towns and cities, well-organized political reform movements were winning widespread support. Corn Laws and Poor Laws, as well as currency and game laws, were all being attacked, while in the industrial north the demand was growing for new laws to protect factory labour. It was in such an atmosphere that the new Whig-led government prepared its promised reform bill.

Early and mid-Victorian Britain

State and society

The implementation of the liberal, regulative state emerging after the Napoleonic Wars involved a number of new departures. The first of these concerned the new machinery of government, which, instead of relying on patronage and custom, involved an institutionalized bureaucracy. This was evident in the development of the factory inspectorate, established by the 1833 Factory Act, though the characteristic way in which the state institutionalized itself was by means of local bodies administering such areas as the fast-developing realm of "public health" and the Poor Law. In fact, towns and cities themselves became very important new locations for the expression of the power of the decentralized state. After the 1835 Municipal Corporations Act, local government, if developing unevenly, was a major part of the new machinery of government. There was a great flowering of civic administration and civic pride during the early and mid-Victorian period in Britain. This was particularly reflected in the architecture and infrastructure of British cities one of the most notable legacies of the period. Magnificent town halls, libraries, concert halls, museums, and, not least, the great civil engineering projects of the time all inculcated the virtues of civic identity and therefore of instituting civic power.

Beyond the machinery of government, the Poor Law of 1834 represented the clearest example of the new ideological departures that characterized the liberal state. Its encouragement of self-supporting actors within the greater scheme of a natural order expressed the mixture of utilitarianism and evangelicalism that was characteristic of the new order. New areas of state action were also evident in education as well as in factory reform, and with these departures a new kind of bureaucratic expertise arose.

Expert bureaucrats from outside of government, including the physician and medical reformer James Kay-Shuttleworth in education and the lawyer Edwin Chadwick in Poor Law and health reform, were brought in to advise the government. Figures such as these indicate the permeability of the Victorian state and its closeness to civil society, for they established their reputations and gained their expertise outside the attenuated structure of the state bureaucracy. From the 1850s onward, however, centralized bureaucracy accrued to itself increasing powers. The reforms of 1853–54 engineered by Charles Edward Trevelyan and Sir Stafford Northcote instituted, by means of public and competitive examination, a system based not on patronage but on merit. In fact, public examination was designed to create meritocracy of a very particular sort, one based on the classically educated Englishman of Oxford and Cambridge universities. For the first time in British history and the history of Oxbridge (the two universities viewed as an institution), though in both cases decidedly not the last time, the ideology of merit was employed to reproduce a particular kind of ruling elite. This elite was built upon the idea of public duty, inculcated by an Oxbridge education, but above all it was based upon the notion that the state and its bureaucracy could be neutral. This neutrality was to stem from the open, competitive examination itself but also from the idea of that the neutrality of the civil service could be guaranteed by the ethics of the Oxbridge-educated English gentleman.

Nonetheless, gentleman of an even higher social station than that of these new civil servants that is, the aristocracy and gentry were still very much a part of government, and, despite all these reforms, the role of patronage remained important. The mid-Victorian implementation of the liberal state by the government of William Gladstone therefore still had considerable work to do. Gladstone, Whig and later Liberal prime minister, was the major single influence on the 19th-century liberal state and arguably the most gifted British politician of his time. The liberal state's attempt to rule through freedom and through the natural order was implemented not merely in social but also in economic terms:

Gladstonian finance, particularly the taxation system, was aimed at encouraging the belief that all groups in society had a responsibility for sanctioning and financing government activity and that therefore they should have an incentive to keep it under control. Economic and social government came together dramatically in the case of the Irish Potato Famine in the late 1840s. The outcome of the famine, a disaster for Ireland involving the death or emigration of millions of people, has to be seen in the context of the long-term agenda of the liberal state, which included Ireland as a sort of laboratory for experimentation in this new kind of government (India was a similar kind of laboratory).

The experimental methods in the Irish case involved an agenda including population control, the Poor Law relief system, and the consolidation of property through a variety of means, including emigration, the elimination of smallholdings, and the sale of large but bankrupt estates. The government measured the success of its relief policies in terms of this agenda rather than its effectiveness in addressing the immediate question of need. The goal of this agenda was the creation of a society of "rational" small-farm production on the model of the natural order of the free market, rather than the "irrational" production of a mass of small peasant proprietors.

However, subsequent implementation of the liberal state for instance, that of Gladstone should not be seen simply as guided by the amoral market. In the third quarter of the century, Gladstone's version of the liberal state represented the apotheosis of the approach to government favoured by the reformer Sir Robert Peel (the Conservative prime minister from 1834 to 1835 and again from 1841 to 1846). This version of the liberal state took the form of an individualism ostensibly based not upon greed and self-interest but upon probity, self-control, and a sense of duty and Christian morality. In this regard, as indeed much more widely in British history, this version of individualism accorded with many of the beliefs of society in general not least those held by the working classes so that the attempt to rule through the moral characteristics of society proved in many respects to be an extraordinarily successful venture in government. Rather like the thinking behind the reformed civil service, the moral rule at the heart of Gladstonian economic reform was designed to establish the neutrality, and therefore the high moral ground, of government: if government were independent of a self-regulating economy, it would also be free from the influence of powerful economic interests. This view of liberal government in the period of Tory power instituted after 1874 changed little and went unchallenged until the late 19th century, even if Tory administrations had a somewhat more positive idea of the state.

The political situation

Whig reforms

Whig interest in parliamentary reform went back to the 18th century, and Grey himself provided a link between two separate periods of public agitation. Yet, in the country as a whole, there were at least three approaches to the reform question. Middle-class reformers were anxious to secure representation for commercial and industrial interests and for towns and cities such as Birmingham and Manchester that had no direct voice in Parliament. "Popular radicals," of both middle-class and working-class origin, were concerned with asserting rights as well as with relieving distress. "Philosophic radicals," the followers of the utilitarianism of philosopher Jeremy Bentham, were strong ideological protagonists of parliamentary reform but were deeply hostile to both the arguments and the tactics of the popular radicals, except when confident that they were in a position to deploy or control them. Agitation in the country kept the reform question on the boil between 1830 and 1832, while an aloof Grey faced unprecedented constitutional difficulties with both the king and Parliament.

The Reform Act of 1832 (see Reform Bill) was in no sense a democratic measure. It defined more clearly than ever before the distinction between those who were and those who were not sanctioned to wield power, and it did so entirely in terms of property ownership, entrenching the power of landed wealth as well as acknowledging new sources of power in the middle classes and the consequent claims upon the rights and virtues of their new political identity. The bill entailed a substantial redistribution of parliamentary constituencies and a change in the franchise. The total electorate was increased by 57 percent to 217,000, but artisans, labourers, and large sections of the lower middle classes still remained disenfranchised. No radical demands were met, even though the manner of passing the bill had demonstrated the force of organized opinion in the country, particularly in the large cities, which were also now given representation.

Returned with a huge majority in the general election of December 1832, the Whigs carried out a number of other important reforms. A statute in 1833 ended slavery in the British colonies; in that same year the East India Company lost its monopoly of the China trade and became a purely governing body with no commercial functions.

The new Poor Law of 1834 turned out to be an unpopular measure in many parts of the country, however, and led to violent outbreaks of disorder. Its basic principle that "outdoor poor relief" (i.e., outside the workhouse) should cease and that conditions in workhouses should be "less eligible" (i.e., less inviting) than the worst conditions in the labour market outside was as bitterly attacked by writers such as Thomas Carlyle as it was by the workingmen themselves.

All of these contentious issues multiplied after 1836, when a financial crisis ushered in a period of economic depression accompanied by a series of bad harvests. Social conflict, never far from the surface, became more open and dramatic. Grey's successor, William Lamb,

Viscount Melbourne, proved incapable of finding effective answers to any of the pressing financial, economic, and social questions of the day, but he did prove adept in his dealings with Queen Victoria, who ascended the throne in 1837.

Chartism and the Anti-Corn Law League

As the economic skies darkened after 1836 and prophets such as Carlyle anticipated cataclysmic upheaval, the two most disgruntled groups in society were the industrial workers and their employers. Each group developed new forms of organization, and each turned from local to national extra-parliamentary action. The two most important organizations were the Chartists and the Anti-Corn Law League. Chartism drew on a multiplicity of workers' grievances, extending working-class consciousness as it grew. The Anti-Corn Law League, founded as a national organization in Manchester in 1839, was the spearhead of middle-class energies, and it enjoyed the advantage not only of lavish funds but also of a single-point program the repeal of the restrictive Corn Laws.

Taking its name from the People's Charter published in London in May 1838, Chartism aimed at parliamentary reform. The charter contained six points, all of them political and all with a radical pedigree: (1) annual parliaments, (2) universal male suffrage, (3) the ballot, (4) no property qualifications for members of Parliament, (5) payment of members of Parliament, and (6) equal electoral districts. These were old demands that would have been supported by 18th-century radicals. Localized Poor Law and factory reform agitations centring on such grievances were subsumed in Chartism because of its commitment to national political action. However, for a variety of reasons not least that the politicians had been able again to convey the sense that the state was benign and neutral and not, as Chartists perceived it, repressive and sectional the mass movement of Chartism ultimately failed.

By contrast, the Anti-Corn Law League, led by Richard Cobden and John Bright, met with success. It employed every device of propaganda, including the use of new media of communication, such as the Penny Post, which was introduced in 1840. The formula of the league was a simple one designed to secure working-class as well as middle-class support. Repeal of the Corn Laws, it was argued, would settle the two great issues that faced Britain in the "hungry forties" securing the prosperity of industry and guaranteeing the livelihood of the poor. So enormous was religion's influence on the league that when it identified the landlord as the only barrier to salvation, it meant religious as well economic salvation. Most Chartists were unconvinced by this logic, but, in a landed Parliament, Peel carried the measure against his own party.

Peel and the Peelite heritage

Peel was the presiding genius of a powerful administration, strictly supervising the business of each separate branch of government; nevertheless, a substantial section of the squirearchy rebelled, roused by the brilliant speeches of a young politician, Benjamin Disraeli, who in his writings had already approached the "condition of England question" in a totally different style than that of Peel. The results of repeal were important politically as well as economically. As a result of the split, party boundaries remained blurred until 1859, with the "Peelites" retaining a sense of identity even after Peel's premature death following a riding accident in 1850. Some of them, particularly Gladstone, eventually became leaders of the late 19th-century Liberal Party, which emerged from the mid-century confusion.

The protectionists, most of whom abandoned protection after 1852, formed the nucleus (around Edward Stanley, earl of Derby, and Disraeli) of the later Conservative Party, but they were unable to secure a majority in any election until 1874. The minority governments they formed in 1852, 1858, and 1866 lacked any secure sense of authority. The Whigs, themselves divided into factions, returned to office in 1847 and held it for most of the mid-century years, but they were often dependent on support from radical and Irish colleagues. There was no time between 1846 and 1866, however, when extra-parliamentary agitation assumed the dimensions it had between 1838 and 1846.

Matters of religion helped divide the limited mid-Victorian electorate, with the Nonconformists (Dissenters) encouraging, from their local bases, the development of liberalism and with the Anglican churchmen often but by no means universally supporting the Conservative Party. Nonelectors' associations (representing the disenfranchised) tried with varying degrees of success to keep radical issues alive, but party divisions remained based on customary allegiance as much as on careful scrutiny of issues, and there was still considerable scope for bribery at election times.

The civil service might be pure, but the electors often were not. The Corrupt Practices Act of 1854 provided a more exact definition of bribery than there had been before, but it was not until a further act of 1883 that election expenses were rigorously controlled. It was then that, quite emphatically, parliamentary representation became not a matter of communities but of individuals, a process taken a considerable step further in 1872 with institution of electoral secrecy by the Ballot Act.

The prestige of the individual members of Parliament was high, and the fragmentation of parties after 1846 allowed them considerable independence. Groups of members supporting particular economic interests, especially the railways, could often determine parliamentary strategies. Nevertheless, contemporaries feared such interests less than they feared what was often called the most dangerous of all interests, executive government. Powerful government and large-scale "organic" reform were considered dangerous, and even those radicals who supported organic reform, like Cobden and Bright, were suspicious of powerful government.

Palmerston

Lord Palmerston, who became prime minister for the first time in 1855, stood out as the dominant political personality of mid-Victorian Britain precisely because he was opposed to dramatic change and because he knew through long experience how to maneuver politics within the half-reformed constitution. In a period when it was difficult to collect parliamentary majorities, he often forced decisions, as in the general election of 1857, on the simple question "Are you for or against me?" He also was skillful in using the growing power of the press to reinforce his influence. At a time of party confusion, when the queen might well have played a key part in politics, Palmerston found the answer to royal opposition in popular prestige, carefully stage-managed. His chief preoccupation was with foreign affairs, and his approach was, on several occasions, diametrically opposed to that of the court.

There was no contradiction between his views on domestic and foreign policy. He preferred the British system of constitutional government, resting on secure social foundations, to Continental absolutism, but, like Canning, his predecessor as foreign secretary, Palmerston was anxious above all else to advance the interests of Britain as he saw them. The supremacy of British sea power, British economic ascendancy, and political divisions inside each of the main countries of Europe before and after the Revolutions of 1848 gave him his opportunity.

His interventions were not confined to Europe. In 1840–41 he had forced the Chinese ports open to foreign trade, and, by the Treaty of Nanjing (1842), he had acquired Hong Kong for Britain. In 1857 he went to war in China again and, when defeated in Parliament, appealed triumphantly to the country. He also intervened in Russia. The Crimean War (1853–56) was designed to curb what were interpreted as Russian designs on the Ottoman Empire and a Russian threat to British power in the eastern Mediterranean. The outcome greatly favoured the British and their main allies, the French and the Ottoman Empire. Although Palmerston's government was defeated in 1858, he was back again as prime minister, for the last time, a year later.

During Palmerston's remarkable ministry of 1859–65, which included Peel's successor as prime minister, Lord John Russell, as foreign secretary and the Peelite Gladstone as chancellor of the Exchequer, it was impossible for Britain to dominate the international scene as effectively as in previous periods of Palmerstonian power. With efficient military power at his disposal, the Prussian prime minister, Otto von Bismarck, proved more than a match for Palmerston. The union of modern Italy, which Palmerston supported, the American Civil War, in which his sympathies were with the Confederacy, and the rise of Bismarck's Germany, which he did not understand, were developments that reshaped the world in which he had been able to achieve so much by forceful opportunism. When Palmerston died, in October 1865, it was clear that in foreign relations as well as in home politics there would have to be what Gladstone described as "a new commencement."

Gladstone and Disraeli

In the large urban constituencies the demand for a new and active liberalism had already been gaining ground, and at Westminster itself Gladstone was beginning to identify himself not only with the continued advance of free trade but also with the demand for parliamentary reform. In 1864 he forecast new directions in politics when he stated that the burden of proof concerning the case for reform rested not with the reformers but with their opponents. A year later he lost his seat representing the University of Oxford and was returned as member of Parliament for a populous Lancashire constituency. The timing was right, because, after the death of Palmerston, the question of parliamentary reform was reopened and the Second Reform Bill was passed in 1867.

The reform of 1867 almost doubled the electorate, adding 938,000 new names to the register and extending the franchise to many workingmen in the towns and cities. The county franchise was not substantially changed, but 45 new seats were created by taking one seat from existing borough constituencies with a population of fewer than 10,000. Disraeli hoped that, in return for his support in passing this measure, urban workers would vote for him. He believed rightly that many of them were Conservatives already by instinct and allegiance, but in 1868, in the first general election under the new system, it was Gladstone who was returned as prime minister.

In both parties, new forces were stirring at the local level, and energetic efforts were under way to organize the electorate and the political parties along new lines. Even though Gladstone resumed power, it became apparent that the popular vote was not Liberal by divine right. In several parts of England, particularly in the industrial north, there developed a strong popular Toryism, which in Lancashire, a great centre of the cotton industry, was based partly upon deference to industrial employers, partly upon dislike of Irish immigrants, partly upon popular Protestant associations with Englishness, and not least upon what to many was a surprisingly strong support for the principles of church and state.

With the development of central party machinery and local organization, the role of the crown was reduced during this period to that of merely ratifying the result of elections. Although the queen greatly preferred Disraeli to Gladstone, she could not keep Gladstone out. Her obvious partisanship made some of her acts look unconstitutional, but they would not have been deemed unconstitutional in any previous period of history. The public during this period was more interested in the political leaders than in the queen, who lived in retirement and was sharply criticized in sections of the press.

Gladstone's first administration had several notable achievements: the disestablishment and partial disendowment of the Irish church, accomplished in 1869 in face of the opposition of the House of Lords; the Irish Land Act of 1870, providing some safeguards to Irish tenant farmers; William Edward Forster's Education Act of the same year, the first national act dealing with primary education; the Trade-Union Act of 1871, legalizing unions and giving them the protection of the courts; and the Ballot Act of 1872, introducing secret voting. Moreover, the Universities of Oxford and Cambridge were opened to Nonconformists, or Dissenters (Protestants who did not conform to the practices of the Church of England), while between 1868 and 1873 the cumbrous military machine was renovated by Gladstone's secretary for war, Edward Cardwell. The system of dual responsibility of commander in chief and secretary for war also was abolished, and the subordination of the former to the latter was asserted. In 1873 the Judicature Act, amended in 1876, simplified the tangle of legal institutions and procedures. Gladstone, throughout his life, preferred cheap and free government to expensive and socially committed government. He was anxious indeed in 1873 to abolish income tax, on which the public finances of the future were to depend.

Many of these reforms did not satisfy affected interests. The Irish Church Disestablishment Act failed to placate the Irish and alarmed many English churchmen, while the Education Act was passed only in the face of bitter opposition from Nonconformists, who objected that Forster's system did not break the power of the church over primary education. Although the act was extended in 1880 when primary education was made compulsory and in 1891 when it became free, there were often noisy struggles between churchmen and Nonconformists on the new school boards set up locally under Forster's act. If the Education Act alienated many Nonconformists, the Licensing Bills of 1871 and 1872 alienated their enemies, the brewers. In the general election of 1874, therefore, months after Disraeli had described the Liberal leaders in one of his many memorable phrases as a "range of exhausted volcanoes," the brewers threw all their influence behind the Conservatives. "We have been borne down in a torrent of gin and beer," Gladstone complained.

In his subsequent ministry, with the assistance of men like Richard Cross, the home secretary, Disraeli justified at last his reputation as a social reformer. By the Employers and Workmen Act of 1875, "masters" and "men" were put on an equal footing regarding breaches of contract, while by the Trade-Union Act of 1875, which went much further than the Liberal Act of 1871, trade unionists were allowed to engage in peaceful picketing and to do whatever would not be criminal if done by an individual. The Public Health Act of 1875 created a public health authority in every area; the Artizans' and Labourers' Dwellings Improvement Act of the same year enabled local authorities to embark upon schemes of slum clearance; a factory act of 1878 fixed a 56-hour workweek; while further legislation dealt with friendly societies (private societies for mutual-health and old-age insurance), the protection of seamen, land improvements carried out by tenants, and the adulteration of food. There was no similar burst of social legislation until after 1906.

If there were significant, though not fully acknowledged, differences between the records of the two governments on domestic issues, there were open, even strident differences on questions of foreign policy. Gladstone had never been a Palmerstonian. He was always anxious to avoid the resort to force, and he put his trust not in national prejudices but in an enlightened public opinion in Europe as well as in Britain. His object was justice rather than power. In practice, however, he often gave the impression of a man who vacillated and could not act firmly. Disraeli, on the other hand, was willing to take risks to enhance British prestige and to seek to profit from, rather than to moralize about, foreign dissensions.

His first ventures in "imperialism" a speech at the Crystal Palace in 1872, the purchase of the Suez Canal shares in 1875, and the proclamation of the queen as "Empress of India" showed that he had abandoned the view, popular during the middle years of the century, that colonies were millstones around the mother country's neck. But these moves did not involve him in any European entanglements, nor did the costly, if brilliantly led, campaigns of Maj. Gen. Frederick Roberts in Afghanistan (1878–80) and the annexation of the Transvaal in South Africa in 1877.

It was the Middle Eastern crisis of 1875–78 that produced the liveliest 19th-century debate on foreign policy issues. In May 1876 Disraeli rejected overtures made by Russia, Austria-Hungary, and Germany to deal jointly with the Ottoman Empire, which was faced with revolt in Serbia. His pro-Turkish sympathies irritated many Liberals, and, after Turkey had gone on to suppress with great violence a revolt in Bulgaria in 1876, the Liberal conscience was stirred, and mass meetings were held in many parts of the country. Gladstone, who had gone into retirement as Liberal leader in 1875, was slower to respond to the issue than many of his followers, but, once roused, he emerged from retirement, wrote an immensely influential pamphlet on the atrocities, and led a public campaign on the platform and in the press.

For him the Turks were "inhuman and despotic," and, whatever the national interests involved, Britain, in his view, should do nothing to support them. Disraeli's calculations concerned strategic and imperial necessities rather than ideals of conduct, and his suspicions were justified when the Russians attacked Turkey in April 1877. Opinion swung back to his side, and in 1878 Disraeli sent a British fleet to the

Dardanelles. London was seized by war fever the term jingoism was coined to describe it which intensified when news arrived that a peace agreement, the Treaty of San Stefano, had been signed whereby Turkey accepted maximum Russian demands. Reservists were mobilized in Britain, and Indian troops were sent to the Mediterranean.

Disraeli's foreign minister, who disapproved of such action, resigned, to be succeeded by Robert Gascoyne-Cecil, marquess of Salisbury, who was eventually to serve as prime minister in the last Conservative administrations of the 19th century. The immediate crisis passed, and, at the Congress of Berlin, an international conference held in June and July 1878, which Disraeli attended, the inroads into Turkish territory were reduced, Russia was kept well away from Constantinople, and Britain acquired Cyprus. Disraeli brought back "peace with honour." But the swings of public opinion continued, and in 1879 Gladstone, starting at Midlothian in Scotland, fought a nationwide political campaign of unprecedented excitement and drama. In the general election of April 1880, the Liberals returned to power triumphantly, with a majority of 137 over the Conservatives. Disraeli, who had moved to the House of Lords in 1876, died in 1881.

Economy and society

Although the Industrial Revolution traditionally has dominated accounts of change over the course of this period, recent research has emphasized the uneven and complex nature of this change. Nevertheless, over the course of the 19th century, the rise of manufacturing industry was striking, with the decisive shift occurring in the first three decades of the century. In 1801, 22 percent of the active British workforce was employed in manufacturing, mining, and construction, while 36 percent was involved in agriculture; by 1851, manufacturing, mining, and construction had increased to 40 percent, while agriculture had dropped to 21 percent. By 1901, agriculture had fallen even farther, to only 9 percent.

Cotton textiles remained the dominant new industry, centred in Manchester, with the textile factory being thought of by one of its contemporary admirers, the Leeds manufacturer Edward Baines, as "the most striking example of the dominion obtained by human science over the powers of nature of which modern times can boast." By 1851 there were some 1,800 cotton factories in Britain. From 1815 to 1851 raw cotton imports had increased unevenly from 101 million pounds to 757 million pounds, while exports of manufactured cotton piece goods increased from 253 million yards to 1.543 billion yards. Manchester was the centre of the cotton industry. During the same period, however, similar steam-driven technology accounted for the expansion of the woolen textiles industry, with Australia, which had provided no raw wool for Britain in 1815, supplying about 30 million pounds in 1851. Bradford and Leeds were the centres of the woolen textile industry. It was the textiles industry more than any other that illustrated Britain's dependence on international trade, a trade that it commanded not only through the volume of its imports and of its manufacturing output but also through the strength of its banking and other financial institutions, as well as the extent of its shipping industry.

The second, capital goods, phase of industrialization, beginning in the mid-19th century, broadened the manufacturing base into areas such as shipping and engineering. In tandem with this advance was the growth of the service industry as the economy expanded over time. The advent of mass consumption in the second half of the 19th-century resulting in the slow development of mass retailing by multiple stores was one consequence of this. While the factory and mechanized production played important roles in the process of industrialization, this process has been usefully described as "combined and uneven development."

Undoubtedly, hand technology and muscle power continued to play a considerable role far beyond the mid-19th century, and, as older forms of production continued alongside new, they were incorporated in, and to some extent regenerated by, factory production. The artisan sector, the conduct of work in people's homes, and subcontracting all remained central to many industries for example, the hosiery industry in Nottingham.

Much production was in fact small-scale and characterized to varying degrees by employers' dependence on the skills and authority of the worker; if in some areas for example, the trades in London capitalism made progress by degrading the status of craft workers, in other areas workers were able to hold their own and adapt to new situations by organizing through the trade unions that gave them leverage over employers. Even in mechanized industries, managerial hierarchies were weakly elaborated, and there was a considerable dependence on worker skill and authority as well as a limited penetration of technology. Also of great importance were domestic service and small shop keeping. The upshot was not a linear process of change in which the end result was de-skilled factory production and the homogenization of the condition of workers but rather a complex set of outcomes in which the relations of capital and labour represented a variegated division of power.

In fact the decentralized nature of industrial production paralleled the decentralized state, and workers' understanding of the economy was in many ways similar to their view of the state namely, one of guarded acceptance. As it did with all other sectors of British life, the state for the most part studiously stayed outside the field of industrial relations; nonetheless, developments in the economy and in labour relations had a decisive role in shaping British workers' views of the state. Within labour itself, there were divisions between "honourable" (traditional, apprenticeship-based, well-paid) and "dishonourable" (low-status, corner-cutting) trades, between those with a trade and those without, between the skilled and the unskilled, between union and nonunion workers, and between men and women. The labour movement itself reflected these divisions, as the increasingly strong trade union movement of this period was in fact largely shaped to meet the interests and demands of the skilled male head of household.

People were concerned too about the rising population as well as the nature and pace of economic change. In the first census of 1801, the population of England and Wales was about 9 million and that of Scotland about 1.5 million. By 1851 the comparable figures were 18 million and 3 million. At its peak in the decade between 1811 and 1821, the growth rate for Britain as a whole was 17 percent. It took time to realize that Thomas Malthus's eloquently expressed fears that population would outrun subsistence were exaggerated and that, as population grew, national production would also grow. Indeed, national income at constant prices increased nearly threefold between 1801 and 1851, substantially more than the increase in population.

The new technology reached its peak in the age of the railway and the steamship. Coal production, about 13 million tons in 1815, increased five times during the next 50 years, and by 1850 Britain was producing more than 2 million tons of pig iron, half the world's output. Both coal and iron exports increased dramatically, with coal exports amounting to 3.3 million tons in 1851, as opposed to less than 250,000 tons at the end of the French revolutionary and Napoleonic wars. Coal mining was scattered in the coal-producing districts; there were few large towns, and miners lived a distinctive life, having their own patterns of work and leisure. Iron production was associated with larger plants and considerable urbanization. In South Wales, for example, one of the areas of industrial expansion, the Dowlais works employed 6,000 people and turned out 20,000 tons of pig iron each year during the 1840s. Birmingham, Britain's second largest city, was the centre of a broad range of metallurgical industries that were organized mainly in small workshops that differed sharply in character from the huge textile mills of Lancashire and Yorkshire.

Industrialization preceded the coming of the railway, but the railroad did much to lower transport costs, to consume raw materials, to stimulate investment through an extended capital market, and to influence the location of industry. The railway age may be said to have begun in 1830, when the line from Manchester to Liverpool, the country's most vigorously expanding port, was opened, and to have gone through its most hectic phases during the 1840s, when contemporaries talked of a "railway mania." By 1851, 6,800 miles (11,000 km) of railway were open, some of which involved engineering feats of great complexity.

There was as much argument among contemporaries about the impact of railways as there was about the impact of steam engines in factories, but there was general agreement about the fact that the coming of the railway marked a great divide in British social history. It was not until the 1870s and '80s that steamship production came to its full realization, and by then British engineers and workers had been responsible for building railways in all parts of the world. By 1890 Britain had more registered shipping tonnage than the rest of the world put together.

Cultural change

The development of private life
It was in this period that private life achieved a new prominence in British society. The very term "Victorianism," perhaps the only "ism" in history attached to the name of a sovereign, not only became synonymous with a cluster of restraining moral attributes character, duty, will, earnestness, hard work, respectable comportment and behaviour, and thrift but also came to be strongly associated with a new version of private life. Victoria herself symbolized much of these

new patterns of life, particularly through her married life with her husband, Albert, and much later in her reign through the early emergence of the phenomenon of the "royal family." That private, conjugal life was played out on the public stage of the monarchy was only one of the contradictions marking the new privacy.

However, privacy was more apparent for the better-off in society than for the poor. Restrictions on privacy among the latter were apparent in what were by modern standards large households, in which space was often shared with those outside the immediate, conjugal family of the head of household, including relatives, servants, and lodgers. Privacy was also restricted by the small size of dwellings; for example, in Scotland in 1861, 26 percent of the population lived in single-room dwellings, 39 percent in two-room dwellings, and 57 percent lived more than two to a room. It was not until the 20th century that this situation changed dramatically. Nonetheless, differences within Britain were important, and flat living in a Glasgow tenement was very different from residence in a self-contained house characteristic of large parts of the north of England.

This British kind of residential pattern as a whole was itself very different from continental Europe, and despite other differences between the classes, there were similarities among the British in terms of the house as the cradle of modern privacy. The suggestive term "social privacy" has been coined to describe the experience of domestic space prior to the intervention of the municipality and the state in the provision of housing, which occurred with increasing effect after mid-century. The older cellular structure of housing, evident in the tangle of courts and alleys in the old city centres, often with cellar habitations as well, resulted in the distinction between public and private taking extremely ambiguous form. In the municipal housing that was increasingly widespread after mid-century, this gave way to a more open layout in which single elements were connected to each other.

Among housing reformers there was a dislike of dead ends, courts, and the old situation where habitations were turned in upon themselves in their own social privacy. In the new order, space became neutral and connective, and, in the new "bylaw housing," streets were regular in layout and width, with side streets at right angles and back alleys in parallel lines. The streets outside were (and remain) surprisingly wide in contrast to the narrow alleys behind. Such streets allowed a maximum of free passage. The street outside was public and communal. The alley or lane behind was less socially neutral than the street, still rather secret. It was not a traffic thoroughfare for the public at large, being reserved for the immediate inhabitants, for the hanging of washing, and perhaps for the playing of football (soccer). In between these public and semipublic spheres and the house within was the space of the yard at the back, which in contradistinction to the street was private and individual (if less so, potentially, than the house itself). In this fashion, municipal authorities sought to inculcate privacy in the lower classes. However, conditions worked against domestic privacy for them, and it was in the homes of the better-off that privacy was most developed.

Within the dwellings of the more privileged, there was a trend towards the specialization of rooms, the separation of the public from the private sides of life, and the development of distinct spheres for women and children. A society based on achieved status, as British society was slowly becoming, was very concerned to regulate and legitimize social relationships of gender and status, and the spaces of the home served as a means of doing this. From about the 1820s a family pattern developed that was conditioned by spatial environments that resulted from the new significance of home and domesticity.

The home was to be a retreat from the stress of the world and a haven of security. This change in perspective was associated with other developments, namely the retreat from the centre of cities to the suburbs evident in Manchester, for example, as early as the 1820s along with a concomitant switch in housing style from the 18th-century terrace (row houses) to the detached or semidetached villa. In the move from the terrace, what was once the common garden of the square gave way to a separate, private garden. The common and more public rooms of the house, which were once for use by all members of the family, were relocated on the ground floor, with the other stories of the house being limited to the use of family members in a distinct domestic sphere.

In terms of the development of working-class domesticity, by mid-century there was a clear gender division of labour between men and women (though it was often contradicted in practice by economic necessity and local employment conditions), based on the assumption that a man was to be the main and preferably sole breadwinner and head of the household. This pattern of gender relationships had profound influence on working-class institutions, not only on the trade union movement but also on the club and association life that was so central to the leisure activity of the less well-off.

However, the Victorian middle-class family should not be confused with the small nuclear family of the 20th century. Families were large and intermarried so that the boundaries between the categories of relative, dependent, and friend were indistinct, recalling an older notion of family as the circle of dependents. The relationship between public and private was therefore similarly complicated. Because the domestic interior could be the site of all sorts of familial and extra-familial interactions and obligations, the nexus of private life might also be distinctly public. Of course, privacy was accelerated by means other than family and domestic arrangements. The spread of reading on one's own and of letter writing, the latter of which increased massively with the development of the cheap Penny Post, were both conducive to privacy.

Moreover, privacy in life led to privacy in death, as what may be called social burial in the old churchyard gave way to the new privacy of the cemetery. An invention of this time (Kensal Green, the first specialist London cemetery, opened in 1831), the cemetery was a new sort of public space, which in theory welcomed all comers, though in practice it was open only to the better-off, at least at first. Communal, spatially particular parish rights of burial were replaced by absolute, abstract property rights, and the hugger-mugger of the old churchyard was replaced by the possibility of the individuation of the dead person, by means of the memorial and the deployment of the clearly demarcated burial site. One could really have eternal rest, instead of being dug up every few decades. The individual had his or her space in death as in life.

Religion

Victorian doubt about inherited biblical religion was as much an acknowledged theme of the period as was Victorian belief. Discoveries in geology and biology continued to challenge all accepted views of religious chronology handed down from the past. Perhaps the most profound challenge to religion came with Charles Darwin's On the Origin of Species (1859). Yet the challenge was neither unprecedented nor unique. In 1860 Essays and Reviews was published; a lively appraisal of fundamental religious questions by a number of liberal-minded religious thinkers, it provoked the sharpest religious controversy of the century.

Behind such controversies there were many signs of a confident belief on all sides that inquiry itself, if freely and honestly pursued, would do nothing to dissolve shared ideals of conduct. Even writers who were "agnostic" talked of the "religion of humanity" or tried to be good "for good's sake, not God's." Standards were felt to count in institutional as well as in private life.

Emphasis on conduct was, of course, related to religion. The British religious spectrum was of many colours. The Church of England was flanked on one side by Rome and on the other by religious dissent. Both were active forces to be reckoned with. The Roman Catholic Church was growing in importance not only in the Irish sections of the industrial cities but also among university students and teachers. Dissent had a grip on the whole culture of large sections of the middle classes, dismissed abruptly by Matthew Arnold as classes of "mutilated and incomplete men." Sometimes the local battle between the Church of England and dissent was bitterly contested, with Nonconformists opposing church rates (taxes), challenging closed foundations, and preaching educational reform and total abstinence from intoxicating beverages. A whole network of local voluntary bodies, led either by Anglicans or Nonconformists, usually in rivalry, came into existence, representing a tribute to the energies of the age and to its fear of state intervention.

The Church of England itself was a divided family, with different groups contending for positions of influence. The High Church movement (which emphasized the "Catholic" side of Anglicanism) was given a distinctive character, first by the Oxford movement, or Tractarianism, which had grown up in the 1830s as a reaction against the new liberal theology, and then by the often provocative and always controversial ritualist agitation of the 1850s and '60s. The fact that prominent members of the Church of England flirted with "Romanism" and even crossed the Rubicon often raised the popular Protestant cry of "church in danger." Peel's conversion to free trade in 1846 scarcely created any more excitement than John Henry Newman's conversion to Roman Catholicism the previous year, while in 1850 Lord Russell, the prime minister, tried to capitalize politically on violent antipapal feelings stimulated by the pope's decision to create Roman Catholic dioceses in England.

The Vatican Hatter, drawing by Joseph Swain, published in Punch, or the London Charivari, Jan. 10, 1874. The hatter, who resembles Pope Pius IX, does not have a hat that will fit Henry Edward Manning, a leader of the Oxford movement who converted to Roman Catholicism in 1851.

The Evangelicals, in many ways the most influential as well as the most distinctively English religious group, were suspicious both of ritual and of appeals to any authority other than the Bible. Their concern with individual conduct was a force for social conformity during the middle years of the century rather than for that depth of individual religious experience that the first advocates of "vital religion" had preached in the 18th century. Yet leaders such as Lord Ashley were prepared to probe some Evangelical social issues (e.g., housing) and to stir men's consciences, and, even if their preoccupation was with saving souls, their missionary zeal influenced developments overseas as well as domestic legislation. There were other members of the church who urged the cause of Christian socialism. Their intellectual guide was the outstanding Anglican theologian Frederick Denison Maurice. The Evangelicals in particular were drawn into substantial missionary activity in the empire and other parts of the world, frequently clashing with settlers and administrators and sometimes with soldiers. They regarded it as their sacred duty to spread the gospel from, in the words of one of the period's best-known missionary hymns, "Greenland's icy mountains" to "India's coral strand."

Beyond the influence of both church and chapel, there were thousands of people in mid-Victorian England who were ignorant of, or indifferent toward, the message of Christianity, a fact demonstrated by England's one religious census in 1851. Although movements such as the Salvation Army, founded by William Booth in 1865, attempted to rally the poor of the great cities, there were many signs of apathy or even hostility. There was also a small but active secularist agitation; particularly in London, forces making for what came to be described as "secularism" (more goods, more leisure, more travel) could undermine spiritual concerns. The great religious controversies of mid-Victorian England were not so much to be settled as to be shelved.

In Scotland, where the Church of Scotland had been fashioned by the people against the crown, there was a revival of Presbyterianism in the 1820s and '30s. A complex and protracted controversy, centring on the right of congregations to exclude candidates for the ministry whom they thought unsuitable, ended in schism. In 1843, 474 ministers left the Church of Scotland and established the Free Church of Scotland. Within four years they had raised more than £1.25 million and built 654 churches. This was a remarkable effort, even in a great age of church and chapel building. It left Scotland with a religious pattern even more different from that of England than it had been in 1815. Yet many of the most influential voices in mid-Victorian Britain, including Carlyle and Samuel Smiles (Self-Help; 1859), were Scottish, and the conception of the gospel of work, in particular, owed much in content and tone, even if often indirectly, to Scottish Calvinism. In Wales there was a particularly vigorous upsurge of Nonconformity, and the Welsh chapel was to influence late 19th-century and 20th-century British politics.

Leisure

Leisure emerged as a distinct concept and activity, at least on a mass scale, only when the hours of labour diminished and became more regular. Before then, work and nonwork activities had been closely related to each other for example, in the popular observance of the weekly "Saint Monday," when furious bouts of working were followed by equally furious bouts of enjoyment on a day supposedly given over to work. In the 1850s, in textiles, the leading sector of the economy, there was a more regular working day and week, and a half-day of leisure, Saturday, also eventually emerged. Hours of labour began to approximate nine per day in the 1870s and eight per day after World

War I. The Bank Holiday Act of 1871 further regularized leisure time. Yet, obviously, for the majority of people, work was the dominant activity.

For the privileged minority, however, leisure defined a good deal of their existence, the model of aristocratic "society" being redeployed in the early 19th century. Even in the 18th century the "middling sort" well-to-do of the towns, the urban gentry, had adopted the assembly room (where the elite had gathered to dance and socialize), the theatre, and the promenade as a means of regulating and enjoying urban life. This growth of a provincial urban culture had a serious side too, in the literary and philosophical societies of the late 18th century. In the first three decades of the new century this more serious aspect became increasingly apparent through the impact of the growth of Evangelical religion and of political events both at home and in Europe, so that there was a shift from the older sociability of propertied urban culture to a new emphasis on the deployment of leisure and culture as means of negotiating social and political difficulties, especially in the new and growing towns and cities.

The idea of "recreation" began to emerge; that is, that nonwork time should be a time of re-creating the body and mind for the chief purpose of work. The idea grew too that this recreation should be "rational." The characteristic institutions of these new initiatives were the Mechanics Institutes for labourers and the Atheneaums for the sons though not the daughters of the more wealthy. Beyond these institutions there was the remarkable growth of those concerned with bringing culture to propertied urbanites, notably art galleries. However, it was not until mid-century that such initiatives began to develop rapidly, as in Manchester in the 1850s, where the Halle Orchestra was established on a professional basis and its concerts opened to anyone who could pay admission, unlike earlier, purely subscription-based music organizations. In the same decade, Owens College, the forerunner of the University of Manchester, was founded.

The development of these institutions marked the emergence a more self-consciously public middle-class culture, one remodelled around a more open and inclusive notion of what public life involved.

In terms of popular culture, a more regularized and less demanding working day and week became part of a new kind of working year, so that old calendrical observances and rituals were lost. At the same time, a number were retained, being transformed to serve new purposes in the changed circumstances of increasing urbanization and industrialization. For instance, the old, established local "feast" and "wake" days of the industrial districts in the north of England were retained, serving many of the old communal functions yet also changing character and obtaining new functions in light of the spread of the railway and the advent of the modern vacation. Communal identities might now be formed by leaving the towns en masse, either for the railway excursion or on holiday, when large sections of the workers from particular towns took their leisure together at the new seaside resorts such as Blackpool. In urban Britain, restrictions upon space as well as upon time shaped the new culture, with old places of congregation, such as common lands on which fairs had been held, now being built over as towns grew. In the process, leisure often moved indoors, becoming more regular and more commercial in its organization. Commercial pressures in fact were most responsible for reshaping what had at least from the late 18th century been identified as popular culture, as opposed to forms of high culture. (Institutions such as the new urban concert halls of the mid-19th century were important in fostering a notion of the sublime and sacral nature of classical music, in contrast to the "low" music of the other sort of urban concert hall, namely the music hall.)

Commercialization of public culture was evident in the music hall from the 1850s, though more so in the late 19th century, with the construction of large purpose-built halls and the development of a nationwide chain of venues and a national "star" system. Before then, even if commercial, organizations were smaller-scale, less commercial, and more locally rooted. Commercial pressures were accompanied by political and moral pressures from above. The civic provision of culture was intended not only for the well-to-do but also for the mass of the population. For example, the public park, from its introduction in the 1840s, was an attempt to reproduce rational recreation among the lower classes through the design of the park as a place where civilized and rational behaviour and deportment could be encouraged. Of course, in practice, parks served other purposes, but their place in what was a widespread and marked reshaping of popular manners should not be underestimated.

This reshaping owed a great deal to the beneficiaries of reform themselves, in that some of the most vocal supporters of the reform of the old order of "superstition and brutality" were radical workingmen whose conception of reason pitted them against the old culture. They were joined by Dissenter workingmen who were equally uncomfortable with traditional culture. Commercial and reform interests combined in the proliferation of reading matter for the "popular classes." Indeed, the creation of a literate population was one of the most striking achievements of the century, but, while journals and books advocating self-improvement reached a surprisingly wide audience, this readership was not as wide as that of the sensational popular literature of the 1830s and '40s. About this time a mass popular press also developed, though at this stage a Sunday press only, in the form of Lloyd's News and Reynolds's Weekly Newspaper. The explosion of the provincial press in the 1850s reached a somewhat different social constituency but was tremendously important in constituting the sense of identity of the towns that it served.

Late Victorian Britain

State and society

From the 1880s a mounting sense of the limits of the liberal, regulative state became apparent. One reflection of this awareness was the increasing perception of national decline, relative to the increasing strength of other European countries and the United States. This awareness was reinforced by British military failures in the South African War (Boer War) of 1899–1902, a "free enterprise war" in which free enterprise was found wanting. One consequence of this and other developments was the growth of movements aimed at "national efficiency" as a means of establishing a more effective state machine. The recognition of social problems at home such as the "discovery" of urban poverty in 1880s in the assumed presence of plenty and increasing anxiety about the "labour question" also raised questions about the adequacy of the state in dealing with the mounting problems of an increasingly populous and complex society. Toward the end of the century, the possibility of a violent outcome in the increasingly intractable problem of Ireland brought existing constitutional methods into question. Behind much of this anxiety was a sense that the

Third Reform Act of 1884 (see Reform Bill) and changes in local government were precipitating a much more democratic polity, for which the classical liberal state had no easy answers. The example of what was called at the time municipal socialism, especially as it existed in Birmingham under the direction of its mayor, Joseph Chamberlain (1873–76), indicated what the local state could accomplish. Instead of the old "natural order" religion that had underpinned the state previously, different currents of thought emerged that saw the state and community as necessary for individual self-realization. German idealism, socialism, and new liberalism (see libertarianism) all encompassed different ways of rethinking the state.

This rethinking revolved around the belief that the operation of the state must incorporate consideration of the collective characteristics of society that is, solidarity, interdependence, and common identity in a much more direct way than hitherto. Indeed, the idea of the "social" came to characterize the entire period and even much later eras. Notions of a distinct social sphere, separate from the economic and political realms, had emerged much earlier, based upon the idea that the characteristics of this social realm were evident in the biological, vital characteristics of populations, so that society was very often understood in organic terms.

The influence of Malthus in the early 19th century and Darwin in the mid-19th century contributed powerfully to this worldview, giving rise to late 19th-century representations of society in the strongly biological terms of "social eugenics" and other variations of "racial" thought, such as the idea of the "degeneration" of the working class. From about the turn of the 20th century, the concept of the social realm as autonomous developed alongside and partly incorporated older understandings. The social question became a sociological question, as indeed it has remained until very recently in British history. Society was now understood, unlike in earlier times, to work according to its own laws and to be divorced from moral questions, although, in practice, political interventions were invariably designed to change moral behaviour.

One major result of this questioning of the state and of new conceptions of society was the extensive social legislation of the Liberal administrations after 1905, which is widely seen as the foundation of the 20th-century welfare state. The new Liberal government embarked upon a program of social legislation that involved free school meals (1905), a school medical service (1907), and the Children's Act (1908). The Old Age Pensions Act (1908) granted pensions under prescribed conditions to people over age 70, and in 1908 the miners were given a statutory working day of eight hours. In 1909 trade boards were set up to fix wages in designated industries in which there was little or no trade union strength, and labour exchanges were created to try to reduce unemployment. In 1911 the

National Insurance Act was passed, whereby the state and employers supplemented employees' contributions towards protection against unemployment and ill health. This act clearly represented a departure from the manner in which government had been carried out, as it began to be executed in supposed accordance with the social characteristics of the governed (age, family circumstances, gender, labour).

Under this new dispensation, individual rights, as well as the rights of families, were secured not by individual economic action but by state action and by the provision of pensions and benefits. These new rights were secured as social rights, so that individual rights were connected to a web of obligations, rights, and solidarities extending across the individual's life, across the lives of all individuals in a population, and between individuals across generations in short, a network of relations that was in fact one early version of society as a sui generis entity.

However, much of this new relationship of state and society was still recognizably liberal in the older sense, constituting a compact of social and individual responsibility. At the heart of this compact was the belief that it was necessary to safeguard the individual from the unfettered operation of the free market, while at the same time making sure that there must be an obligation to obtain gainful employment. Contributory pension schemes required individuals to make regular payments into them rather than providing social insurance from general taxation.

The National Insurance Act provided a framework within which workers were to practice self-help, and, although involvement was mandatory, the administration of the legislation was largely through voluntary institutions. David Lloyd George, who did most to push the legislation through, himself combined these characteristics of old and new liberalism. At the same time, in practice this new formula of government emerged in a very piecemeal and haphazard way, often driven by the circumstances of the moment, not least the circumstances of party politics. Moreover, the circumstances of war were of overwhelming importance. It was World War I in particular that fostered the idea of the increased importance of the interventionist, collectivist state.

The demands of winning the war required an unparalleled intervention in a running of the economy and in the operations of social life, particularly when the radical Liberal Lloyd George took power in 1916. Perhaps the most important factor legitimizing the increased role of the state was conscription in the armed services, and the most important general outcome was the idea that "planning" (understood in many different ways) was from this point forward a fully legitimate part of governmental enterprise. Nonetheless, despite the piecemeal nature of the change, what is striking is how this understanding of the relationship between state and society obtained across the whole political spectrum and how it lasted so long. This increased role of the state was accompanied, after World War I, by the increasing specialization and professionalization of an expanding civil service.

The political situation

Gladstone and Chamberlain

Gladstone's second administration (1880–85) did not live up to the promise of its election victory. Indeed, in terms of political logic, it seemed likely in 1880 that the Gladstonian Liberal Party would eventually split into Whig and radical components, the latter to be led by Joseph Chamberlain. This development was already foreshadowed in the cabinet that Gladstone assembled, which was neither socially uniform nor politically united. Eight of the 11 members were Whigs, but one of the other three Chamberlain represented a new and aggressive urban radicalism, less interested in orthodox statements of liberal individualism than in the uncertain aspiration and striving of the different elements in the mass electorate.

At the opposite end of the spectrum from Chamberlain's municipal socialism were the Whigs, the largest group in the cabinet but the smallest group in the country. Many of them were already abandoning the Liberal Party; all of them were nervous about the kind of radical program that Chamberlain and the newly founded National Liberal Federation (1877) were advocating and about the kind of caucus-based party organization that Chamberlain favoured locally and nationally. For the moment, however, Gladstone was the man of the hour, and Chamberlain himself conceded that he was indispensable.

The government carried out a number of important reforms culminating in the Third Reform Act of 1884 and the Redistribution Act of 1885. The former continued the trend toward universal male suffrage by giving the vote to agricultural labourers, thereby tripling the electorate, and the latter robbed 79 towns with populations under 15,000 of their separate representation. For the first time the franchise reforms ignored the traditional claims of property and wealth and rested firmly on the democratic principle that the vote ought to be given to people as a matter of right, not of expediency.

The most difficult problems continued to arise in relation to foreign affairs and, above all, to Ireland. When in 1881 the Boers defeated the British at Majuba Hill and Gladstone abandoned the attempt to hold the Transvaal, there was considerable public criticism. And in the same year, when he agreed to the bombardment of Alexandria in a successful effort to break a nationalist revolt in Egypt, he lost the support of the aged radical John Bright. In 1882 Egypt was occupied, thereby adding, against Gladstone's own inclinations, to British imperial commitments. A rebellion in the Sudan in 1885 led to the massacre of Gen. Charles Gordon and his garrison at Khartoum (see Siege of Khartoum) two days before the arrival of a mission to relieve him. Large numbers of Englishmen held Gladstone personally responsible, and in June 1885 he resigned after a defeat on an amendment to the budget.

The Irish question

The Irish question loomed ominously as soon as Parliament assembled in 1880, for there was now an Irish nationalist group of more than 60 members led by Charles Stewart Parnell, most of them committed to Irish Home Rule; in Ireland itself, the Land League, founded in 1879, was struggling to destroy the power of the landlord. Parnell embarked on a program of agrarian agitation in 1881, at the same time that his followers at Westminster were engaged in various kinds of parliamentary obstructionism. Gladstone's response was the Irish Land Act, based on guaranteeing "three fs" fair rents, fixity of tenure, and free sale and a tightening up of the rules of closure in parliamentary debate. The Land Act did not go far enough to satisfy Parnell, who continued to make speeches couched in violent language, and, after a coercion act was passed by Parliament in the face of Irish obstructionism, he was arrested. Parnell was released in April 1882, however, after an understanding had been reached that he would abandon the land war and the government would abandon coercion. Lord Frederick Charles Cavendish, a close friend of Gladstone and the brother of the Whig leader, Lord Spencer Hartington, was sent to Dublin as chief secretary on a mission of peace, but the whole policy was undermined when Cavendish, along with the permanent undersecretary, was murdered in Phoenix Park, Dublin, within a few hours of landing in Ireland.

Between 1881 and 1885 Gladstone coupled a somewhat stiffer policy in Ireland with minor measures of reform, but in 1885, when the Conservatives returned to power under Robert Arthur Salisbury, the Irish question forced itself to the forefront again. Henry Herbert, earl of Carnarvon, the new lord lieutenant of Ireland, was a convert to

Home Rule and followed a more liberal policy than his predecessor. In the subsequent general election of November 1885, Parnell secured every Irish seat but one outside Ulster and urged Irish voters in British constituencies a large group mostly concentrated in a limited number of places such as Lancashire and Clydeside to vote Conservative.

The result of the election was a Liberal majority of 86 over the Conservatives, which was almost exactly equivalent to the number of seats held by the Irish group, who thus controlled the balance of power in Parliament. The Conservatives stayed in office, but when in December 1885 the newspapers reported a confidential interview with Gladstone's son, in which he had stated (rightly) that his father had been converted to Home Rule, Salisbury made it clear that he himself was not a convert, and Carnarvon resigned. All Conservative contacts with Parnell ceased, and a few weeks later, in January 1886, after the Conservatives had been defeated in Parliament on a radical amendment for agrarian reform, Salisbury, lacking continued Irish support, resigned and Gladstone returned to power.

Split of the Liberal Party

Gladstone's conversion had been gradual but profound, and it had more far-reaching political consequences for Britain than for Ireland. It immediately alienated him further from most of the Whigs and from a considerable number of radicals led by Chamberlain. He had hoped at first that Home Rule would be carried by an agreement between the parties, but Salisbury had no intention of imitating Peel. Gladstone made his intentions clear by appointing John Morley, a Home Rule advocate, as Irish secretary, and in April 1886 he introduced a Home Rule bill. The Liberals remained divided, and 93 of them united with the Conservatives to defeat the measure. Gladstone appealed to the country and was decisively beaten in the general election, in which 316 Conservatives were returned to Westminster along with 78 Liberal Unionists, the new name chosen by those Liberals who refused to back

Home Rule. The Liberals mustered only 191 seats, and there were 85 Irish nationalists. Whigs and radicals, who had often seemed likely to split Gladstone's 1880 government on left-right lines, were now united against the Gladstonians, and all attempts at Liberal reunion failed.

Chamberlain, the astute radical leader, like many others of his class and generation, ceased to regard social reform as a top priority and worked in harness with Hartington, his Whig counterpart. In 1895 they both joined a Salisbury government. The Liberals were, in effect, pushed into the wilderness, although they held office briefly and unhappily from 1892 to 1895. Gladstone, 82 years old when he formed his last government, actually succeeded in carrying a Home Rule bill in the Commons in 1893, with the help of Irish votes (Parnell's power had been broken as a result of a divorce case in 1890, and he died in 1891), but the bill was thrown out by the Lords. He resigned in 1894, to be succeeded by Archibald Primrose, earl of Rosebery, who further split the party; in the general election of 1895, the Conservatives could claim that they were the genuinely popular party, backed by the urban as well as the rural electorate. Although Salisbury usually stressed the defensive aspects of Conservatism, both at home and abroad, Chamberlain and his supporters were able to mobilize considerable working-class as well as middle-class support for a policy of crusading imperialism.

Imperialism and British politics

Imperialism was the key word of the 1890s, just as Home Rule had been in the critical decade of the 1880s, and the cause of empire was associated not merely with the economic interests of businessmen looking for materials and markets and the enthusiasm of crowds excited by the adventure of empire but also with the traditional lustre of the crown. Disraeli had emphasized the last of these associations, just as Chamberlain emphasized the first. In the middle years of the century it had been widely held that colonies were burdens and that materials and markets were most effectively acquired through trade. Thus, an "informal empire" had been created that was as much dependent on Britain as the formal empire was. Nonetheless, even during these years, as a result of pressure from the periphery, the process of establishing protectorates or of acquiring colonies had never halted, despite a number of colonial crises and small colonial wars in Africa, Asia, and the Pacific. Most of the new acquisitions were located in tropical areas of the world and were populated mainly by non-Europeans.

There were further crises during the 1880s and '90s, when the Liberals were divided on both tactics and objectives, and public opinion was stirred. When Chamberlain chose to take over the Colonial Office in 1895, he was acknowledging the opportunities, both economic and political, afforded by a vast "undeveloped estate." The same radical energies that he had once devoted to civic improvement were now directed toward imperial problems. The argument about empire assumed an increasingly popular dimension. Boys' books and magazines, for example, focused on the adventure of empire and the courage and sense of duty of empire builders, and textbooks often taught the same lessons. So also did the popular press. In consequence, the language of imperialism changed.

However, it was difficult to pull the empire together politically or constitutionally. Certainly, moving toward federation was a challenging task since the interests of different parts were already diverging, and in the last resort only British power above all, sea power held the empire together. The processes of imperial expansion were always complex, and there was neither one dominant theory of empire nor one single explanation of why it grew. Colonies that were dominated by people of British descent, such as Canada or New Zealand and the states of Australia, had been given substantial powers of self-government since the Durham Report of 1839 and the Canada Union Act of 1840. Yet India, "the brightest jewel in the British crown," was held not by consent but by conquest. The Indian Mutiny of 1857–58 was suppressed, and a year later the East India Company was abolished and the new title of viceroy was instituted. Imperial control was tightened too, through the construction of a network of railways. Thomas Macaulay's dream that India would one day be free and that such a day would be the happiest in British history seemed to have receded, although the nationalist movement that emerged after the first Indian National Congress in 1885 was eventually to gain in strength. Meanwhile, given the strategic importance of India to the military establishment, attempts were made to justify British rule in terms of benefits of law and order that were said to accrue to Indians. "The white man's burden," as the writer and poet Rudyard Kipling saw it, was a burden of responsibility.

It was difficult for the British voter to understand or to appreciate this network of motives and interests. Chamberlain himself was always far less interested in India than in the "kith-and-kin dominions" (populated primarily by those of British descent) and in the new tropical empire that was greatly extended in area between 1884 and 1896, when 2.5 million square miles (6.5 million square km) of territory fell under British control. Even he did not fully understand either the rival aspirations of different dominions or the relationship between economic development in the "formal" empire and trade and investment in the "informal" empire where the British flag did not fly.

Queen Victoria's jubilees in 1887 and 1897 involved both imperial pageantry and imperial conferences, but, between 1896 and 1902, public interest in problems of empire was intensified not so much by pageantry as by crisis. British-Boer relations in South Africa, always tense, were further worsened after the Jameson raid of December 1895, and, in October 1899, war began. The early stages of the struggle were favourable to the Boers, and it was not until spring 1900 that superior British equipment began to count. British troops entered Pretoria in June 1900 and Paul Kruger, the Boer president, fled to

Europe, where most governments had given him moral support against the British. Thereafter, the Boers employed guerrilla tactics, and the war did not end until May 1902. It was the most expensive of all the 19th-century "little wars," with the British employing 450,000 troops, of whom 22,000 never returned. Just as the Crimean War had focused attention on "mismanagement," so the South African (Boer) War led to demands not only for greater "efficiency" but also for more enlightened social policies in relation to health and education.

While the war lasted, it emphasized the political differences within the Liberal Party and consolidated Conservative-Liberal Unionist strength. The imperialism of the Liberal prime minister, Lord Rosebery, was totally uncongenial to young pro-Boer Liberals like Lloyd George. A middle group of Liberals emerged, but it was not until after 1903 that party rifts were healed. The Unionists won the "khaki election" of 1900 (which took its name from the uniforms of the British army, a reflection of its occurrence in the middle of the war) and secured a new lease of power for nearly six years, but their unity also was threatened after the Peace of Vereeniging, which ended the war in May 1902. Salisbury retired in 1902, to be succeeded by his nephew, Arthur Balfour, a brilliant man but a tortuous and insecure politician. There had been an even bigger break in January 1901 when the queen died, after a brief illness, at age 81. She had ruled for 64 years and her death seemed to mark not so much the end of a reign as the end of an age.

There were significant changes in terms of the impression organized labour made on politics. Some of the new union leaders were confessed socialists, anxious to use political as well as economic power to secure their objectives, and a number of socialist organizations emerged between 1880 and 1900 all conscious, at least intermittently, that, whatever their differences, they were part of a "labour movement." The Social Democratic Federation, influenced by Marxism, was founded in 1884; however, it was never more than a tiny and increasingly sectarian organization. The Independent Labour Party, founded in Bradford in 1893, had a more general appeal, while the Fabian Society, founded in 1883–84, included intellectuals who were to play a large part in 20th-century labour politics.

In February 1900 a labour representation conference was held in London at which trade unionists and socialists agreed to found a committee (the Labour Representation Committee), with Ramsay MacDonald as first secretary, to promote the return of Labour members to Parliament. This conference marked the beginning of the 20th-century Labour Party, which, with Liberal support, won 29 seats in the general election of 1906. Although until 1914 the party at Westminster for the most part supported the Liberals, in 1909 it secured the allegiance of the "Lib-Lab" miners' members. Financially backed by the trade unions, it was eventually to take the place of the Liberal Party as the second party in the British state.

The return of the Liberals

The Liberals returned to power in December 1905 after Balfour had resigned. Between the end of the South African War and this date, they had become more united as the Conservatives had disintegrated. In 1903 Chamberlain had taken up the cause of protection, thereby disturbing an already uneasy balance within Balfour's cabinet. He failed to win large-scale middle- or working-class support outside Parliament, as he had hoped, and the main effect of his propaganda was to draw rival groups of Liberals together. In the general election of 1906, the Liberals, led by Sir Henry Campbell-Bannerman, a cautious Scot who had stayed clear of the extreme factions during the South African War, won 377 seats, giving them an enormous majority of 84 over all other parties combined. The new cabinet included radicals and Liberal imperialists, and when Campbell-Bannerman retired in 1908, H.H. Asquith moved from the Home Office to the premiership.

Social reform had not been the chief cry at the general election, which was fought mainly on the old issues of free trade, temperance reform, and education. In many constituencies there was evidence of Nonconformist grievances against the Balfour-engineered education act of 1902 that had abolished the school boards, transferred educational responsibilities to the all-purpose local authorities, and laid the foundations of a national system of secondary education. Yet local and national inquiries, official and unofficial, into the incidence of poverty had pointed to the need for public action to relieve distress, and from the start the budget of 1909, fashioned by Lloyd George, as chancellor of the Exchequer, set out deliberately to raise money to "wage implacable warfare against poverty and squalidness." The money was to come in part from a supertax on high incomes and from capital gains on land sales. The budget so enraged Conservative opinion, inside and outside Parliament, that the Lords, already hostile to the trend of Liberal legislation, rejected it, thereby turning a political debate into a constitutional one concerning the powers of the House of Lords. Passions were as strong as they had been in 1831, yet, in the ensuing general election of January 1910, the Liberal majority was greatly reduced, and the balance of power in Parliament was now held by Labour and Irish nationalist members. The death of King Edward VII in May 1910 and the succession of the politically inexperienced George V added to the confusion, and it proved impossible to reach an agreement between the parties on the outlines of a Parliament bill to define or curb the powers of the House of Lords.

After a Liberal Parliament bill had been defeated, a second general election in December 1910 produced political results similar to those earlier in the year, and it was not until August 1911 that the peers eventually passed the Parliament Act of 1911 by 131 votes to 114. The act provided that finance-related bills could become law without the assent of the Lords and that other bills would also become law if they passed in the Commons but failed in the Lords three times within two years. The act was finally passed only after the Conservative leadership had repudiated the "diehard peers" who refused to be intimidated by a threat to create more peers.

In the course of the struggle over the Parliament bill, strong, even violent, feelings had been roused among lords who had seldom bothered hitherto to attend their house. Their intransigence provided a keynote to four years of equally fierce struggle on many other issues in the country, with different sectional groups turning to noisy direct action. The Liberals remained in power, carrying important new legislation, but they faced so much opposition from extremists, who cared little about either conventional political behaviour or the rule of law, that these years have been called by the American historian George Dangerfield "the strange death of Liberal England."

The most important legislation was once more associated with Lloyd George the National Insurance Act of 1911, which Parliament accepted without difficulty but which was the subject of much hostile criticism in the press and was bitterly opposed by doctors and duchesses. Nor did it win unanimous support from labour. The parliamentary Labour Party itself mattered less during these years, however, than extra-parliamentary trade union protests, some of them violent in character "a great upsurge of elemental forces." There was a wave of strikes in 1911 and 1912, some of them tinged with syndicalist ideology, all of them asserting, in difficult economic circumstances for the workingman, claims that had seldom been made before.

Old-fashioned trade unionists were almost as unpopular with the rank and file as they were with capitalists. In June 1914, less than two months before the outbreak of World War I, a "triple alliance" of transport workers, miners, and railwaymen was formed to buttress labour solidarity. In parallel to labour agitation, the suffragists, fighting for women's rights, resorted to militant tactics that not only embarrassed Asquith's government but tested the whole local and national machinery for maintaining order. The Women's Social and Political Union, founded in 1903, was prepared to encourage illegal acts, including bombing and arson, which led to sharp police retaliation, severe sentences, harsh and controversial treatment in prison, and even martyrdom.

The issue that created the greatest difficulties, however, was one of the oldest: Ireland. In April 1912, armed with the new powers of the Parliament Act, Asquith introduced a new Home Rule bill. Conservative opposition to it was reinforced on this occasion by a popular Protestant movement in Ulster, and the new Conservative leader, Andrew Bonar Law, who had replaced Balfour in 1911, gave his covert support to army mutineers in Ulster. No compromises were acceptable, and the struggle to settle the fate of Ireland was still in full spate when war broke out in August 1914. Most ominously for the Liberals, the Irish Home Rule supporters at Westminster were losing ground in southern Ireland, where in 1913 a militant working-class movement entered into close alliance with the nationalist forces of Sinn Féin. Ireland was obviously on the brink of civil war.

The international crisis

The seeds of international war, sown long before 1900, were nourished between the resignation of Salisbury in 1902 and August 1914. Two intricate systems of agreements and alliances the Triple Alliance of Germany, Austria-Hungary, and Italy and the Triple Entente of France, Russia, and Britain faced each other in 1914. Both were backed by a military and naval apparatus (Britain had been building a large fleet, and Richard Haldane had been reforming the army), and both could appeal to half-informed or uninformed public opinion. The result was that a war that was to break the continuities of history started as a popular war.

The Liberal government under Asquith faced a number of diplomatic crises from 1908 onward. Throughout a period of recurring tension, its foreign minister, Sir Edward Grey, often making decisions that were not discussed by the cabinet as a whole, strengthened the understanding with France that had been initiated by his Conservative predecessor in 1903. An alliance had already been signed with Japan in 1902, and in 1907 agreements were reached with Russia. Meanwhile, naval rivalry with Germany familiarized Britons with the notion that, if war came, it would be with Germany. The 1914 crisis began in the Balkans, where the heir to the Austro-Hungarian throne was assassinated in June 1914. Soon Austria (backed by Germany) and Russia (supported by France) faced off. The British cabinet was divided, but, after the Germans invaded Belgium on August 4, thereby violating a neutrality that Britain was committed by treaty to support, Britain and Germany went to war.

Economy and society

Changes in economic conditions during the last decades of the 19th century were of crucial importance. Mid-Victorian prosperity had reached its peak in a boom that collapsed in 1873. Thereafter, although national income continued to increase (nearly quadrupling between 1851 and 1911), there was persistent pressure on profit margins, with a price fall that lasted until the mid-1890s. Contemporaries talked misleadingly of a "great depression," but, however misleading the phrase was as a description of the movement of economic indexes, the period as a whole was one of doubt and tension. There was anxious concern about both markets and materials, but the retardation in the national rate of growth to below 2 percent per annum was even harder to bear because the growth rates of competitors were rising, sometimes in spectacular fashion.

The interests of different sections of the community diverged between 1870 and 1900 as they had before the mid-Victorian period. In particular, grain- and meat-producing farmers bore the full weight of foreign competition in cereals, and many, though not all, industrialists felt the growing pressure of foreign competition in both old and new industries. As a result of improved transport, including storage and refrigeration facilities, along with the application of improved agricultural machinery, overseas cereal producers fully penetrated the British market. In 1877 the price of English wheat stood at 56 shillings 9 pence a quarter (compared with 54 shillings 6 pence in 1846); for the rest of the century, it never again came within 10 shillings of that figure. During the 1890s, therefore, there was a sharp fall in rent, a shift in land ownership, and a challenge to the large estate in the cereal-growing and meat-producing areas of the country. The fact that dairy and fruit farmers flourished did not relieve the pessimism of most spokesmen for the threatened landed interests.

In industry, there were new forms of power and a trend toward bigger plants and more impersonal organization. There were also efforts throughout the period to increase cartels and amalgamations. Britain was never as strong or as innovative in the age of steel as it had been in the earlier age of iron. By 1896 British steel output was less than that of either the United States or Germany, while the British textile industry was declining sharply. Exports fell between 1880 and 1900 from £105 million to £95 million.

Yet the country's economic position would have been completely different had it not been for Britain's international economic strength as banker and financier. During years of economic challenge at home, capital exports greatly increased, until they reached a figure of almost £200 million per annum before 1914, and investment income poured in to rectify adverse balance of trade accounts. Investing during these years in both "formal" and "informal" empire was more profitable, if more risky, than investing at home. But it also contributed to domestic obsolescence, particularly in the old industries. Thus, ultimately, there was a price to pay for imperial glory. During the last 20 years of peace before 1914, when Britain's role as rentier was at its height, international prices began to rise again, and they continued to rise, with fluctuations, until after the end of World War I. Against this backdrop, the City of London was at the centre of international markets of capital, money, and commodities.

Meanwhile, whether prices were falling or rising, labour in Britain was increasingly discontented, articulate, and organized. Throughout the period, national income per capita grew faster than the continuing population growth (which stayed at above 10 percent per decade until 1911, although the birth rate had fallen sharply after 1900), but neither the growth of income nor the falling level of retail prices until the mid-1890s made for industrial peace. By the end of the century, when pressure on real wages was once again increasing, there were two million trade unionists in unskilled unions as well as in skilled unions of the mid-century type, and by 1914 the figure had doubled.

In terms of the distribution of the labour force in this period, among the most striking changes was the development of white-collar occupations. Between 1881 and 1921, of male workers, those in public administration, professional occupations, and subordinate services, along with those in commercial occupations, increased from some 700,000 to 1,700,000 (out of a total workforce of some 9,000,000 in 1881 and 13,500,000 in 1921). Those in transport and communications almost doubled in number to 1,500,000, while those who worked in the manufacture of metal, machines, implements, and vehicles increased from almost 1,000,000 to over 2,000,000. Those in mining also doubled in number, to 1,200,000 in 1921. These were the real growth areas in the economy. The number of individuals involved in the agricultural sector, on the other hand, declined but exceeded 1,250,000 in 1921 and thus made up a still important component of the occupational structure of the country. All other sectors remained stable or lost workers, with the growth industry of the early 19th century, textiles and clothing, decreasing from about 1,000,000 to 750,000 workers in 1921.

The economy lost a good deal of its old artisan character. Accompanying this erosion of artisan power at the point of production were some tendencies toward increases of scale in factory production. To some degree there also was a decline in the old hierarchies of skill, most notably in the erosion of the position of artisans, the mid-Victorian labour aristocracy. At the same time, the characteristics of the social structure of production in the preceding period were still apparent, namely "combined and uneven" development, whereby old and new forms of industrial organization and production methods were often combined, and overall development was not uniform.

The result was that skill and authority were still distributed in a very complex way throughout industry. Older historical accounts concerning the late 19th- and early 20th-century formation of an increasingly de-skilled and uniform labour force have given way to a more nuanced picture, so that the rise of the Labour Party is no longer interpreted, as it earlier was, simply as a consequence of the supposed emergence of this de-skilled labour force. Moreover, in line with more recent scholarship, the emergence of the Labour Party in the late 19th and early 20th century is no longer viewed as a reflex reaction to economic conditions or to the situation of workers; instead, it is understood in terms of the role of political intervention and political language in shaping what was indeed a new sense of class unity and not as a direct expression of the labour force itself, which was in fact still strikingly divided not only by skill but by many other characteristics of workplace experience.

The number of women in professional occupations and subordinate services doubled to 440,000 in 1921, out of a total workforce of some 5,500,000 women. This shift did much to reshape women's changing understanding of themselves, particularly among the middle classes, where the more public world of work called into question exclusively domestic definitions of femininity. Women's employment in textile and clothing manufacture was, however, still massive, with the real decline in the production of textiles not coming until after World War I. In 1881 the textile and clothing industry employed nearly 1,500,000 women; though by 1921 this number had shrunk, it remained considerable, at 1,300,000. Within the textile industry, women's trade unions made some headway, but it is testimony to the power of traditional paternalist understandings of gender relationships among workers that male authority still obtained for the most part in both the home and the workplace, where women were excluded from the better-paid and more-skilled jobs. Domestic service was still the bedrock of women's employment, comprising some 1,750,000 workers in 1881 out of a total of 3,900,000, though by 1921 this number had grown to 1,800,000 but shrunk in relative importance.

Family and gender

The structure of families in this period was still relatively diverse and significantly unlike 21st-century versions of the nuclear family based upon co-residing parents and young children. There is some evidence to suggest that industrialization strengthened rather than weakened kinship ties and intergenerational co-residence, because of the practical help resident grandparents could render to working mothers. Relationships across generations, both within and outside the household, continued to be important. Despite the migration of production from home to factory, the traditional identity of the family as a productive unit survived quite strongly into the 20th century, notably among shopkeepers and other self-employed workers, among tenant farmers, and particularly among the still important area of "homework" production, which, as a component of the late 19th-century clothing industry, went through a massive revival. The family retained many residual economic roles and acquired some new ones.

For example, there was still a strong tendency for occupations to pass from father to son in all classes. The economy of workers, however, was much more likely to involve the collective earnings of father, mother, and children, compared with the family economy of those who were better-off.

In mid-19th-century England and Wales (Scotland had its own divorce, custody, and property rights), a husband had absolute right of control over his wife's person, as well as considerable rights over her property. He also had sole responsibility for the rearing and guardianship of children, and the common law gave him absolute freedom to bequeath his property outside his family. A wife, in contrast, had neither legal duties nor enforceable legal rights, and, indeed, under common law her juridical personality was totally submerged in that of her husband. During this period, the situation was to undergo remarkable changes as the law began to make inroads into not only the rights of husbands but also the rights of parents generally. By the end of this period, legal intervention had largely eroded the absolute paternal rights enshrined in the common law, although sexual relations between husbands and wives remained largely untouched by legal change. However, cultural changes were to lag behind legal ones.

For the better-off in society, marriage was gradually transformed from what was in large measure a property contract into a union in which companionship and consumerism played a larger role. That women were increasingly becoming consumers was reflected in the Married Women's Property Acts of 1882, which allowed women to control their own income. The period was therefore to see changes within marriage in the direction of greater independence for women, as well as changes in the status and independence of women outside marriage. At the same time, the legal and administrative code remained decidedly biased against women; for instance, income tax was framed as a duty of the male head of household. In terms of what might be called upper-middle-class society, traditional gender roles were still extremely powerful: girls were educated at home up to World War I and were trained for the social conventions of home life and home management; boys were sent to school, often to boarding school; and more companionate versions of spousal relationship were accompanied by the preservation of distance between parents and children, with much child care still being left to servants. Lower down the scale, things were much the same, although few middle-class households could afford a wholly idle wife.

In this period it was widely established that natural processes no longer gave an adequate account of motherhood, which was increasingly seen as an activity of great moral, intellectual, and technical complexity that had to be learned artificially like any other skill. Indeed, there was an unprecedented concern with the nature of motherhood, which was not seen as a private matter but as something involving the future of society, the country, the empire, and indeed the "race." This concern was an expression of changing gender roles; but, while on one hand it embodied a reaction against forces of change, in some respects it also signaled the movement toward greater gender equality. The role of the state was to reflect these changes, as its intervention in family life also reached unprecedented levels.

From the 1860s to the '80s, the agitation surrounding the Contagious Diseases Acts an attempt to control venereal disease in the armed forces that involved state regulation and inspection of prostitution laid the foundations for subsequent feminism. The campaign for the repeal of the acts generated public discussion of the double standard of licence for men and chastity for women. This agitation brought women into the public sphere much more directly than before and in new ways. Moreover, it served to complement changes in education, charity work, political organization, and associational life (which for women expanded considerably in this period), all of which took women outside the home, especially better-off women. This was also the case with the growth of women's role as consumers, with shopping and the new department stores further increasing women's involvement in public urban life.

The discussion generated by these acts resulted in a series of feminist responses varying from the more socially, sometimes politically, conservative emphasis on traditional family roles and on maternalism, seen in the "social purity" campaigns of the late 19th century (with their links to "social hygiene" movements espousing hygiene as the gateway to moral betterment), to the more radical, egalitarian political feminism of the early 20th century. The latter form was itself split into radical, socialist, and constitutional variants. In 1903 the women's suffrage movement split dramatically over the issue of the parliamentary vote, some pursuing the vote as merely one item on a long list of political and extra-political reforms and others concentrating on the single aim of obtaining the vote.

These agitations also influenced men's conception of themselves, notably in response to the social purity movement's emphasis on the importance of chastity for men as well as women. Male roles were further defined in the 1880s with the consolidation of male homosexuality as a distinct social identity, given legal definition at the time (in the Labouchere amendment of 1885, which criminalized homosexuality as gross indecency), not least in the famous case involving the arrest and imprisonment of Irish poet and dramatist Oscar Wilde. From this time the rise of "scientific" understandings of sexuality, including the science of sexology, also served to redefine gender roles. However, there as in so many other realms, recognition for women lagged behind that for men, and it was not until the 1920s that a similar delineation of lesbian identity became fully apparent.

Mass culture

Class distinctions in cultural life continued to be very important. "Rational recreation" (productive and socially responsible recreation) remained an aim of those who wished to reform the culture of the lower classes. However, it also came to characterize the provision of recreation for the upper classes too. The idea of "playing the game" and "the game for its own sake" represented an extension of rational recreation into the sphere of sports, particularly as developed in the public schools, which in this period were reformed so as to institute a sense of public duty and private responsibility among the propertied classes.

The cult of the disinterested amateur was part of the notion of the classically trained English gentleman, whose education and sense of moral duty purportedly created a moral superiority and disinterestedness that uniquely fitted him to rule. The development of popular forms of literature aimed at boys in this period served to glorify this particular manifestation of gentlemanly rule. More broadly, the model of the reformed public school itself, as well as a reformed Oxbridge (the Universities of Oxford and Cambridge had been restructured in large part somewhat earlier to meet the needs of a changing, moralized civil service), came to have a considerable influence on educational institutions in Britain. The masculine emphasis in sports was complemented by the club life of the upper classes, which, while always decidedly masculine, in the 1880s and '90s, in terms of the development of London clubland, served even more to emphasize expressions of masculine identity in leisure activities.

The move from the sociability that characterized upper-class culture in the 18th century to the more didactic, socially concerned interventions of the early and mid-19th century gave way to a gradual involvement in hitherto forbidden forms, forms now suitably sanitized and made rational (or, as in the case of classical music, made sacred). It was not only music that became respectable but also the reading of novels, the playing of cards, and theatre attendance. The growth of the "legitimate" theatre from the 1880s, in distinction to more popular, melodramatic forms, is indicative of this development.

Institutions and locations that were defined by associations with class especially harboured these changes, most notably the school and the suburb. As the transport system developed, especially the expansion of railway commuting from the 1870s and '80s, suburban life grew in importance, most notably in London. However, it was not only the propertied in society who sought to create rational recreation: in continuance of earlier attempts to influence change from within the labouring population, the reform of low culture was sought by the appeal to high culture in radical and socialist movements such as the Cooperative movement, the Workers Educational Association, and, after World War I, the Left Book Club. Radical rationalist recreation took the form of rambling, bicycling, and educational holidays.

However, this very negotiation of the hitherto forbidden cultural forms also represented a qualification of the class character of culture and the development of what came increasingly to be called "mass culture." In part this represented a nationalization of cultural life that reflected the increasing importance of a mass polity. Britain also became a more centralized, homogeneous national society. But a simple, linear development toward uniform experience had not characterized British history. The earlier development of modern British society had seen an emphasis on the significance of local and regional cultures, which echoed and reflected the relationship between state and society. While the four nations of the British Isles had constituted a unitary state since the end of the 18th century, Britain remained in the early and mid-19th century a society that was highly diverse and localized.

Different cultural, religious, and legal traditions reinforced the very diverse occupational and manufacturing structure that industrialization brought with it. The importance of political decentralization was reflected in very strong municipal cultures, so that the centre of gravity of a good deal of British artistic and literary life long continued to remain in the English provinces and within each of the constituent nations. The growth of organized sports reflected not only the social separation between classes but also the strength of regional and local attachments.

Nationalization was apparent in an increasingly elaborate and integrated communications structure represented in the railway, the telegraph, the postal service, and later the telephone. By the beginning of the 20th century, the local press, while strong, was beginning to give way to mass-circulation newspapers, most famously the Daily Mail. The nationwide retailing revolution apparent from the 1880s, along with the development of an increasingly nationally coordinated and centrally based entertainment industry, which could be seen, for example, in the development of music hall, were part of the process too. So was the migration of intellectual life into the universities, which tended to be dominated by Oxbridge and University of London colleges, despite strong provincial resistance and pride. London itself became the cultural centre of the country and therefore the cultural centre of the British Empire. A fundamental influence on this change was the shift in the British economy from manufacturing industry to international finance and, with it, the migration of wealth, prestige, fashion, and social status away from the provinces to London.

While organized sports might express regional loyalties, their increasingly organized and commercialized basis whereby rules were drawn up, leagues founded, and competitions inaugurated served to coordinate local loyalties on a national basis. National bodies were created, along with national audiences. Spectatorship gave way to participation among all classes. In this sense, a "mass" culture was evident. This culture, however, might occur within and across class lines. For example, professional football (soccer) and county cricket, the best-known instances of mass sports, particularly in the early days, witnessed the class distinction between "gentleman" and "players," as well as north-south differences. Particular sports developed along class lines: tennis and golf, at least in England, were played by the higher orders of society, and rugby was divided along the class lines, with rugby union for the higher classes and rugby league for the lower classes. (See rugby for the history and development of both traditions.) Indeed, professional football has only relatively recently lost its working-class character in Britain. Nonetheless, in the 20th century, developments of mass culture across class lines were increasingly important with cultural and social homogeneity increasingly going hand in hand.

www.ingramcontent.com/pod-product-compliance
Lightning Source LLC
Chambersburg PA
CBHW021051080526
44587CB00010B/208